ILLUSTRATING ASIA

Comics, Humor Magazines, and Picture Books

ConsumAsiaN Book Series

edited by

Brian Moeran and Lise Skov

The Curzon Press and The University of Hawai'i Press

ILLUSTRATING ASIA

Comics, Humor Magazines, and Picture Books

Edited by

John A. Lent

UNIVERSITY OF HAWAI'I PRESS
HONOLULU

Editorial Matter © 2001 John A. Lent

Published in North America by
University of Hawai'i Press
2840 Kolowalu Street
Honolulu, Hawai'i 96822

First published in the United Kingdom
by Curzon Press
Richmond, Surrey
England

Printed in Great Britain

Library of Congress Cataloguing-in-Publication Data

Illustrating Asia : comics, humor magazines, and picture books /
edited by John A. Lent.
     p. cm. – (ConsumAsiaN book series)
    Includes bibliographical references and index.
    ISBN 0–8248–2471–7 (alk. paper)
    1. Comic books, strips, etc.–Asia–History and criticism.
  I. Lent, John A. II. Series.

  PN6790.A78 I45 2001
741.5'095–dc21

                                    00-054498

CONTENTS

CONTENTS

Part II Representations and Portrayals

ACKNOWLEDGEMENTS

This book is the latest in a series of works I have authored or edited to focus attention on Asian cartooning and cartoonists. Others are *Themes and Issues in Asian Cartooning: cute, cheap, mad, and sexy* (Popular Press, 1999), *Pulp Demons: international dimensions of the postwar anti-comics campaign* (Associated University Presses, 1999), *Comic Art in Africa, Asia, Australia, and Latin America: a comprehensive international bibliography* (Greenwood, 1996), the forthcoming *Asian Animation* (John Libbey) and *Asian Comics and Cartoons* (University of Mississippi Press), and special numbers of *Philippines Communications Journal, Southeast Asian Journal of Social Sciences, Journal of Asian Pacific Communication*, and *Asian Thought & Society*. Contributors to the edited volumes among these helped me better understand the world of cartooning and comic art in Asia and to them, I am grateful.

Throughout the more than past decade, I have had the privilege of interviewing hundreds of cartoonists, illustrators, and animators in Africa, Asia, the Caribbean, Europe, and North and South America (about 250 in Asia alone), all of whom increased my knowledge of and appreciation for the profession. Acknowledging all of them singly is not possible here, but I would like to mention Winnie Hettigoda, K. M. K. Madagama, S. C. Opatha, Camillus Pereira, and W. R. Wijesoma, who were helpful while I was in Sri Lanka gathering data for the chapter in this book.

At Temple University, I was fortunate to work with a coterie of graduate students who shared my belief that cartooning in Asia can be a worthy and serious area of study; all six chose an aspect of this topic for their Ph.D. dissertations. I thank Dr. Hongying Liu-Lengyel, Dr. Wendy Hsiao, Dr. Rei Okamoto, Dr. Kie-Un Yu, and soon-to-be Ph.D.s Aruna Rao and Asli Tunç, for helping make these among my most fulfilling and productive years in the academy.

The ConsumAsiaN and its editors, Brian Moeran and Lise Skov, deserve the thanks of all in Asian popular culture for their dedication to building this series as an excellent outlet for our work.

I am in debt to Daiwon Hyun, Rei Okamoto, Aruna Rao, and Asli Tunç for the technical assistance they rendered to make this book possible; to all nine

ACKNOWLEDGEMENTS

authors who without complaint revised their manuscripts on at least three occasions, and to copyright holders of illustrations who granted permission for their use. Every effort has been made to trace the copyright of the illustrations reproduced in this book. In the one or two cases where this has been impossible, the author and publisher would be pleased to hear from any copyright holders whom they have been unable to contact, and to print due acknowledgements in subsequent editions.

A NOTE ON JAPANESE AND CHINESE NAMES

The names order of Japanese contributors to this volume is given in both ways, depending on the preference of the individual. Thus, two authors have their surnames last (Fusami Ōgi and Rei Okamoto) and one (Shimizu Isao) chooses to use the Japanese style. All Chinese authors preferred using their surnames last. But, names in the text are given surname first, the common style in China, Japan, Korea, and Taiwan.

INTRODUCTION

John A. Lent

Development of Asian Illustration

Illustrating has been a preoccupation of Asians for many millennia and a vehicle for storytelling and mirthmaking for centuries.

Grotesque figures taking on characteristics of contemporary cartoons adorned Chinese burial paraphernalia as early as the Yangshao Culture (5000–3000 B.C.E. [Before Contemporary Era]) (see Lent 1992), and more than 2000 years ago, narrative images were drawn on the walls of the Ajanta cave temples of India. Described by Rao (1995:164) as 'vibrant, full of life and vitality', the latter resemble contemporary comic art in that they contain 'topical morals, depict sequential images, and contain a wealth of expression in each scene'.

About the same time the Ajanta drawings were executed, in China during the Western Han Dynasty, the tradition of telling a story with cartoon-like illustrations was conceived. Up through the sixth and seventh centuries, picture stories appeared on coffins, doorguards, stone slabs, and frescoes (see Zhu 1990 and Peng 1980), and in the Song (960–1279) and Yuan (1279–1368) Dynasties, in books. Artists were asked to decorate popular storybooks flourishing at the time, with illustrations at the tops of the pages. One author has said Song book paintings had cartoon characteristics (Shi 1989:12).

An important medium of storytelling, with roots in India before 325 B.C.E., was the picture scroll which eventually spread widely to Iran, Turkey, China, Japan, and parts of Europe. Scrolls, usually long, horizontal depictions of sequential stories, were often carried from village to village by storytellers who spun their yarns while unfolding them. Often sensational in content (about murders and other crimes), some carried inscriptions above each frame describing the action. In China, called *chuan-pien*, they appeared as early as the T'ang Dynasty (618–906); the much older Indian version, *pat* or *pata*, was the medium of *patuas*, who sang the mythological stories while uncurling the highly illustrated sequences. Much later in the eighteenth century, the patas became more secular in theme and satirical in tone. Similar unrolled scrolls (*wayang bèbèr*) are known to have existed in Indonesia 800 to 1000 years ago.

1

Just as in Rajasthan (India), picture storytellers (*dalangs*) lugged the wayang bèbèr from place to place as they wove humor – sometimes light, sometimes ribald, but always funny – into their stories (see Mair 1988).

Japan had narrative picture scrolls by the twelfth century, when Bishop Toba created the *Chōjūgiga* (Animal Scrolls) depicting animals behaving in human fashion. Some early Japanese scrolls were of a sacred nature, but when they were not religious, they were very uninhibited. Examples of the wilder ones included *Hōhigassen* (Farting Contests) and *Yōbutsu Kurabe* (Phallic Contests), the latter showing men comparing their huge erect penises and using them in unbelievable feats of strength. Describing a picture scroll, obviously not in the latter category, Schodt wrote:

> As one untied the string that bound it and began unrolling the scroll from right to left, hills faded into plains, roofs of houses dissolved to show the occupants inside, and, like the comics of today, changes in time, place, and mood were signified by mist, cherry blossoms, maple leaves, or other commonly understood symbols.
>
> (1983:28–29)

Playful and humorous art was sometimes part of these picture story books and scrolls, as it was integral to Chinese wall paintings, Indonesian wayang bèbèr, or Indian royal portraiture. During the first half of the Qing Dynasty, political satire and caricature were notable in works of painters such as Zhu Da (1626–1705) and Luo Liangfeng (1733–1799) and in the colored woodblock prints (*nian hua*). The latter, popular during the New Year, were put on walls as symbols of luck, or on doors to ward off evil. In thirteenth-century Mughal India, caricature appeared in psychological portraiture commissioned by Jahangir, who believed he could determine the loyalty of each of his courtiers by the peculiarities depicted in these exaggerated paintings (Rao 1995:165). Caricature was also plentiful in portraits of Deccan and Rajput rulers in the seventeenth century, and in Japanese floating world woodblock prints (*ukiyo-e*) from 1600 to 1867. When ukiyo-e artist Ōoka Shimboku bound together some prints in 1702 and created *Tobae Sankokushi*, Japan had its (and perhaps the world's) first cartoon book. Yellow-cover booklets (*kibyōshi*) served in the same capacity at the end of the eighteenth century. The metamorphosis of Japanese cartoon books was not very different from how the first United States comic books were fashioned from bound comic strips, or, as Berman tells us in these pages, how *cergam* were made in post-World War II Indonesia.

In the nineteenth century, European (followed later by American) influences affected the development of comic and narrative art of Asia. Humor magazines, often modeled after and named for *Punch* and *Puck*, found their way to India and Japan about the mid-nineteenth century, the Philippines in the 1890s–1900s, and China in the 1920s–1930s. American-style comic strips were imported by various Asian newspapers in the early twentieth century and their local copies followed soon after (see Lent 1995).

Dimensions of *Illustrating Asia*

Illustrating Asia: comics, humor magazines, and picture books brings together elements of this rich tradition of pictorial storytelling, most notably those connected to comic art – narrativity, sequence, humor, satire, and dialogue. Various forms of picturetelling and comics are analyzed, including comic books, comic strips, pictorials, and fan magazines, and although a large portion of the book is historical in approach, other methods of research, such as interviews and content and textual analyses, are plentifully employed. The main thrusts of *Illustrating Asia* are comic art in its historical and socio-cultural environments and the representation and portrayal of topics such as ancient Chinese philosophy, gender, and the enemy in Asian cartoons and comics. Three East Asian (China, Japan, and Taiwan), two Southeast Asian (Indonesia, Malaysia) and two South Asian (India, Sri Lanka) countries are dealt with in these chapters. Seven of the chapters concentrate on East Asia, and although this may seem to be a disproportionate representation, it can be justified because both the comic art profession and the study thereof are more developed in this region than most other parts of Asia.

Reading these essays will not render an answer to what is Asian about picture books and comic/cartoon books in Asia; such has not been the purpose of *Illustrating Asia*. Instead, an attempt has been made to introduce concepts and data about media normally not deemed worthy of scholarly scrutiny and, in the process, to mark some commonalities linking picture books and comics/cartoons from country to country in Asia.

Some Common Themes

A consistent theme that comes through many chapters of this book relates to the influences of colonialist and other outside forces. Japanese *manga*, American comic books and syndicated comic strips (newspaper funnies), and *Mad* magazine have been perceived as helpful or harmful at various times to the development of comic and narrative art in Asia. Manga are readily available in most parts of East and Southeast Asia and are credited or blamed for affecting the ways cartoonists conceptualize and draw stories. Genres that depend upon stories of ancient warrior classes, techniques that sequence panels in cinematic fashion, and sex and violence subject matter that is rather explicit, are characteristics that can be traced to manga. In fact, variants of the word manga have entered the Chinese (*manhua*) and Korean (*manwha*) lexicons to denote comics and cartoons.

As those in comics industries in neighboring countries such as South Korea, Taiwan, and China (including Hong Kong) witnessed Japan's success in the globalization of manga and *anime*, they tried to enter the foreign arena too, by displaying their works at comics conventions in the United States and elsewhere, by creating characters and stories with universal appeal, and by soliciting government and other support to upgrade the profession, lower taxes, and make for more profitable trade arrangements.

The prevalence of manga in such large numbers across Asia sparked much protest, as parents and governmental bodies in South Korea, Taiwan, Thailand, and Hong Kong vilified them for their sex- and violence-laden content and portrayals of ways of life anathema to these Asian cultures. The Korean government had banned comics (actually all Japanese cultural products) after World War II, but over the years, it also censored them through an ethics committee, a strange twist of logic since they were not supposed to be there in the first place. In 1966, the Taiwanese government began to regulate comics, with the result that the censors were accused of holding a double standard, with manga given much more leeway than Taiwanese comics. In both South Korea and Taiwan, manga pirates dominated production and distribution until the 1990s.

Cartoonists in these Asian countries also decried the manga invasion as part of Japan's continuing economic and cultural imperialism in the post-colonial era. They pointed out how indigenous comics and cartoons almost disappeared at one time or another in Indonesia, Taiwan, South Korea, and elsewhere, because of the easy accessibility of manga.

Western (mainly American) influences were also prominent, with early Japanese and Filipino newspaper comic strips appearing as clones of 'Bringing Up Father', 'Tarzan', 'Popeye', and others, and as mentioned before, with the first cartoon and humor magazines in India, Japan, and China established by westerners and carrying already-established American or European periodical names such as *Sketch*, *Punch*, or *Puck*. In more modern times, humor magazines have taken on characteristics and the name of *Mad* magazine, for example, *Unmad* in Bangladesh and *Gila-Gila* (Crazy about Mad) in Malaysia; similarly, Filipino comic books (*komiks*) did not deviate far from American comics in plot or name (*Lastik Man* for *Plastic Man*, *Kapteyn Barbell* for *Captain Marvel*, or *Flash Ter* for *Flash Gordon*).

In quite a few countries, American comic books themselves still hold sway. Indonesian companies publish American (and French) comics as part of their full line of periodicals, while Vietnamese cartoonists redraw and translate Disney (as well as Japanese and French) titles, appending their own names as creators to the finished works. In Singapore, most comic book stores sell primarily foreign (mainly American) books, perhaps part of the reason local comics have not gained a foothold. Certainly western comic strips distributed very inexpensively through United States-based syndicates have made it difficult for local cartoonists to compete.

Westernization was evident in other aspects of cartoon and graphic art as authors of *Illustrating Asia* discuss: the early picture books of Taiwan read like European tales and carried Continental styles; the first Sri Lanka newspaper strip was a copy of one from England; some cartoons of Republican China reflected a 'Parisian tradition of erotic eye'; and *shōjo* comics of 1970s Japan idealized westernized romantic images.

4

Oftentimes, westernization is appropriated into a traditional context; in other words, Asian artists have taken this basically western form and subsequently reconnected it to their construct of 'traditional' Asian culture. Hybridization of this type has been applied to all aspects of popular culture, such as film, television, dance, music, fast food, drinks, sports, and of course, cartoons and comics. Thus, Chinese cartoonists use ancient brush and ink techniques to make drawings on modern themes and often base gag cartoons on folktales; Malaysian, Indonesian, Chinese, Hong Kong, Japanese, and other Asian artists employ ancient warrior stories; and still others reinvent comics with more appropriate Asian topics such as martial arts, mah-jong, or science fiction with ancient China or Buddhism plots. Sometimes the twists given to characters and stories during the process of hybridization are more than unique – perhaps even ludicrous. Rao in this book tells how Indian comics superstar Bahadur wears western blue jeans with an Indian shirt (*kurta*), to show he is both modern and aware of his roots, and how plots are mixed so that masked superheroes go home to their parents at night and villainesses seek to destroy the universe because they cannot find a suitable husband.

Another common thread connected to the previous discussion and weaving in and out of cartoons/comics and picture books of Asia are religions, cultural forms, philosophies, and political systems that found their way from one part of the continent to the next. Examples are Buddhism which has left its imprint of humor and playfulness on ancient Asian art, Confucianism which has reified leaders and elders beyond the reach of satirists and cartoonists, and cultural migrations that have carried with them artifacts such as picture books, wayang, and so forth. Long-standing Chinese communities in most of Asia brought in art and visuals that had an impact on what eventually became comic art.

Also affecting comic and narrative art of Asia is the rapid growth and dispersion of 'new' media in most countries, brought on partly by their newly-industrialized and urbanized nature, the growth of middle classes with purchasing power, the privatization and deregulation of national media systems, and concomitant tie-ins with American and European conglomerates eager to tap into the huge Asian market. Cartoon and picture book personnel from Korea to Sri Lanka bemoan the incalculable harm that they believe satellite and cable television, the Internet, and video have done to their markets. In the Philippines, serialized comic books (*nobelas*) have all but disappeared because of competition from other media for readers' attention (and because of economic downswings); in Sri Lanka, comic newspapers have dwindled in number and circulation over the past decade as the national television service increased its schedule of foreign animation shows, and in India, Indrajal Comics folded and *Amar Chitra Katha* quit publishing new titles, unable to meet the challenge of action-adventure shows on television and video.

On the other hand, Asian cartoons and comics have benefited from cross-fertilization other media have provided. This has been a worldwide phenomenon from the beginnings of the comic strip in the United States more than a century ago. In Taiwan and China, distinctions between picture books and comics were not very clear, and often stories were adopted from novels, operas, and films. Shen explains that quite a few Chinese cartoonists of the 1930s were famous in the picture book (*lianhuanhua*) field, that they adopted their themes from novels, historical romances, and operas, and that adaptation of novels to cartoon format was often preceded by a movie version. Philippine movie directors told me in the 1980s that about 50 per cent of their films were taken from the komiks, and Hong Kong cartoonists related how they based an entire genre of comic books on movie themes. In Japan, manga and anime are very closely entwined, usually with the animated story following the comic book. The works of other Asian print cartoonists (most recently, Lat of Malaysia and Park Jae-Dong of South Korea) have been animated for television or the theatre.

The global trend towards extreme commodification of cultural forms has hit Asia, although not to the extent that it has overwhelmed the western world. Comics, cartoon, and picture-book characters have been fashioned into a number of merchandised items in Japan, South Korea, Singapore, Malaysia, and Hong Kong, among others.

Common to parts of Asia is a less-than-enthusiastic reception – even a disdain – for comics and cartoons, some people dumping them into the ashcan of 'low culture', others snubbing them as children's fare. South Korea, Sri Lanka, and Taiwan stand out as countries where comics have been relegated to such a lowly status. But, contrary to this belief, more often the readers are adults, as Berman indicates while discussing Indonesia. Following on the heels of the 1950s anti-comics campaign in the United States (and subsequently, a couple of dozen other countries of the world), parental, religious, and governmental groups in at least the Philippines, Taiwan, South Korea, Hong Kong, Thailand, and Japan pushed to rid their societies of what they perceived to be the pernicious effects of comic books. Like their counterparts in the western world, they were part of the maximum effects school, believing that a medium such as comic books could cause juvenile delinquency (see Lent 1999).

At other times, criticism of comics and cartoons has followed the cultural/ media imperialism discourse. Although some of the concern has been about American, and by extension, capitalistic and materialistic, values permeating Asia, the bigger fear expressed by the South Koreans and Taiwanese had to do with Japanese 'soft colonialism' relayed by manga.

Various authors in *Illustrating Asia* allude to comics/cartoons being the bane of governments because their political context threaten authority. Berman relates how both Presidents Soekarno and Soeharto of Indonesia denounced comics, the former accusing comic artists of subversion and their works as being 'garbage and a western induced poison', and how a type of underground comic book emerged. In most countries of Asia, strong censorship of all mass media has been the rule for decades, with some loosening of restrictions in the 1990s. Noted Taiwanese cartoonists of the 1960s abandoned the profession for as long as 20 years because of martial law and censorship restrictions, and in South

Korea, cartoonists were arrested and jailed, harassed by the Korean Central Intelligence Agency, and censored under about 40 years of dictatorship. Philippine cartoonists labored under severe conditions during the Marcos regime, and in Burma, China, North Korea, Singapore, and Vietnam, their colleagues steer away from political topics, even in what they term political cartoons. The Sri Lankan situation relative to freedom of expression is also very restrained, as cartoonists have been threatened with death, beaten, harassed, and censored. In India, the constraints placed on comics came from women's and religious groups who, practicing 'political correctness', protested against the way historical and mythological characters were portrayed in the *Amar Chitra Katha* series. Cartoon artists have resisted in a variety of ways – starting underground comics in Indonesia, publishing in exile as in the case of some Burmese cartoonists, and employing innuendo and other subtleties as in South Korea, Philippines, and other places. As Shen states, cartoonists in China during the Japanese invasion of the 1930s formed a Cartoon Propaganda Team that through their cartoons told of Japanese atrocities and sought financial help to support the struggle for national salvation.

Like other print media, comics and picture books have been pigeonholed by location and class; for the most part, they are urban phenomena purchased by the middle class. Emanating from cities which have the production capabilities, the books usually depict urban settings, characters, and lifestyles. As a result, their audience is more often made up of city, rather than rural, readers because the stories relate to them, they have more purchasing power and higher education and literacy levels, and the books are accessible, which they often are not in remote areas hampered by poor transport services and adverse weather conditions.

For years, across Asia, comics have been made available to those without purchasing power through rental shops and book stalls. Shen in this volume describes the street book stalls of Shanghai that rented out picture books in the 1920s and 1930s, and Shimizu tells about the establishment of 'lending libraries' in Japan in the 1950s, when the popular red comic books increased their prices and children had to resort to renting them. The rental system became an important means of distributing comics and picture books in Japan, as well as elsewhere (for example, Hong Kong, Taiwan, Singapore, South Korea), even though parents and education officials denounced rental shops for being havens for juvenile delinquents. In the early 1990s, South Korean officials ruled that a comic rental shop could not be within the range of 200 meters of a school. In recent years, rental shops have faced the threat of extinction because of legislation such as that in South Korea, the increased purchasing power of young people who can now buy their own comics, and the aforementioned swing of interest to television, video, and computer entertainment.

In South Korea, production of comic books has been tiered to account for the rental market. Comic books about the size of a popular paperback are created in so-called 'comic book factories', where an assembly-line operation based on the master–apprentice system is in place. They are produced in limited press runs (under 3000 copies) for the rental shops. Competing with the comic books in the 1990s have been comics magazines of a larger format for sale in bookstores. The master–apprentice division of labor and its assembly-line approach to making comic books found favor over the years in other parts of Asia, notably China, Hong Kong, and Japan. The other major approach to comic book production is the use of a small editorial staff that hires work out to a team of regular freelance artists and writers, a practice common in the Philippines.

The Authors and Their Contentions

Contributors to *Illustrating Asia* hail from a number of disciplines and a wide range of backgrounds and career stages. One of the pitfalls of this diversity is an unevenness in tone; a strength is that it allows for tracking the thinking of Asian intellectuals based in the west as well as in Asia and western scholars residing in Asia, and of those researchers long acquainted with Asia and popular culture and those new to the field. Some authors emphasize the continuity or importance of traditional Asian forms of graphic representation feeding into the development of comics and cartoons; others take notice of the west as a decisive formative influence. Basically, two approaches are used: either a chronological order or an espousal of an ideological viewpoint scheme (comics as reflection of modern social reality, a feminist questioning of gender categories, and so forth).

Laine Berman, in her socio-political analysis of Indonesian comic books, highlights external impacts of Japanese and American comic books, most notably the feeling of inferiority that resulted among local cartoonists, and the way that wayang had been incorporated into comic art. She devotes considerable attention to political and economic restrictions on comic books and shows how even the underground comics published by art school students or non-government agencies are rather tame affairs.

Looking at Indian comic books, Aruna Rao also discussed foreign influences and how they convinced one Indian nationalist, Anant Pai, that he had to start the *Amar Chitra Katha* series, based on Indian traditions. She also traces the fall of the series and recounts criticisms that the stories stereotyped women as perpetually self-sacrificing wives and mothers, and Muslims as 'cruel and untrustworthy' invaders. The chapter provides an overview of the art form in India – how it originated and who makes and reads the comics.

In the first of her two contributions, Shu-chu Wei discusses the evolution of picture books, among which she subsumes cartoons and comic books. Examining what she considers the most important texts chronologically, she also shows political connections – that in the post-World War II era, comics were used as anti-communist propaganda. Taiwan experienced an anti-comics backlash in the 1960s, when teachers and parents blamed them for poor academic performance and the government censored them severely. Wei treats other picture books, especially those funded by UNICEF and Xinyi Foundation.

All types of Sri Lankan comic art are examined by John A. Lent, who surveys key cartoonists about their careers and working conditions and the field more generally. He discusses the decline of comic papers since the 1980s, resulting from the introduction of new media and increased teacher disdain for comics, culprits responsible for harming comics elsewhere. Lent relates the precarious existence of cartoonists in the realm of Sri Lanka's violence-riddled politics.

Kuiyi Shen looks at picture books (lianhuanhua) and comic books (manhua) in Republican Shanghai of the 1920s–1930s. He traces the history of picture books to nineteenth-century illustrated story books (*lianhuan tuhua*) and shows how picture books sprouted at the same time artists began submitting comic strips to newspapers and magazines and shortly before the first cartoon magazines appeared in the 1910s. He, too, points to the political factor, describing the itinerant Cartoon Propaganda Team which between 1937–1940 carried out anti-Japanese propaganda. Shen believes picture books and comics catered to the needs of the middle and lower classes.

Republican China of the 1910s–1940s is also the setting for Yingjin Zhang's contribution. After giving the historical precedents for the narrative function and visual style of cartoons and pictorials, Zhang then focuses on recurring motifs of prostitution and modeling and discursive modes of fetishism and voyeurism, through which he connects seemingly unrelated photographs, cartoons, illustrations, texts, cartoonists, writers, editors, publishers, and readers. He concludes that the pictorial and cartoon magazines, through the circulation of nude and erotic images, provided an alternative public space where erotic imagination was given a corporeal form.

Shimizu Isao concentrates on the 20-page red comic books that mushroomed in pre- and post-war Japan. Claiming that despite the prevalence of *ponchi* (a type of comic book for children) in the 1890s, as well as cartoon magazines and, after 1917, comic strips, the red comic books were the real beginnings of the genre. He credits manga 'god' Tezuka Osamu with originating 37 red comic books, which were blatantly copied by other artists.

The second part of *Illustrating Asia* deals with various representations and portrayals in the comics.

Shu-chu Wei analyzes the work of prominent Taiwanese cartoonist Tsai Chih-chung, noted worldwide for his representations of ancient Chinese philosophy in some of the highest-circulated comic books of all time. She tells us how Tsai tackles the difficult tasks of making the serious, abstract thoughts of Confucius, Laozi, and Zhuangzi interesting without distortion and then marketing them. Wei says Tsai never expected his comic books to replace the original classics. Thus, in his books, he includes the original text and notes on every page.

In the first of two chapters on gender representation, Fusami Ōgi studies Japanese girls' comics (*shōjo manga*) mainly for the 1970s, a turning point in women's representation and participation in manga. She states that during that decade, Japanese women developed a clear self-identity, as did shōjo manga. Although Tezuka Osamu probably wrote the first shōjo narrative, it was a group of women cartoonists born in postwar Japan, called the 'Magnificent 24s', who fashioned them into a genre very different from boys' comics (*shōnen manga*). Ōgi states that shōjo evolved differently over the years, and today, use multiple dimensions of gender.

Ronald Provencher uses popular Malay humor magazines to track images of men and women in Malaysia. After detailing the popularity of the magazines (*Gila-Gila* tops *all* Malaysian magazines in circulation), he interprets a series of *Gila-Gila* and *Cabai* (humor magazine exclusively for women) cartoons and gender humor. One myth dispelled by Provencher's analysis of the nine cartoons relates to the submissiveness of Malaysian women.

As do almost all contributors to *Illustrating Asia*, Rei Okamoto sets her study in an historical perspective. Her focus, however, is on *Manga* magazine, 1941–1945, and how it characterized the enemy. She says that Japan's premier cartoon magazine served key propaganda roles in antagonistic and derogatory satires of the enemy (symbolically represented by Franklin D. Roosevelt, Winston Churchill, and Chiang Kai-shek) and depictions of wartime life in Japan. Okamoto finds Roosevelt usually pictured as a weary old man or a demon with a human face, in both cases obsessed with money; Churchill as a fat, evil man with a cigar, a male chauvinist, or a helpless woman clinging to Roosevelt; and Chiang as a pathetic, wily loser with a feeble body, always in deep trouble.

Illustrating Asia adds to the literature in the budding field of comic art, which in the past decade has been favored with university courses, academic interest groups, and a number of books, videos, conference presentations, and journal and periodical articles. More importantly, this book helps to fill a void in Asian studies where, for reasons such as snobbishness and ethnocentrism of the American scholarship, inattentiveness of Asian scholars (for the same reasons), and poorly collected or otherwise inaccessible research materials, pictorials, cartoons, and comics, and popular culture more generally, were not studied (see Croizier 1998).

The Asian scene has been changing in the 1990s, with academic efforts to study Asian popular culture and art, the depoliticization of artistic and other cultural discourses in repressive countries, the freer access to Asian artists and art, the growing popularity of cultural studies, the burgeoning market worldwide for Asian cultural artifacts, and the determined efforts of a group of academic researchers, of which the contributors to *Illustrating Asia* are an integral part.

Part I

Overviews and Case Studies

1

COMICS AS SOCIAL COMMENTARY IN JAVA, INDONESIA*

Laine Berman

Under the tightly controlled rule of former President Soeharto, certain classes of Indonesians thrived and actually enjoyed what can best be termed a highly materialistic life style. A great part of this new consumerism extended itself to the comic book. Toward the latter part of the Soeharto era, not only had the comic book flourished in sales and respect, it was also reclaimed by artists and activists as a new medium of protest and self-expression. Since the great economic crisis has hit Indonesia with a wrath unfelt in other parts of Asia, economic hardship and rising prices have taken over from censorship and oppression to prevent the comic from developing as it seemed it would in the latter half of the 1990s. This chapter examines the comic book through its struggle for identity. I trace this struggle by locating the comic as a tool for protest and self-expression, which I then extend as a reflection of Indonesian youths' parallel struggle for identity in a changing world.

The connection between comic books and social commentary, let alone protest, is not a very direct one in Indonesian contexts, nor is it simple to trace. This is because of Indonesia's long history of imperialism, problems of identity, and authoritarianism. Imperialism, of course, refers to the Dutch period (from about 1600 to 1945) where the presses tended to reflect Dutch rather than indigenous concerns. In the post-independence era (after 1945), what I call problems of identity refer to the broad rejection of indigenous comics for anything imported. The authoritarian control and censorship of the mass media during the Soeharto period (1966–1998) prevent any true 'protest' comic from reaching any but a small minority of the population. Comics none the less have a special value and influential power in Indonesia that deserves to be studied in far more depth than has yet been done. Thus, by piecing together information from the recent comic convention in Jakarta (February 1998), my own Indonesian comic collection, personal acquaintances with the artists, the few articles available, and the memories of Indonesians, I have attempted to present a brief commentary on the Indonesian comic book as a genre for social analysis within the boundaries of the island of Java.

Why Comics?

To understand the role of comics in the mass media is to understand them as a part of the social relations they report, and not as an objective force separate from them. Ever since the invention of mass-produced images through words or pictures, printing has served its huge clientele by providing our daily doses of political, ideological or social information. Print media is used and often controlled by the powerful for their self-glorification and as an instrument of political propaganda. Protest media on the other hand cry out against injustice, condemn the abuses of power, and teach the masses new social ideas. Even in the most authoritarian of nations, the comic is used as a weapon of the weak in denouncing injustice (Phillippe 1982). In their various forms, from the editorial cartoon, the strip, to the comic book, comic images have the potential to throw a different light on a people's conceptions of themselves and their politics than do the more formal media (Anderson 1990).

With a background in linguistic anthropology, my main concerns are to recognize the styles and purposes of direct human interaction, particularly within contexts of inequality and oppression. Direct human interaction includes the everyday conversations, gossip, rumors, jokes, and so on that people tell each other, while inequality often determines who has the right to say what and under what circumstances. These are the very aspects of social information that are neglected in most social and political analyses. Yet, as we all know, they form a very significant aspect of understanding for perhaps a majority of a people. Comics in this respect have the potential to fill the void as symbolic dialogue since they tend to be regarded as a people's medium, often reflecting common concerns and complaints. The most attractive feature to me about comics is the fact that their interpretation, like social discourse, is based on context, meaning that they are visually significant and verbally dependent on specific moments in time. Within the visual and verbal, we find an intertextual quality that links these story worlds with real worlds. It is this link between supposed fantasy and real experience that makes the comic a significant source for understanding modern populist perspectives on local events. The comic in Indonesia then is a type of social and political communication that, as Anderson (1990) has pointed out, presents the low, intimate, informal perspective on Indonesian experience, which stands in sharp contrast to the formal, polite, or high official perspectives we see in the press and in many scholarly analyses.

What then does the mainstream Indonesian comic book tell us about modern populist perspectives?

Defining the Genres

In order to clarify my focus, I differentiate cartoons in the mass media from comic books. Cartoons in the media refer to comic editorials and strips as a part of the press (news or magazines), while the comic book is marketed and sold on its own right. The central difference within Indonesian contexts would be that comic books are almost entirely imported, whereas cartoons are partially and increasingly indigenous creations, reflecting indigenous concerns within and despite all the political pressures preventing freedom of speech. Whether or not each attracts a different audience remains to be investigated[1]. Indonesia has a varied and diverse press with over 240 daily or weekly newspapers, commanding a total circulation of some 10.5 million copies. More than 100 magazines are published with a total circulation of over five million copies. But despite this huge popular newspaper market, only around fourteen use cartoons (Lent 1993). Of the newspaper dailies, only *Suara Merdeka* and the Jakarta tabloid *Pos Kota* have color cartoon sections each week. Over the years, these cartoon strips have changed from imported and translated adventure stories to almost entirely indigenously drawn, locally relevant issues. The only other main use of cartoon material is the fortnightly magazine called *HumOr*[2].

What do Indonesian cartoons describe? In contemporary Indonesia readers will find the pages of the press and other public media full of quotations from government officials and prominent leaders. These officials from the President, to the Minister of Information, to religious figures, and prominent professors proclaim the press as free and open. Yet, at the same time, a vast battery of laws prevents criticism, and a practice of telephone calls to media editors assures self-censorship is the rule. Similarly, the Indonesian president proudly describes his nation as a democracy and the elections in which he runs unchallenged a 'Festival of Democracy'. This type of authoritarian, hierarchically structured power in the shaping of popular meaning is a common source of humor within contemporary cartoons.

The most widely read of the weekly news magazines, *Tempo* (banned since June 1994 for publishing information on taboo topics[3]), presented one editorial cartoon at the beginning of the magazine along with letters from readers. While the letters, one can only assume, were uncensored and actually reflected a rare opportunity for some members of the population[4] to publicly express their views, Figure 1.1 presents a good example of what that view of freedom of expression was meant to be. Taken as a premonition of what was to come, we are shown through cartoon form exactly what the Authority defines as the freedom to express differences of opinion. The picture shows a group of young boys all singing quite happily and with full intensity to the same tune. Meanwhile the boy on the right seems to have gotten things wrong where he takes the Authority's words too literally. He is being reprimanded and told, 'Now *that's* what's meant by difference of opinion!' Less than one year later when *Tempo* was banned for printing a difference of opinion from that of the Authority, see how this conflict between the Authority's words and their contradictory deeds appeared in the *Jakarta Post*:

PRESS BANS SPUR NEW DEBATE ON OPENNESS
The government, facing accusations of turning back the clock on democracy yesterday said the ban against three news magazines would

Figure 1.1

not have happened if they had used their newly gained freedom more wisely. Minister/State Secretary Moerdiono gave his assurances that the government remains committed to the present course of political openness. On a separate occasion last night, Moerdiono said that everyone should shoulder the responsibility of maintaining the current momentum of openness. 'Don't let anyone slip out', he said

(*Jakarta Post* 1994).

The article maintains that freedom of expression still exists and that all infractions are the result of a breach of responsibility toward this paternal Authority. Thus, *Tempo's* own history reveals what can happen to the boy on the right if he is foolish enough to make the same mistake again.

The *Panji Koming* strip (Figure 1.2 (1992)) appears each Sunday in *Kompas*, the most popular of the daily national newspapers, along with three imported strips. The name *Panji Koming* can tell us a bit about its perspective. *Panji* is an old Javanese title for mid-ranking royalty. *Koming* means stunted or small-minded in the Javanese language. By adorning the hero with this obscure title preceding a comic given name, its creator is matching elite position with ignorance in this strip set in the past, as seen through clothing and hair styles. The hero Panji is barefoot, meaning that despite the title he is a peasant. Yet he is also someone able to show the obsequiousness expected by his betters. Status is often reflected through basic, broadly recognized symbols. The powerful wear shoes; they are fat; and they are treated with deference despite their foibles. Here

16

Figure 1.2 (1) I want to build a temple here. But, sir, our land is not for sale. (2) Narrow minded! Ignorant! You're selfish! Stubborn! Hard headed! (3) Stuck in the past! Can't see around you! (4) That's right!

too, the powerful say things that reflect certain truths, although not necessarily the ones they intended.

In this strip, hierarchical expectations of deference and the abuse of power are set in the past, which permits an element of freedom in presenting a social commentary that is relevant now. In modern news media, the powerful often cite the ignorance of the common people as a justification for their paternal, authoritarian role, 'for the good of the masses'. As Panji's less deferential associate states, it is not the peasants who are looking stupid.

Social issues such as guarding one's appearance or place in the social hierarchy and particularly gender problems are also common topics of humor. The Semarang-based (North Central Java, the regional capital) daily *Suara Merdeka* prints a Sunday color cartoon section where the misadventures of Mr. Bei reflect the concerns of common, contemporary working people. Poor Mr. Bei, despite his innocence and perfectly good intentions, is sure to get something wrong. Reflecting very Javanese scenarios, the strip reveals honest, working-class values and how these vary between gender or social rank.

In Figure 1.3 Mr. Bei is innocently off to the market and picks up some vegetables for his wife. Mr. Bei runs into a neighbor just as he reaches home. As typical neighborly (male) chatter, he comments on the huge bundle of greens. Mr. Bei's response is referentially unclear. It could mean 'they're [the greens] to eat with goat', as in 'we're having goat meat for dinner', or it could mean 'it's goat food'. Cassava greens quite often are given to the goats, and it is more manly in Javanese society to buy food for the goat than to run errands for one's

Figure 1.3 (1) I'm off to the market mum. In that case, buy me some cassava greens. I'm making rendang [a spicy meat dish]. (2) Wow for just 500 [US$.20] get as much as this, cheap! Mother Bei is certain to be thrilled! (3) Wah, such a big bunch, what'dya buy it for Mr. Bei? It's to eat with the goat. (4) Why give food to a goat when you can butcher it and enjoy it yourself! How dare he! (5) Here mum, your cassava greens . . . Just a minute! (6) Here, I'll add banana leaves and other greens so that your goat grows big and fat! Oh no! Angry again!

wife. The neighbor assumes the greens are for the goat and jokingly says, 'Why give food to a goat when you can butcher it [the goat] and enjoy it yourself!' This comment infuriates Mother Bei and readers laugh at the differences in male and female perceptions and the hostility these cause. Why? Mother Bei knows that the greens are for her family, not a goat, and she is highly insulted at being compared to an animal.

Under the very heavy hand of what is locally called self-censorship, these strips and editorial cartoons are able to take a far more relevant and hence humorous stance than comic books, which are almost entirely imported and thus

18

have little if any social meaning within localized contexts. Gender and social hierarchy issues are a safe bet, whereas politics is always dangerous ground[5]. Yet, it is precisely this rather huge discrepancy between cartoons and comic books in terms of cost, storyline, and social relevance that needs further discussion. To say each is popular is an understatement. Each does, however, reflect a very different aspect of local society. Before we can dig a bit deeper and discuss some ways in which government regulations are avoided in independent comics, we will first look briefly at the historical development of mainstream comics.

History of Comics and Cartoons

Cartoons in the mass media are the strips appearing in the funny pages of the news or the one shot visual condensation of political communication, the editorial cartoon. The editorial cartoon has a very long history while the cartoon strip did not exist in indigenous form prior to World War II. All types of comics depend upon sophisticated printing technology and an economy in which people are able and willing to buy daily, weekly, or monthly publications. During the Dutch Occupation, editorial cartoons were widely used in the Dutch-controlled Jakarta print media, but these reflected Dutch not indigenous interests, and would have only been available to a few Indonesians[6]. During the Japanese occupation in 1943–45, the war for independence in 1945–48, and the early years of freedom, posters were used for propaganda, which had an influence on the later development of the genre (Anderson 1990; Zaimar 1998).

Once the cartoon strip became established, these imported and translated strips eventually spurred on the indigenous cartoon. Bind a string of strips together and you have the comic book, referred to locally as *cergam*, an acronym for *cerita bergambar* or story with pictures. The comic book made its debut in Indonesia in the 1950s but all I can find on them is that they were American look-alikes (*Jakarta Post* 1996). In the 1960s and up till the 1970s, Indonesian cartoons finally found their place. These were almost entirely adventure, *silat* (kung fu) stories of which the artist Oto Suastika was one of the early heroes. His artwork and stories were considered among the best in Indonesia after they appeared as a cartoon strip in the *Starweekly* in 1954. Praised for the quality of the drawing and general attractiveness, Oto adapted his stories from Chinese legends, with Chinese settings and Chinese details. Despite his popularity, his pay (rupiah 750 per page and rupiah 3000 per month, about US$10 then) was never adjusted for inflation over the almost ten years his cartoon strips were printed (*Tempo* 1988:90).

Because of economic difficulty in the post-revolution era, the indigenous comic did not develop until the 1950s. American strips had already begun flooding the local markets. But in 1954, inspired by these American comics, an Indonesian artist named Kosasih printed *Sri Asih*. What followed was a proliferation of locally produced copies of foreign comics, the adaptation of

Chinese legends, silat adventure stories, and a surge in their sales during the 1960s to the 1970s. This era is referred to as 'the golden age of Indonesian comics'. Everybody was reading them! During this time, a brilliant scheme for evading the problem of economic difficulty appeared through the comic rental kiosk which blossomed throughout Java (Wirosardjono 1998). Many Indonesians have described for me their memories of that time through images of people sitting under trees beside the huge piles of comics they had just borrowed from the rental kiosk! As popular culture, then, the comic book is highly valued by locals who seem more than prepared to become entirely involved in these often epic narratives.

During the 1970s, the theory of comics as a reincarnation of past oral traditions met its modern economic reality where Chinese silat stories eventually led to a revival of local legends in comic book form. The most notable of these were the *Mahabarata* and *Ramayana* comics by Kosasih. Other famed Indonesian comic artists were Ganes TH who created *Si Buta dari Gua Hantu* (the Ogre from Ghost Cave), and Hans Jaladara, who wrote *Panji Tengkorak* (Panji Skull) back in the 1970s. The Chinese influences were obviously still strong since this comic story was later turned into a Hong Kong adventure film (*Suara Merdeka* 1996a). This taste for epic legend comics prevails today. Ride any bus in Java now and you are sure to be offered miniature comic books on Mohammad, the Buddha, or Jesus.

Since much of the comic material was extracted from adaptations of myths and legends, their huge significance for local readers makes one wonder what exactly it means to transform profound texts with their deep ethical and religious messages into comic book form. Does the comic format turn the Pandawa brothers from the epic Mahabarata into a lesser type of super hero than they are because of the Indonesian misconception that the sole purpose of the comic is to entertain children? Western intellectuals bemoan these comics as superficial and simplistic, 'crude comic [...] replacement of the skillfully demanding, enduring, elegant and aesthetically whole style of the *wayang kulit*' [shadow puppet theater] (Lindsay 1987). Meanwhile, in a country as sensitive and as prone to religious violence as Indonesia, the proliferation of the Prophet Mohammed and other religious super heroes into comic book form would never be locally evaluated as crude, caricatured stereotypes that fail to be highly significant educational models. Yet, Lindsay's (1987) serious concerns lead us to questions that are impossible to answer. Is the altering of context from sacred text to comic a means of liberating an elitist genre in order to reach as wide an audience as possible, truly supporting a notion of comics as the people's art? Or are real values only conveyed through original books and performance genres such as wayang and lost through transference to the comic book?

Both Presidents Soekarno and Soeharto have taken a position on these questions, first when President Soekarno accused comic artists of subversion and denounced their work as garbage and a western-induced poison in the 1960s. Schools and kiosks were raided and the comics confiscated and burned. Later, in the Soeharto era, comics were again attacked for fostering laziness and having no educational value (*Jakarta Post* 1996). The 'Golden Age' of comics with its new mass produced and consumed versions of old traditions is herein put to rest. Strangely, this rejection of the industry by the presidents rarely appears in writings on comics. What constantly does appear in the media now is a lament for the death of the national comic along with an admission that anything local quite simply is not as good as the foreign variety[7]. Yet, one still wonders why this hugely popular medium was destroyed. As comic artists themselves admit, Indonesian comics suffer from 'writing problems' and Ganes TH adds that 'readers need something new. Offering the same old thing just won't do' (*Jakarta Post* 1996). This leads us back to questions of censorship and the limitations on new topics that will be discussed later.

Meanwhile, with such strong forces denouncing the local comic industry, the desire for comics has been met by a flood of foreign comics. Beginning with the 1980s, translations of Donald Duck, Spiderman, Flash Gordon, and other American and European favorites have begun to fill the book shop shelves, while the Indonesian natives wallow in the dust of neglect, if, that is, they can even be found in the storage bins. Translations of American cowboy and especially Indian stories and other western legends take over where local and Chinese legends once ruled. Comics such as *Musuh dalam Selimut* (Enemy in a Blanket, 1982) reveal where the local industry has gone. While the comic was sold as a western import in translation, often it concealed an indigenous (illegal) copy inside. In my issue of *Musuh*, behind the cowboy story I was surprised to find *Tigra* (a Marvel title), a local adaptation of the western super hero genre. Tigra contains Indonesian bad guys, Caucasian good guys, and a super hero who is female, young, beautiful, wild, mute, a great kung fu fighter, very responsive to (Caucasian) handsome men, and wears very skimpy clothing.

The extreme popularity of these local legend and kung fu comics in the 1970s is obvious because of the extent to which they are easily located in any of the Javanese homes I have ever visited. Yet, despite the obviously huge numbers sold in the recent past, these comic book legends remain largely unavailable in the book shops today[8]. Such a fact is hard to explain since the come-back of the 1970s comic hero, Panji Tengkorak, as a film star in the mid 1980s. Other comic artists (*komikus*) had also tried their hand at breathing new life into the dead industry by riding in Panji's cinematic wake. In the latter half of the 1980s, many of the old favorite artists like Jan Mintaraga made a valiant effort by digging up Javanese legends such as *Jaka Tingkir, Ramayana,* and *Imperium Majapahit.* The mass popularity of these comics is evident from their full color serialization in strip form in every one of the Javanese language weekly magazines and newspapers. In 1994 some of the Indonesian language newspapers also began reprinting these old legend serials. But they never appeared in comic book form and their popularity pales in comparison to the foreign imports. Indonesian markets seem to be demanding something new, and these demands are not being met by local artists.

By the end of the 1980s, translations of Japanese comics such as *Dragon Ball*, *Candy*, and *Kung Fu Boy* entered the local scene with their eastern styles of story-telling. They are also praised for a quality of drawing that was deemed vastly superior to the local efforts. Indonesian-made comics are now reduced to pretty much only the cartoon editorial variety and those strips that appear in newspapers. In the 1980s and well into the 1990s, about two thirds of these newspaper weekly cartoons were translations of foreign strips. Since nothing new was to emerge, according to official sources, the national comic was dead (*Hai* 1995a).

It is not just the success in sales of foreign comics that has squeezed the local varieties off the shelves. Since production expenses are much greater than buying the rights to established foreign comics, local comics actually cost more than the imports do. All things considered, producers have little incentive to support local artists. Furthermore, Indonesian comic artists seem to have had too narrow a repertoire: either the familiar traditional story or copies of foreign comics. Local artists have told me that the Indonesian comic neglects indigenous perspectives on humor or traditions of story-telling because they are boring[9]. Yet, quite realistically, Indonesian artists cannot offer comics about real, modern, social issues and contemporary concerns since many of these would be deemed subversive. No comic books have ever appeared on everyday common topics such as youth gangs, teen love, coming-of-age problems, and criminal elements within local contexts. In Indonesia, there are no comparisons to Malaysia's Lat and his highly acclaimed *Town Boy* or *Kampung Boy* comics. In the 1990s, there is not one Indonesian comic book that looks at local reality the way the Mr. Bei strip does, for example.

What is obvious within the current Indonesian comic world is that any indigenous efforts are deemed inferior in comparison to the slick, trendy overseas super hero comic. The one recent challenger to the overseas onslaught is from the super hero *Caroq* produced by *Qomik Nusantara*, the effort of a group of fourteen art students from the Bandung Institute of Technology in West Java. In an interview with the teen magazine *Hai* (1995a:58–60), the artists insist their heroes are all modeled on Indonesian details. The hero, named Sarmun, is an ethnic Baduy (West Java) who wears Madurese (an island located just off the north east coast of Java) style of clothing and fights with Madurese blades. In fact, the characters are direct copies of the ultra muscular American comic heroes such as Batman, Captain Marvel, and others easily recognizable by comic buffs[10].

Despite their new attitudes, dependence on teamwork instead of the lone comic artist, and their slick, futuristic stories and artwork, the kinds of criticism *Caroq* is receiving can help us understand how difficult it is for local efforts. Within the Indonesian internet comic network, *Caroq* is condemned for being just like the import comics. Meanwhile, other local comics such as *Patriot* or *Captain Bandung* are harshly criticized for not being as slick and attractive as the imports. With such finicky buyers, the Indonesian comic is in a no-win situation. Add on the fact that they are more expensive than the imports and it is easy to see why Indonesian fans buy the imports.

22

Thus, with little support from local buyers, little opportunity for publication, an apparent fear of tackling modern issues, and a local tradition murdered by foreign marauders, Indonesian comic books seem destined to fade from existence. Meanwhile, there still remains a small group of local heroes that retains its place in local hearts.

Wayang Influences

In the early 1970s characters from the shadow-puppet theater (*wayang*) started to appear in cartoon strips in various forms and roles. While so many lament the subversion of wayang into crude, simplistic comic form, the wayang clowns more than any other aspect of this sacred art have had the strongest influence on modern Javanese art forms, including comics. It is believed that the Javanese added clowns to the epic Hindu myths before 600 C.E., and in local syncretic style, the clowns have become wholly adapted into the Mahabarata and Ramayana legends. The wayang clowns, named Semar and Togog, were originally gods but because of their bad behavior were banished from heaven to live among mortals on earth. Semar and his sons, Petruk, Gareng, and Bagong, have their roles in these tales as servants to the Pandawa brothers, the princes of the Kingdom of Amarta. While we have already mentioned the legend comics and heard how foreign researchers and Indonesian presidents found these transformations from sacred text into profane comic lacking, it may well be worth explaining further what these wayang legends actually mean in Javanese contexts.

The Javanese arts, including wayang, dance, music, as well as the Javanese language and styles of interaction, are elegant, graceful and highly controlled (Peacock 1968). The wayang has been maintained in Java for over a thousand years as a venerable dramatic tradition, and regarded as the most important vehicle for teaching and preserving the complex treasure of local mystical beliefs (Peacock 1968) through highly ritualistic performances from the great Hindu epics, the Mahabarata and Ramayana. The wayang is also a means through which to teach proper ways of speaking and behaving through the Javanese speech levels, the most elaborate of any known language. The Javanese language too, as scholars describe, is a form of high art whose inherent decorum and graciousness create a world of intense beauty. Scholarly descriptions focus on elegance and decorum rather than content and social inequality and state that refined language is a way of avoiding all conflict where speakers compete to bestow a calm graciousness upon their interlocutors rather than express personality and feelings. From these very brief descriptions of Javanese art, language, and behavior, we should begin to piece together a picture of a people who value above all else an external display of self as calm and graceful. How this self-control translates into the day-to-day lives of real people, their successes, their failures, and their comics is a topic begging for deeper investigation. These social rules of harmonious order and calm acquiescence that border on the sublime, especially within a political order that depends on self-censorship and in many respects terrorism as a means for maintaining social inequality as the status quo (e.g. Berman 1999, 1998a; Heryanto 1990), assure us of the existence of numerous issues that grind away in silence beneath serene surfaces. Thus, for centuries the clowns from these magnificent ancient tales have been a thoroughly Javanese creation and the much-loved voice of the common people. Why? Because clowns can speak their hearts and minds in the presence of their masters.

One of the first incarnates of the wayang clown in cartoon strips appeared in the form of *Djon Domino*, a long-nosed, canvas-capped, T-shirted hero in the Jakarta tabloid, *Pos Kota*. Djon is utterly unlike most western comic characters, since he has no clear-cut social role or status, no friends, no enemies, and no identifiable associates. What is consistent is his appearance and iconographic similarity to Petruk, the long-nosed clown of the wayang shadow puppet theater (Anderson 1990) (Figure 1.4).

Why Petruk? As Anderson (1990:167) points out, the wayang clowns perform a dual function. They are characters embedded within the story's space and time, but they are also the mouthpieces for satire and criticism directed toward the audience and thus outside the story's space and time. The wayang world is a world of masters and servants in which clowns as dependents never challenge that social order. It is precisely this obvious difference in status, the clowns' coarseness to their masters' elegance, ugliness to graceful appearance, crude to exquisite speech, that allows the clowns to laugh at their betters but never undermine them. Clowns cannot be masters and this accepted fact between performance and audience makes the clowns so appealing to other subordinates in hierarchical Javanese society.

Servants becoming kings make for humorous themes as in the wayang story titled *Petruk Dadi Ratu* (Petruk Becomes King). The Djon Domino strip,

Figure 1.4 A view of Petruk as wayang figure, in the Djon Domino incarnate, and in the Petruk/Gareng series (*Cergam Petruk/Gareng* 1986).

24

however, creates a universe whereby *Ratu Dadi Petruk*, or the King Becomes Petruk. As Anderson describes, this is an inconceivable world in Javanese terms because moral status is indistinct, everyone is a clown, and subordinate and master are linked in complicity.

While I cannot locate a history for the *Petruk* series of comic books from the Gultom Agency in Jakarta, these more blatantly wayang clown figures are caught in scenes of violence, social frustration, and class alienation as they try to enjoy very simple pleasures such as fishing in *Gara-Gara Sepatu* (All Because of Shoes, 1986). Petruk can't even fish properly and hooks a pair of boots instead of a fish. Since he does not own any shoes, this seems like a good thing. In these storylines, humor is found where Petruk seizes enjoyment out of situations marked by unfairness and cruelty. Violence is inevitable since Petruk the barefoot peasant now sports a pair of shoes which he is carrying over his shoulder. He is beaten to a pulp by villagers who accuse him of stealing those boots because he looks like a thief: in other words, everyone knows peasants don't have shoes so he must have stolen them. Help arrives but only in the form of a more refined character who in a few polite words is able to stop the violence and set the world right. Thus, the humor of the story is based on symbolically accepting the social order. Peasants must be shoeless, villagers must violently protect their meager possessions, and only the refined can return the world to its proper place. Raise the status of the clown through shoes or attention and he finds crude pleasures which inevitably offend his betters.

The social order in Javanese society is fixed within the cosmic order. Where we each fit within this order is predetermined and hence cannot be altered. The acceptance of fate through acquiescence and refinement leads to respect and praise from others. To strive for more than one deserves is greedy and results in chaos, which becomes a recipe for humor. Thus, the beatings Petruk receives are funny, as is his ludicrous behavior. As the fool, he inappropriately responds with glee to the attention he gets as a thief. In addition to their symbolic behavior, clowns dress as either peasant or servant in a sarong, or khaki pants, a servant's coat, a cap, and they are often barefoot. His movements are coarse, he scratches his buttocks, nudges with his elbow, he grins and jerks, he's raucous and lewd, and he says the things many Javanese wish they could say but do not (Peacock 1968). Crude actions are combined with the odd so clowns wear odd make-up, odd clothes and have odd movements (Siegel 1986). These stereotypes result in laughter when they come into conflict with the breakdown of social and deferential expectations. Thus, surreal humor is located where the boss loses control, the clown servant ridicules his betters, and the clown attempts to rise above his station.

The Comic as Social-political Commentary

In terms of their value as commentary then, comic books and cartoons reveal wide differences in what the genre as symbolic commentary is able to say.

Throughout the regime of President Soeharto, censorship had been the rule for all publications. Thus, comic books or strips and editorial cartoons in the press are constrained. The comic book even more so because it depends only upon itself for sales and survival. Thus, indigenous efforts are deemed too risky economically or politically. Yet by attempting to identify what makes a cartoon funny, we gain access to an intimate perspective on local meaning. The people's art, just like the coarse humor of the wayang clowns, shines through the limitations of censorship in ways that can and do criticize the political order. But as we have also seen, many of the modern comics also reveal why such a powerful social order still exists. As long as individuals' actions aimed at subverting the social order are considered surreal and funny, we can assume that order is still defended by those who are most oppressed by it.

It is not just the indigenous comic book that remains such a rarity in Indonesia, but the comic's officially neglected, rejected, and maligned cousin, the independent publication, is even worse off. The independent comic is extremely limited in its distribution because by name and content it is easily branded illegal. With government fears that freedom of speech is a threat to national stability, and their insistence that alternative perspectives confuse the masses and must be avoided, there is reason to raise issue with the Indonesian comic book as a type of people's art. What kind of people's art avoids contemporary contexts in favor of the historical and the formulaic? Even the independent comics, which specifically do deal with modern issues, fall into this shady category because they are unregistered, hence illegal publications. Regardless of the potential popularity of their storylines, anyone caught in possession, distribution, or creation of these comics is at risk. Any unregistered comic showing signs of political commentary, in other words, anything critical, or not in line with official representations, is illegal as evidenced by police confiscation of Athonk's *The Bad Times Story* (discussed below) in 1994, the censorship and confiscation of his epic comic illustrations on land rights issues, police confiscation of the cartoons on military abuses of power by Marto Art, the arrest of the printers of the calendar containing comic lampoons of the president and his wife[11], and more.

Since all the information I have found in researching comic books in Indonesia comes from the mainstream press or a national seminar, we can expect it to reflect these dominant biases and never mention the independents. While everyone complains about the lack of anything new or relevant in Indonesian comics, the blame falls on the comic artists or publishers, never the political conditions of self-censorship. Thus, in line with government limitations on free speech, the comic books readily available in Indonesian book shops have no political commentary and reflect nothing of relevance to Indonesian contexts – which in itself is a reflection on local culture. These translations of *Donald Duck*, *Superman*, and *Spiderman* (US), *Asterix*, *Tintin*, and *Bobo* (Europe), *Gen Si Kaki Ayam* (Gen the Chicken Foot, Japan) and the whole range of adventurer stories fill the shelves. What's more, Indonesians are lapping them up! The president of Gramedia, Indonesia's largest book chain, has reported that imported comics are now their strongest sales with 90 per cent of these from Japan. Shop windows are full of Japanese super hero figures and the vast comic displays have been moved from the rear up to the front of the stores (*Suara Merdeka* 1996b). Two active Indonesian internet networks devote themselves entirely to discussion of comics. The majority of these discussions are limited to praising the imported comics and denouncing the indigenous as just not interesting, sharp or well designed. With prices of these imports up around the rupiah 10,000 (US$5.00) range per comic, these are clearly no longer working or lower middle class readers, historically the prime target for comics and comic strips. So if the people within this so-called people's medium are not reading them, can the comic book in Indonesia be compared with comic books and their social positions as described elsewhere?

While officially speaking, the national comic is dead, underground comics do exist. But, the kinds of intimate self, historical, social, political, or cultural criticism found in many free-world independent and mainstream comics are rare in Indonesia. Often lacking reflection and self-questioning at either a personal or political level, the epic traditional comic, as well as the underground efforts, both add to, as well as reflect, the current atmosphere of guarded reserve and increasing isolation. The message in these comics is often acquiescence (*nrimo*) and no longer acquiescence based on awareness and knowledge (*eling lan nrimo*). In some of the activists' comics, the message is resist (*lawan*) but also without the awareness and knowledge of self and context required for a people to truly understand freedom from oppression (*eling*). What I have termed problems of identity, then, refers to a widespread avoidance of expressing a self within – and even minimally in contact with – the current socio-political environment. Instead, contextual realities are replaced by translations of not just western stories but also western perspectives and ideal solutions within indigenous contexts. The results are often quite surreal but without the sense of playful intention expected from chance encounters.

Yet, in all fairness, the harshness of my criticism reflects my own frustration more than local realities. Take into consideration the economic pressures faced by young artists and the social pressures to conform with received standards within the art academies and galleries and we are better able to understand why they are increasingly forced to sell-out. In the face of real-world pressures, then, very few have the funding, social flexibility, or courageous inclination to discover what free expression really means. This also can explain why such a seemingly large number of young artists in the art center of Yogyakarta end up taking mainstream jobs to support their families, while others resort to drugs, alcohol, social behaviors intended to shock and, all too frequently, insanity.

Regardless of their limited distribution, the independents are all we have as a representative of the uncensored indigenous comic book. They are most definitely worthy of discussion.

Independent Comic Books

Independent comic books fall into two main categories, the art school and the NGO independent. We will take them in that order. The art school indies would be the most limited in terms of accessibility and distribution. These comic books are often weird (*waton aneh*), have little if any story, and tend toward the pornographic. In terms of students at the Yogyakarta campus of the Art Institute of Indonesia, the work of the art school drop-out, Athonk, is what triggered the new interest in comic book production.

Athonk's first self-published comic, called *The Bad Times Story*, is a playful mix of the idealism of youth with biting social and political commentary, all of which are concealed behind local peculiarities. First inspection of *The Bad Times Story* reveals that all the main characters are devils. Yet, a demonic appearance does not necessarily signify evil just as Athonk's own appearance, a fondness for punk gear, chains, and a Mohawk haircut, does not signify a rejection of his Javanese heritage. Nothing is necessarily what it would seem and all things must be taken for their own merit. But what have devils with halos, punks in conservative Java, and questions of good and evil have to do with Indonesian comics or politics? As the artist writes, *The Bad Times Story* is 'a story of an endless warfare'. But where is this war? It is a war of independence from oppression, the battle to be an individual, to speak freely and question the rules of order. In the narrow confines of local society, this translates as a battle for the right to choose one's own means of expression in a world where such freedoms are illegal. Thus, as in Athonk's everyday life, the idealism of youth, the social pressures to conform, and uncertainty over good and evil despite all appearances, ring throughout this story. True to the social hierarchy in which he grew up, Athonk takes the Authority's perspective in framing his story: he and his friends caught up in the fight for freedom are the devils. The cruel and oppressive Authority is the angel.

Linguistically, *The Bad Times Story* is written in an English that reflects Jalan Sosrowijayan, the tourist center of Yogyakarta. Athonk learned English through tourists and the other local youths who make their living serving them in the Sosro area. This comic is, then, written in what is termed 'Sosro' English. Regardless of how odd the language may seem, English is the language of free speech and expression, and as such, it is the language of choice even for those who may not be very proficient. Clearly, proficiency is not Athonk's concern, while careful reading displays a much more biting social criticism than could ever be expressed in a more conventional language.

In terms of visual symbols, the story is located in a tropical island paradise guarded by huge stone heads with the facial features of Salvador Dali. The island is called 'Daliland'. Why Dali? Firstly, Athonk's father's name is Dalijo. Second, one of the major art influences in Indonesia is Surrealism. Daliland then is symbolic of the Indonesian art circles that have censored Athonk's artwork as too political, preventing him from public exhibition. Thus, as in his own life, these icons are huge, ever-present military figures, scrutinizing everything that occurs on Daliland. Regardless of his own brushes with the Authority, the idealism of youth prevails in these attempts at understanding what freedom of expression may mean. Fortunately Athonk remains very close with his friends and colleagues at the Art Institute and in Javanese hierarchical fashion he is considered an elder brother to these younger generations of student artists. Many have followed Athonk in taking up the calls for both activism and comics.

One of the earliest (1996) in the recent comic output from the Art Institute is *Selingkuh* (dishonesty, deception, corruption). This comic-cum-manual is entirely devoted to weighing out the pluses and minuses of deception with the ultimate goal of luring someone into sexual engagement. Success or failure both lead to the same ending: a fight with the wife, financial debt, unwanted children, divorce, misery, suicide, and the comfort and joy of imagining and/or doing the whole sex scene again. Regardless of the consequences, sex as the reward for a good deception heavily outweighs the negatives, at least in terms of its presentational build-up within the comic.

Is there a message here? Is this a mockery in the form of crude values or an honest depiction of social norms? Ben Anderson has said that sexuality in Indonesian comics is a device for exposing vulnerability and complicity (Anderson 1990:171). Unlike the fine examples set by the heroic brothers of the *wayang* traditions[12], *Selingkuh* places sexuality as the ultimate goal. In Anderson's terms then, the emphasis on sex affirms the absence of self-control and power in contemporary life. The comic contains absolutely no sense of Javanese culture or perspective as it is supposed to be, no sacred Javanese civilization, and nothing refined, graceful, elegant (*alus*). None of the discursive politeness expected in Javanese interactions is apparent either. Instead, formulaic phrases reflect what is significant for youths on a type of self-inflicted exile from the lofty expectations of their elders (and foreign scholars).

English functions here, not as the language of free speech, but as the medium for insipid 'pick-up' conversation. English is also used in the listing of required *selingkuh* accessories: performance, transport, bar, doping, hotel. While all the actual steps leading up to sexual conquest are in English, the sex act as well as the hefty bill, the brief rush of guilt, and the final fight with the wife are all described through Indonesian words. Interestingly, the *'Ending Perselingkuhan'* (the End of Deception) is in English with the choice of ways to reach the *'Suicide Alternatif'* listed in Indonesian. Interpretation of this linguistic code-switching can take many directions. Is this evidence of western vulgarity destroying traditional values, or praise for modern economic and social advances as a means of simplifying a tradition of predatory male sexuality? English here shows how selingkuh practitioners benefit from increased accessibility to selingkuh partners via tourism, bars, hotels, and so on, while the Indonesian language brings the whole experience back down to earth via the expense in real terms within the home. Is this an exposé of modern change, or of a tradition ignored through our preference for the more sacred readings of Javaneseness? Is this comic an insult to Javanese culture and values or is it playful and imaginative? Finally, is it simply *waton aneh* (weird for the sake of being weird)?

Core Comics (1996) launched their first efforts through a series called *Berteman dengan Anjing* or Befriending Dogs. As with *Selingkuh*, this is a group venture among art students. Each volume contains compilations of many individual and group efforts that all conform to one of three specific themes. The similarities end there. The introductory collection of three volumes takes all of its themes from dogs in an Islamic-influenced society that vilifies dogs. *Dogfight* contains stories of violence, where dogs fight dogs, humans destroy dogs, dogs become human soldier heroes, and even the worms that survive in dogs' feces are allowed to feed on humans. *Stairway to the Dog* is full of science fiction stories with dogs as mad scientists, dog heaven where the dog gets to curse at and abuse people, space dogs fall in love with earth women, and other stories too weird to identify. *Tanggaku Kirik* (My Neighbor is a Puppy) compiles stories based in human worlds where dogs coexist in various roles, in dog worlds where humans are the beasts, stories about dogs' dreams and aspirations for love, to become human, or to just survive. Since the Core Comic series[13] contains such a variety of artists and styles, some obviously very talented while others are weird and vulgar, it is quite difficult to 'analyze' in terms of humor, style, meaning. Some efforts are clearly well crafted while others seem spur of the moment and rather shoddy. Some are thoughtful, while others are intentionally tasteless. As a whole, there is no clear underlying social or political commentary, unless one wants to apply the symbolism of man beats dog or dog aspires to greatness and fails to the social hierarchical themes of rigid place we have seen repeated elsewhere. The fact that nearly every story has a sad ending may be as revealing as the series can get.

Activist comics are a very different category from the one described previously. Despite the fact that many activists are also art students, these comics are independently produced through funding from development organizations often to highlight particular social issues rather than as a showcase for art or imagination. Most of these comics are translations of activists' comics produced internationally without redrawing the pictures to give relevance to Indonesian contexts. This is not always the case though. Combining art, narrative, and social activism within the people's genre, these comic books theoretically would attract the broadest audience for the most relevant of society's needs. In terms of the activist comic as a meaningful art form, the great Indonesian poet and performer, Rendra has stated that 'freedom of expression is dependent on the artist's degree of contact with the people, life, and nature [as] an indication of his or her ability to express the truth, or soul of society' (cited in Miklauho-Maklai 1991:81). Thus, if commitment to society is based on stories that have a direct involvement with the everyday world of common people (*wong cilik*), these activists' comics then have the potential to reflect social and political freedoms way beyond those of the other comic book types. In short, are these activist comics the socially relevant models of contemporary culture we would expect to see in such a genre? The first challenge to answering such a question is in locating original Indonesian comics.

Ontran-Ontran ing Muria (Chaos in Muria 1993) was written by Brotoseno and drawn by Marto Art (graduates of the Art Institute in Yogyakarta[14]) and funded by an independent environmentalist organization in North Central Java as part of a broad anti-nuclear campaign. The comic, as well as anti-nuclear T-shirts (designed by Athonk), were for distribution to villagers in the Muria district, the proposed site of the first Indonesian nuclear power plant. The comic is written in Javanese, the regional language spoken by these villagers in their everyday contexts, and not Indonesian, the language of officialdom. The comic shows villagers how to recognize the quality of information being communicated to them by specifically reproducing the kinds of jargon used by the Authority as they praise nuclear power. The narrative stresses ethical values through which the morally righteous villagers are rewarded for not being stupid enough – despite their rural ignorance – to be duped by their crooked village head, a pawn of the Authority. While the peasant villagers know nothing about nuclear energy, they do recognize the one-sided nature of the information they are being given. But they have no means or ability to access alternative sources either intellectually or culturally. Since modern interpretations of Javanese cultural expression assure the prevention of any type of conflict as a threat to the social hierarchy, the public forums staged by the Authority do not permit Muria villagers to raise concerns about the nuclear power plant. Instead, they retreat to their own private worlds, the only context available within which to question Authority and its decisions.

When a local boy suddenly returns home as a university-educated super hero, the required leader emerges. This young leader is assisted by the local priest and mullah, quotes from the Bible and Koran, and formal Javanese discourse as a way to smooth his entry into this world of less educated but older male superiors. Through these opposing dialogues of official deception and university-learned savvy, local villagers and comic readers are taught the alternative perspectives on nuclear energy. They are also taught exactly what the legal steps are to reject authoritarian abuses of power, how to protest correctly, and how to stand up to military threats. At the end of this comic narrative, the villagers win over adversity and they all go back to their fields and live happily ever after.

As a comic book, *Ontran-Ontran ing Muria* is beautiful. It contains good pictures and a great dialogue. But placing it within the context it was meant for, the comic is worrisome because it presents an idealistic and unrealistic view of the righteous as victorious. As history shows, this is rarely the case in contemporary Indonesia. Furthermore, rather than teach villagers to make their own decisions about their lives, this comic does no more than present a counter ideology to that of the Authority. Someone must always speak for the villagers, either the village head or the student leader, maintaining a wide discrepancy between who can speak and who cannot, who knows and who does not. Replacing one set of correct answers for another does not help rural villagers to understand any of the freedoms the activists claim they are fighting for (see Freire 1993 for discussion of survival in oppressive regimes). As other cases have revealed, the fight for one's legal rights in Indonesia often results in far greater losses.

31

In terms of communication then, activists' comics are pedantic, and usually designed by students who have studied or adapted western approaches to the specific problem. Thus, they also follow aggressive western trends which are often inappropriate in Indonesian contexts. Additionally, the government has not only placed severe limitations on the distribution of these activists' comics, it has also been building up its campaign to obliterate informal sectors of the economy and the poor and marginalized classes who depend on them for their livelihood. These independent organizations are then forced to compete with not only the laws that often brand their written efforts illegal, but also the dominant ideologies that train the population to dislike and distrust many of the poor their comics are attempting to defend. Comic books geared toward educating the masses on topics such as violence towards women, street children, rubbish scavengers, wandering street sellers, prostitutes and more, find themselves in direct conflict with national ideologies and indoctrination programs. In light of all these obstacles, it is a miracle that Indonesian comics exist at all and an affirmation of the true power of the comic as a means of expression.

As one final tribute to the comic in Indonesian contexts, this last example comes from the one group who does very clearly use comics to describe its unique day-to-day realities. It is not surprising that this particular group is more oppressed, marginalized, and persecuted than any other. Since January 1993 an NGO in Yogyakarta has been publishing a monthly newsletter written by and for the community of street children. As a street society, these kids identify themselves as a well-formed and special community. The proof of such exclusivity is obvious in their creative use of language. Its members have rejected their alienation by the dominant classes through creating their own exclusive vocabularies, strengthened and spread through the publication of their monthly newsletter called *JeJAL*[15]. *JeJAL* was initially intended to encourage and support literacy and community empowerment by allowing the children a means through which to express themselves creatively. Within these pages, many of the children's everyday activities are described through their own terminology which specifically avoids the psychological self-positioning and acceptance of marginalization the dominant order attempts to impose. Such creativity in linguistic expression is naturally a threat to the Authority who have proclaimed *JeJAL* illegal, confiscated it, harassed its publishers and even conducted frequent raids to rid the streets of these unwanted children.

Each issue of *JeJAL* contains comic strips that are drawn entirely by the children. In a community that varies in literacy abilities, the comic serves to bridge the gap between the literate and the illiterate, introduce the issue's main theme, and act as an incentive for the lesser literate to improve his skills. The comic figures that appear each month are *Mbah Mboro* (Father Boro) or *Mas Malio* (Elder Brother[16] Malio) where Boro and Malio are truncated forms of Malioboro, the main street of Yogyakarta. This is where many of the children ply their various trades, sleep, meet their friends, locate, recruit, and protect other children new to the streets. Mbah Mboro or Mas Malio then function as the spiritual father figures in the children's lives. They advise, respond, joke, and always represent an insider, yet adult, perspective on the life of the street child.

As a reflection of the life, experiences, words and perspectives of street children, these comics actually fulfill the definition of freedom of expression noted by Rendra. In these pages, freedom of expression is seen through the (street) artist's degree of contact with the (street and mainstream) people, (street) life, and nature as they 'express the truth or soul of society'. The comics are drawn by people who are so outside of mainstream society that they are mainly invisible (see Figure 1.5). The irony lies in the fact that those considering themselves recognized because of their adherence to the rules of society are permitted to be inhumane to others.

The street children, as exiles from recognition, are ironically able to be far more in touch with humanity. Thus, these unrecognized but humane street kids are able to speak very openly about topics most would be afraid to utter. Figures 1.5 and 1.6 show that to be recognized does not necessarily guarantee one's humanity by showing how the recognized can indeed act with extreme cruelty toward her own children. In the real Indonesian world, poor people, street people,

Figure 1.5 *Mbah Boro*, July 1994 – (1) hey . . . what's your name? You're a new street kid? Hang out here then, lots of friends. (2) (university) (5) Mbah, they say we have lots of friends here but it sure seems untrue. (6) It says in the wayang wait for official recognition. But always show your humanity.

33

Figure 1.6 *Mas Malio*, Feb 1994 – (1) Mas Malio, where is Mbah Boro? We want to say goodbye. We're going back home. (2) Hmm yesterday there was a police roundup. Maybe he got caught. (3) Several days later. Hey mas, I went home but my dad had gone without leaving word. (4) My village mas, has been transformed into a huge shopping center. Crazy! Nobody knows where the villagers have gone. (5) Maybe they transmigrated (to an outer island)? As for me, I did meet my father but he ordered me to leave again. (6) That's right mas. I'm sure he's patient, never disappears without a word. So then, let's just consider him our father!

prostitutes and beggars are made to disappear through official police or military cleansing operations. Family members disappear without a trace or throw away their unwanted children as the disposable evidence of their problems. Economic development permits those with more recognition than others to confiscate land and evict residents. Forced to grow up in a world dependent on these notions of legitimacy, Mas Malio suggests the children select the policeman at a busy intersection as their father, because unlike their own families, he is always around. Like the huge stone figures on Daliland, Authority figures maintain the status quo with relative ease. A tradition of deference assures mass acceptance of these symbols of social place and self-censorship becomes a highly potent means of stamping out creativity and dissent – but not entirely.

Final Remarks

As a symbolic reflection of social or political reality, this discussion has shown how the comic can present us with a rich store of social commentary, providing the medium is viewed through the lens of authoritarian control as the extremely narrow channel through which cultural identity is squeezed. Thus, unlike others that praise the comic as a tool of the weak, the mainstream comic book market or press has little place for this. The independent comics, which should come closer to Rendra's definition of free speech than other means of communication, display a jumbled blend of constrained expression or frenzied imagination, wayward identity and feudal hierarchies, pedantic control and misplaced hope, depression and desperate sexuality. Is this modern society? Looking at the street kid comics, which focus on the major themes in their lives, such as their own humanity within an inhumane world, I dare to say yes.

In this world in which printed materials are carefully scrutinized by a Minister of Information, where permission to publish must include no less than 20 official letters on top of a stamp from the local police attesting to the lack of political content or motivation, indigenous comics (or for that matter creativity), are not able to flourish. Meanwhile, the cartoon strip or the editorial cartoon often does reflect contemporary concerns as wrung through historical settings or the faux pas of clowns. The Mr. Bei (*Suara Merdeka*), Panji Koming (*Kompas*), or Doyok (*Pos Kota*) strips, which seem to come closer to social reality than other strips, have as their heroes well-intentioned but naïve middle-aged men. Despite their good intentions, the final panel often pictures the hero fallen silent, put back in place by the wife or a bureaucrat. Thus, he is a clown-like figure destined to lose.

Under these tightly constrained circumstances, this look at comics in Java reveals how political pressures on freedom of expression, in combination with the extended economic crisis and the increased costs of producing comics, are major factors in crushing what should be a thriving industry. There is little investment in local work, because it is not worth the economic or political risk. While the writings on the import comic boon all blame the victim, that is, they attack local artists for their inferior work, no one questions why local artists constantly revamp old themes. As Indonesian artists themselves have stated, nothing new comes out in local comics, and when it does, no one buys it. These areas need to be further investigated. When self-reflection is exchanged for indirectness and irrelevance because creativity is subversive, what happens to cultural identity?

Notes

* An early version of this paper was presented for the Seminars in Southeast Asian Studies, Monash University, Australia on 27 March 1997. The author wishes to thank Barbara Hatley, Anthonk, John Weeks, the Yogyakarta and Melbourne comic artists community for their comments and support.
1 I have no statistics on who buys what but it is obvious that both the press and comics attract huge numbers of readers. I also suspect, and this has been confirmed by Indonesians, that adults are the main readers of comic books.
2 I will not discuss *HumOr* again here, opting instead for more 'working class' humor and the work of artists/activists from Yogyakarta in Central Java. See Lent (1993) for discussion on this slick magazine.

3 Taboo topics are generally disclosures about the Soeharto family wealth and business dealings or disclosures about shoddy business dealings at public expense undertaken by high-ranking officials.

4 The magazine was expensive (around US$2.00 per issue) pricing it above the means of the majority of the population for whom $2.00 can feed a family for a few days.

5 Yet see Warren (1998) for discussion of political cartoons in the Balinese press.

6 Some Indonesians claim their comics originated in the relief sculptures that decorate their ancient temples, and in other traditions of communicating ancient texts such as *wayang bèbèr* (scrolled picture stories) and *lontar* (manuscripts on palm leaves, see Kusuma 1998; Tabrani 1998; Zaimar 1998). Whether these texts reflect indigenous concerns or Hindu imports is beyond the scope of this chapter. More significantly, these texts were not available to wide audiences. Thus, they will not be discussed here.

7 Meanwhile, the papers presented at the National Comic Seminar in Jakarta (7 February 1998) deny this and instead praise the national flavor of local comics as they stress its thousand year history by linking it to earlier means of creating stories with pictures. I was surprised to see at the conference that Balai Pustaka (Indonesia's oldest publishing house) prints some wonderfully professional, local comics. These comics, however, do not appear in the Balai's catalogue and apparently cannot be found in local book shops (see Berman 1998b for discussion).

8 The Gunung Agung book shop in Blok M, Jakarta actually sold some in 1993, when I bought the Baratayudha series (from the *Mahabarata*). These were old, but not second hand. In later trips (1996, 1997, and 1998) I searched again but none was available. There are two sources in Yogyakarta where people sell the comics they hid during the comic blitzes of the 1960s and 1970s.

9 No less than ten young artists from the Yogyakarta Art Institute have said this.

10 During a recent trip to Indonesia, I searched all over for a copy of this comic and found none. None of my *komikus* friends had one either. *If* it is still being published, it is certainly suffering distribution problems too.

11 The artist is still living in exile in Holland and the distributor was arrested and jailed.

12 In other respects this is thoroughly untrue. In the original version of the *Mahabarata*, all the Pandawas are married to Drupadi and none is survived by children, favoring aestheticism over sexuality. In the Javanese version, however, Arjuna is a great lover with many wives and lovers and spending much of his time in heaven among the goddesses (Zaimar 1998:6).

13 As of 1997, Core Comics has ceased to exist. Some of the artists who have graduated from the Art Institute, most notably Bambang Toko, are now creating comics independently and selling them through limited distribution. With the rise in paper and photocopy costs during the crisis of 1998, it is extremely likely such activities will be effected.

14 The artist and writer are senior to Athonk, who in turn is senior to the *Selingkuh* and *Core* artists. This hierarchy is very obvious to these artists who still look up to their elders with deference and for leadership. Even among activists, the social order is upheld.

15 *JeJAL* is an acronym for *jerit jalanan* or 'screams from the streets'. *Jejal* itself means crowded, jammed.

16 The Javanese use kinship terms as polite terms of address. Thus, *Mbah* and *mas* are both respectful terms for an elder person. Mbah is not gender specific, whereas mas refers only to males.

FROM SELF-KNOWLEDGE TO SUPER HEROES: THE STORY OF INDIAN COMICS

Aruna Rao

Comic books are hawked all over India, from large bookstores patronized by affluent customers, to roadside bookstalls protected from sunshine and rain by ragged canvas covers. Grocery stores in suburban neighborhoods and villages display comics alongside the new shampoos and sacks of rice, and small mom- and pop-operated 'lending' libraries rent out comics by the day. Middle-class children go to bookstalls in crowded markets to buy used comics for a few cents, and bubble gum and soft drink manufacturers give away comics with each purchase. Comics are now a ubiquitous part of contemporary India, but little is known about who makes them, and even less about who reads them. A similar situation exists with respect to most popular media in India, where the usual arrogant distinctions are made about what is 'Culture' and what is ephemeral 'trash'.

The urgency of the need for research into popular media lies in the fact that Indians consume vast amounts of media products everyday, yet very little is known about the content and effects of these media. As Reddi (1985) notes: 'Whether modern Indian youth will become the engineers, doctors, politicians and administrators of tomorrow, or whether the frustrations and despair of a developing society will lead to destabilization, social unrest, and new socio-political structures will be partially determined by the influences of the mass media'. The systematic study of Indian comics is difficult, mainly because they are part of the often ephemeral popular street culture. They are not considered important enough to be included in any archives, and even publishers rarely stock older issues. Many of the comics used for this author's analysis came from the lovingly preserved personal collections of comics writers, and illustrators[1] who were generous enough to loan their comics.

Armed with one survey of comics readership in India (Joshi 1986), I conducted a series of interviews with comics creators and publishers (Pai 1993, 1995; Puri 1993, 1995; Fernandes 1993; Subbarao 1993, 1995; Halbe 1993; Waeerkar 1993, 1995; Rai 1995; Kumar M. 1995; Surti 1995; Bhramania 1995; Uppal, 1995), collected all available comics reviews, and read a few hundred comics in order to answer the questions: how did comics originate in India; who makes them, and who reads them? All the answers are not forthcoming yet, but the broad picture made available is outlined in the following pages.

Comics as Self-knowledge

India has a long and varied tradition of pictorial art used for story telling, ranging from the cave paintings of Ajanta and Ellora to the scandal-mongering Kalighat paintings (*patas*) of nineteenth-century Bengal (Rao 1994). However, the modern comic book came into India rather late. The only comics available before the early 1970s came from the west. Cowboys and Indians in westerns, soldiers in trenches in World War II comics, *Archie*, *Phantom*, *Tarzan*, and *Mandrake the Magician* – these were the fantasy characters that peopled most children's imaginations. One comics writer (Surti 1995) recalled running after trains at railway crossings during World War II as British soldiers flung American comics at the screaming children pursuing the train.

In the 1970s, all this changed dramatically. As with all sudden media trends, this one has its own myths of origin and apocryphal stories. Everyone agrees, however reluctantly, that it all started with one man's infectious enthusiasm for cultural nationalism. Anant Pai, now a loquacious comics icon in his late sixties, was a young man in newly independent India in 1960. He was part of a generation of young men who arrived in India's big cities with little money, but plenty of ambition and big ideas. Pai was from a prominent family of southern industrialists, but had been orphaned at an early age, and reared by relatives. He had been infected with the heady patriotism of the time, when people believed that anything was possible in modern India. Pai trained as a chemical engineer, but chose to enter publishing, and in 1961 was employed by the publishing division of *The Times of India*, one of the oldest and largest newspapers in the country. Noticing that the press was not being used to its full capacity, he suggested to his supervisor that they print comic books. Since imported comics were popular, *The Times of India* decided to publish a comics series. His manager was a *Superman* fan, but Pai interviewed potential readers and recommended Lee Falk's *Phantom* comics as the series to be published. He decided that the *Phantom* series set in a steamy, tribal Africa would probably be a good bet, as the milieu might seem familiar to Indians. The comics sold very well, and Pai started putting together this fact with something close to his heart; the lack of interest and knowledge that middle-class children demonstrated about India's culture and history.

The legacy of a colonial school system, based on Macaulauy's notorious assertions (one being that a shelf of a good English library was enough to replace the entire literature of the Orient, and the other that Britain's purpose in colonizing India was to create a race of men English in every way, except for the color of their skin) had been readily accepted in the missionary schools where the middle and upper classes chose to send their children. When Pai asked a group of children to create a prototype for a comics magazine, he found that all their stories and pictures were derived from stereotypes of the British children's literature[2] that formed the staple reading matter for most urban, middle-class children. The stories involved daffodils and English boarding schools, but nothing from the immediate reality that these children experienced. On another occasion, he watched a TV quiz show through the display window of a store in Delhi in 1967, where contestants racked up scores when asked about Churchill and Socrates, but fell silent when asked to name Rama's mother[3].

He tried to interest *The Times of India* in his idea of an indigenous comic book for children, one that would gain the approval of parents and teachers by providing information on Indian myth and history, but met with little success. In 1967, he finally sold his idea to a Bombay-based publisher, India Book House. He decided to name the series *Amar Chitra Katha*, which translates as 'Immortal Picture Stories', or alternately, 'Our Picture Stories'.

Together with illustrator Ram Waeerkar, Pai produced the first issue of *Krishna* in 1969, followed by *Shakuntala*, *The Pandava Princes*[4], and various other mythological stories. Sales were slow initially (20,000 copies in the first three years), but by the late 1970s, *Amar Chitra Katha*, published in five regional languages and English[5], was selling about five million copies a year, and had a peak circulation of about seven lakhs (700,000) a month (Kapada 1986). India Book House began bringing out at least one comic a month by 1975, and sometimes even brought out as many as three in a month. While Pai initially wrote the first few stories himself, he soon hired a core team of writers and editors, including Subbarao, Luis Fernandes, and Kamala Chandrakant. This team was largely responsible for the attempt at authenticity and balanced portrayal of history in comic books that became the hallmark of *Amar Chitra Katha*.

Pictures and stories: how the comics look and sound

Amar Chitra Katha illustrations emphasize a pictorial, realistic style, and are usually static, with more talking heads than action. A peculiarity of most comics artwork in India is the lack of attention to backgrounds. Instead, characters are carefully drawn and colored, with great attention to period costumes and jewelry (see Figure 2.1). This attention to detail was part of the larger effort to make these comics authentic, or at least to avoid the error of omission in depicting actual historical events, or mythical figures with popular appeal. The *Amar Chitra Katha* style became an established convention, and is still visible in the current crop of comics that have little to do with history.

The quality of the artwork is often uneven, and reflects either the talents or inadequacies of the freelance artists employed. Comics illustrators often refuse to identify themselves as such, as much of their income comes from providing illustrations for advertising or magazines. An interesting exception to this rule is Pratap Mullick, a veteran comics illustrator who now runs his own comics studio and training workshop in Pune, Maharashtra, and provides illustrations to every

Figure 2.1 *Tales of Durga*, *Amar Chitra Katha* (Courtesy of India Book House).

major comics publisher in India. Most illustrators, such as Mullick and Ram Waeerkar[6], have developed a vigorous, cinematic style that resembles calendar art, or film posters, but do not depart radically from western styles. Perhaps the only illustrator who drew strongly from indigenous traditions of painting was Kavadi, who died a few years ago. His characters, with their rounded faces, plump bodies, and enormous, expressive eyes, are distinctly Indian, and recall the image of classical Bharatanatyam dancers.

The content of speech balloons in *Amar Chitra Katha* is often stilted and didactic, obviously stemming from the 'serious' educational approach writers have (see Figure 2.2). The attempt is more to instruct than entertain, and writers take pride in the fact that they do not use colloquialisms or slang (Puri 1995).

40

Figure 2.2 *Tales of Durga, Amar Chitra Katha* (Courtesy of India Book House).

Kamala Chandrakant, the writer who shaped this way of writing, made the interesting observation that she was writing for an audience that spoke an Indian language at home, but wanted their children to read English (Subbarao 1995). All Indian languages have a formal written form, and an informal spoken form, and perhaps the comics try to mimic this feature in English.

The rise of Amar Chitra Katha: *marketing strategies and cultural nationalism*

The 1970s and early 1980s were the peak of *Amar Chitra Katha* popularity. Their success can be partly attributed to clever marketing strategies, and the publicity that Pai managed to generate. The marketing was directed towards urban centers, where Pai has an enormous following among children as 'Uncle Pai'[7]. He organized quiz contests and fancy-dress competitions, gave away prizes, and flooded petrol pumps and bookstores with displays. He received press coverage by asking famous people to release new comics. This was a very clever marketing tactic, as being associated with prominent nationalists, politicians, and government officials lent an air of official sanction for the publication, and the comics themselves reached the status of revered cultural icons. For instance, the Prime Minister at the time, Rajiv Gandhi (who received a lot of flak by admitting in Parliament that comics were his favorite reading material), released *March to Freedom* based on the independence movement. The Archbishop of Bombay, Simon Pimenta, released *Jesus Christ*, a comics biography of Jesus. By 1980, *Amar Chitra Katha* had acquired fame even among Indians abroad, and been translated into 38 languages, including French, Swahili, and Serbocroat.

In 1980, riding on the comics boom generated by *Amar Chitra Katha*, India Book House started publishing a fortnightly comic called *Tinkle*[8], a comics magazine for children that included short humorous fiction, as well as educational non-comics sections dealing with history or science. It developed a very popular interactive format, in which children sent in a story, which was then edited and illustrated by *Tinkle* staff, and published with the child's name and photograph. Subbarao (1995), the man who initiated this format, notes that

> some of these stories, which grandparents know, some uncle knows, some old man knows, the idea is somehow if children hear about it, they will bring such stories to our notice, and then we give it in comics format. That was our plan. That's why we gave *Reader's choice*. And then it was a huge success. We used to receive 200 stories in a month, from our readers.

Tinkle built on the success of *Amar Chitra Katha* by moving beyond history and mythology to depict contemporary situations for children, as well as providing humor in the comics.

The reasons for the enormous popularity of *Amar Chitra Katha* are not hard to explain. The unique historical and political circumstances of the times made these comics an important part of the emerging national identity of India. Immediately after independence in 1947, there was a political upheaval that resulted in a power struggle between the earlier feudal power structure preserved by the British, and the newly elected socialist government (Spear 1965). By the end of the 1970s relative political and social stability had been achieved, and children of this generation grew up with a fairly stable idea of the nation as a geographical and cultural unit, with undisputed boundaries. There was a democratically elected government in power, and there were distinct goals for the children of the middle class. Technology and science were all-important in terms of formal education, as per the Nehruvian[9] model of development, but Gandhi's legacy[10] was an uneasy reminder that there was more to nation-building than industrial-economic strength.

The solution was to weld scientific rationalism to a sort of cohesive Hinduism modeled on Christianity and Islam (Fuller 1992), while also incorporating the traditional family structure. While progress increasingly meant westernization of the outer domain of politics and lifestyle, the inner domain of religious belief and family was less amenable to change (Chatterjee 1986, 1990). In this context, comics filled an important void in the life of families. Parents wanted their children to learn English, and be ready for an increasingly westernized world, but were also uneasy about the lack of traditional cultural knowledge that this lifestyle resulted in. *Amar Chitra Katha* provided a way for parents to accomplish the task of cultural education with little effort. In this way, *Amar Chitra Katha* played an important part in the transmission of traditional stories and myths.

Issues of representation

The widespread popularity of *Amar Chitra Katha* led to public interest in its content to an unprecedented degree. Elite newspapers and magazines that previously would not have concerned themselves with comics began to examine the phenomenon. The initial surge of approval for comics diminished somewhat as different agendas began to surface. Criticism of the comics largely revolved around two issues; the portrayal of women, and the portrayal of minorities.

Women's groups protested the stereotyping of female characters. Moralists in a notoriously puritanical society were concerned about the sexual content, which was largely limited to the depiction of women in costumes that showed more skin than contemporary attire did. It was pointed out that men outnumbered women in the comics, and also had more active roles. Women were shown most often as wives or mothers, and were nearly always shown as self-sacrificing. These findings were in tune with studies of media representation of sex roles worldwide, which have suggested that women are outnumbered by men in the mass media, and are primarily shown in a domestic or sexual context (Gallagher 1981, 1983; Signorelli 1986; Krishnan and Dighe 1990). Men, on the other hand, tend to be shown as employed, often in high-status, traditionally male occupations (Craig 1992). Most media studies, however, have been conducted with mainstream media such as television or newspapers.

The issue that raised the most controversy was the depiction of *satis*, or widows who voluntarily or involuntarily committed suicide by immolating themselves on their husband's funeral pyre. Sati[11] was an upper-caste Hindu practice that was outlawed in the nineteenth century by the colonial British administration in response to the demands of Indian social reformers. In this context, the depiction of sati in *Amar Chitra Katha* was offensive. In the *Amar Chitra Katha Ranak Devi*, the title character entreats her brother to bring back the body of her dead husband, who was killed in a confrontation with a Muslim ruler, so that she can commit sati. The comic ends with a picture of Ranak Devi seated tranquilly on a pyre, holding her husband's head on her lap, surrounded 'by flames. In another comic, *Padmini*, the title character is a beautiful queen whose husband is killed by a Muslim king who lusts after her. She leads the women of her court in *jauhar*, a practice similar to sati where all of the women of a court commit mass suicide by burning alive rather than submit to a conqueror.

Other areas of controversy involved religious and cultural representations in *Amar Chitra Katha*. Some groups complained that either the comics departed too drastically from their mythological and historical sources, and others that they had not gone far enough in removing the prejudices of their sources. For example, Pai's effigy was burnt in the state of Punjab after the publication of the comic *Ramayana*, as followers of Valmiki, the sage (*rishi*) credited with authoring the well-known Hindu epic poem of the same name, objected to his portrayal as a reformed thief in the comic. More seriously, *Amar Chitra Katha* was accused of promoting the superiority of a Bhramanical Hindu culture at the expense of other Indian cultures. The stories tend to be told from the point of view of brave, nationalistic Hindu warriors (although there was no cohesive Hindu kingdom on the lines of the modern nation at the time being depicted [Spear 1965]), while Muslim invaders are depicted as cruel and untrustworthy. Another factor is the depiction of characters according to popular standards of beauty that reflect Aryan notions of hierarchy. Heroes are fair-skinned and straight nosed, while villains are dark-skinned and aboriginal in appearance.

Violence, depicted with splattered blood and headless bodies, is common, and war is usually shown as a noble and righteous activity undertaken in service of religion, nationalism, or even as part of a cosmic plan. The caste hierarchy is usually depicted uncritically, with low-caste characters shown as morally repugnant because of their caste-based professions, such as carrying nightsoil, tanning leather, or cremating the dead (see Figure 2.3). For example, in *Harishchandra*, a king dedicated to telling the truth is tested by the gods. He loses everything he owns, and even sells his wife and child in his pursuit of truth. He reaches the very last level of wretchedness when he is forced to work as a servant to a Chandala, a member of an untouchable caste who cremate the dead. While the Chandala eventually turns out to be the god of death in disguise, the depiction of untouchability as a justified social practice is deeply troubling.

While issues dealing with non-Hindu topics have been published, they are few and far between; for instance, 50 out of 436 titles are about primary characters who are Muslims. In the recent past, *Amar Chitra Katha* has brought out limited editions of its 50 best-selling titles. Of these, 21 are stories of Hindu gods, fourteen deal with stories taken from Hindu mythological sources, thirteen deal with actual historical personages, of which one each is Muslim, Buddhist, and Jain, and only two are not religious figures. The remaining two deal with popular animal folktales from Buddhist sources. Even in an informal survey, these titles are not inclusive of the vast range of stories of the different regions and people of India.

In this context, it is instructive to hear Subbarao's (1995) recollection of a comics character he created in *Tinkle*, a comic magazine which did not have the burdens of historical or mythological authenticity to carry. While editing the

Figure 2.3 *Harishchandra, Amar Chitra Katha* (Courtesy of India Book House).

stories that children sent in, he noticed the paucity of non-Hindu characters in the stories. Additionally, even when Muslim children sent in stories, they used Hindu names for the characters. In his words:

I noticed that 100% stories had Hindu names. Including stories sent by children in Hyderabad[12], by Muslim kids. A Muslim child writing the story, his own story, he would give the name like Ramu, Krishna, or Govinda or Radha[13], there was no Hussein. Apparently, they were shy, or it never occurred to them. The cultural domination of the Hindus is so high. Like maybe convent educated kids would think of writing a story in New

York or London, here Muslim children would use Hindu names. So I created a character called Anwar, a Muslim boy, his parents were educated Muslims, and I used to write under the name Appaswamy. Anwar became a big hit. And that gave *Tinkle* a kind of image that nothing else did. The first time Muslim children took part in large numbers when Pai went to Hyderabad. And *Tinkle* is popular with Muslim community. I think we have to thank Anwar for it. It is very significant for anybody wanting to make a sociological study, you know. Anwar is still a popular character.

When faced with criticism, the writers of the comics initially argued (Subbarao 1993, 1995) that they cannot factually distort the classics, and that they merely reproduce a historical text as it exists. The writers had a generally unfavorable opinion of the 'intellectuals' who criticized their work. As far as they were concerned, the comic had to have a strong plot, a story that entertained, and be true to its source. The fact that the source could be reinterpreted for contemporary thought had not occurred to them.

Then, fueled by the good intentions of the editorial team, India Book House began to develop a response. They made an effort to find stories depicting women and minorities as protagonists. Then, they began an extensive process of self-censorship, examining each comic to ensure that it was as fair as possible to all protagonists. After a while, an unfortunate consequence of self-censorship was that the comics began to seem as dry and dusty as the historical texts they were based on. Wary of criticism, and conscious of their juvenile audience, *Amar Chitra Katha* began to pursue documentation and fairness to all parties to such a degree that the comics looked like illustrated versions of history textbooks, complete with reference lists. The motives of the *Amar Chitra Katha* creators were more than laudable; they wanted to make comics that were fair to all protagonists, and were willing to consider perspectives that were not currently popular. However, this textual orientation began to undercut the efficacy of the medium. The visual power of the comic was diluted by a reliance on large amounts of printed text. As Subbarao (1995) puts it,

> Around that time I think we started taking *Amar Chitra Katha* too seriously. It ceased to be an entertaining medium. Maybe we thought that whatever is in *Amar Chitra Katha* becomes the gospel truth for readers. Possibly we made mistakes. We are much better than some of the history textbooks. Still, it may not be very entertaining.

How Amar Chitra Katha ended

At this time, *Tinkle* continues to be successful, despite the competition from other comics and television. *Amar Chitra Katha* has not been as fortunate; after sales dropped to below 40,000 in a month, India Book House stopped issuing new titles. Presently, the comics are being repackaged in a glossier format to be sold as limited editions. The conventional wisdom is that the decline of *Amar Chitra Katha* by the beginning of the 1990s signals the increasing impact of commercial television on the urban schoolchildren who constituted their basic audience. On the other hand, former employees of India Book House and competitors suggest that *Amar Chitra Katha* had exhausted its source of popular historical and mythological stories (Uppal 1995). Additionally, former employees point to internal dissent within India Book House, based on disagreement with Pai's controlling management style.

The breakup of India Book House has resulted in a new and differently organized comics industry. Subbarao and Luis Fernandes, both former writers for India Book House, attempted to start a new comic series, but did not have much commercial success. They now market syndicated comic strips to newspapers and magazines. New entrants to the comics market, mostly based in Hindi-speaking north India, are significantly different from *Amar Chitra Katha* in style and content. *Amar Chitra Katha* continues to have a loyal following, especially among the young adults who grew up with these comics as their main source of information on Indian history and mythology, and in turn, want to give the same resource to their children. They also appeal to the Indian diaspora in countries such as Britain and the United States.

While acknowledging and addressing the issues of representation in the comics, *Amar Chitra Katha* still remains the most original and dynamic contribution to comics in India. Its commitment to creating an audience for age-old stories and to educating children in their cultural history has not been matched by any other comics publisher in India.

The Arrival of the Super Hero: Bahadur

While *Amar Chitra Katha* was the trailblazer in terms of publishing comics in India, other publishers also saw the potential for comics. The *Phantom* series published by *The Times of India* did so well that they established the *Indrajal Comics* series, and brought out other action-adventure titles like *Mandrake the Magician*. In 1976, *Indrajal* published its first indigenous series, based on the action-adventure hero, Bahadur ('The Courageous One' in Hindi).

In this popular series, created by cartoonist and artist Abid Surti, Bahadur is a vigilante in the tradition of the Phantom and Mandrake. Respected by the police for his abilities, he is often called in for help. However, he dispenses with masks and secret identities for an image of modernity with rural roots. Bahadur's appearance represents the Indian appropriation of westernization into traditionalism – he is tall and mustachioed, and always wears blue jeans with a saffron *kurta*, a homespun Indian shirt (see Figure 2.4). Surti (1995) notes that each item of clothing has its own associations. The blue jeans indicate Bahadur's western style modernity, while the kurta shows his affiliation to his Indian roots. Saffron, which appears on the Indian flag, is also the ancient color of renunciation and purity, and is often worn by holy men and monks.

47

Figure 2.4 *The Web of Hatred, Indrajal Comics* (Courtesy of The Times of India Publishing Division).

Bahadur's work on the right side of the law represents how he transcended the circumstances of his birth. His father was a bandit (*dacoit*) who was killed by the police, and though he initially sought revenge, he was won over by the very police inspector who shot his father. This convoluted beginning is typical of the Hindi film (Chakravarty 1993), where paternal legacies are often overcome through personal effort, as they rarely are in real life. Also similar to the Hindi film is the clouding or outright omission of factors that Indians deal with and place great importance on every day. Issues of religion, caste, family origin, and class are not given importance, as the omission of Bahadur's last name and his lack of explicit religious affiliation show.

48

ARUNA RAO

Figure 2.5 *The Ill-Fated Outlaws*, *Indrajal Comics* (Courtesy of The Times of India Publishing Division).

Another interesting feature of the *Bahadur* series is the recurring role of Bela as Bahadur's girlfriend, who is allowed an active role that women in comics rarely are (see Figure 2.5). At first, she was presented only as Bahadur's girlfriend, an ambiguous mixture of demure sari clad Indian woman and resourceful companion. Gradually, she became the center of many of the comics, with some featuring her on the cover alone as the karate-chopping nemesis of the villains. She was also presented as a student, with wide-ranging interests in areas such as ecology and history. Such interests made her a catalyst for change in the stories, allowing her to bring up issues that became the focus of the story. There may be some autobiographical element to this transformation in Bela. Jagjit Uppal, the

49

writer who made Bela an important feature of the comics, speaks frequently of his wife as a companion in creating stories, and was perhaps drawn to create a similar companion for Bahadur. She was the ideal woman, 'a research scholar in chemistry or bio-chemistry' and also 'a black belt in karate' (Uppal 1995).

The series was aimed at pre-teens, and through most of the first ten years, Bela was always treated somewhat bashfully. She was fashionably dressed, but rarely depicted as a sex object. If a villain made leering comments about her, or even grabbed her, such acts of disrespect quickly dissolved into apology as she beat him up. Similarly, she was a perpetual girlfriend, sharing a seemingly blissful, asexual relationship with Bahadur without seeking any more intimacy than was considered appropriate for a pre-teen readership. By the 1990s, social attitudes towards sexuality had changed a little, and other comics that had risen as competitors were far more explicit. Additionally, long-time illustrator Govind Bhramania was replaced by his son, Pramod Bhramania. So, Bela was made into a more sexual figure. In many of the later comics, Bela is a teenage boy's dream, with endless panels of her jogging into the sunrise, or posing as a snake charmer's apprentice in skimpy costumes (see Figure 2.6). Bela and Bahadur began to talk in a more grown-up fashion, and in the final comic, there is a near-proposal. As Uppal (1995) puts it,

> They were always together. In fact, we were on the verge of getting them married. We were planning that. They went to one *Adivasi* (tribal) place ... Bela and Bahadur's place. I was planning to take them there for their wedding ... So, in that story, Bela says, is this a proposal? And he says, well, I don't know, and suddenly, when they come home, and chief (police inspector) is waiting. So he says, okay, there goes the proposal.

The *Bahadur* series context reflects the dominant motifs of the 1970s and 1980s in India. Bahadur's enemies are dacoits, or bandits, who made a living by raiding surrounding villages in the Chambal Valley (a mountainous area of Madhya Pradesh state in North India). The spare, dusty, sparsely populated Chambal Valley is similar to the American 'wild west', and captured the popular imagination of Indians in much the same way[14]. Bahadur, with the blessings of local police too far away from remote areas to be of immediate help, forms the Citizens Security Force (CSF), a 'voluntary organization engaged in self-protection' (*Indrajal Comics*, No. 364) or a militant, armed, paramilitary force that protects the villagers from the dacoit raids. In Bahadur's many battles with evil, it is increasingly obvious that he is a role model for the young Indian. He lectures captured dacoits on the values of hard work and honesty and extols the virtues of being Indian. In one comic the chief of police addresses Bahadur in front of a village audience: 'We're all proud of you, Bahadur, to have brought this awakening amongst villagers. Today they are not only aware of their rights, but are conscious of their duties towards the state and country' (*Indrajal Comics*, Vol. 21, no. 11).

The message of the *Bahadur* series is positive in many ways; it suggests that people can transform their future through their own efforts, a redemptive

Figure 2.6 *The Snake Charmer's Bait, Indrajal Comics* (Courtesy of The Times of India Publishing Division).

message for a society that is rigidly hierarchical. It also suggests, however, that violence is a natural enough manner in which this change can be made, and occasionally, that class privileges are fixed.

The rise and fall of Indrajal Comics

The creation of the *Bahadur* series has been credited to *Indrajal Comics* manager, A. C. Shukla, as well as Abid Surti, the writer responsible for the early success of *Bahadur*. Surti, who considers himself an artist rather than a comics creator, now makes stained glass for a living. Besides Bahadur, he also created other comic strips based on characters such as Shuja, a Tarzan-like tribal action hero, and detective comics like *Inspector Vikram* and *Inspector Azad*. Surti is unique in the Indian comics industry for being adept in both writing and illustrating comics. He soon tired of a management attitude that did not allow him control over his creations, and cut himself off from comics after the 1980s. He was one of the few people involved in Indian comics who saw them as a medium with potential for artistic experimentation, besides being a straightforward way to tell a story. His comics have an energy and appeal that few others manage to emulate.

After Surti's departure, *Bahadur* was written and illustrated by others, most prominently including Jagjit Uppal, now a celebrity astrologer. Uppal, who has set up shop in the famous Taj Hotel in Bombay (the hotel store carries an elegantly lettered sign urging guests to consult the in-house astrologer), is now far-removed from the comics, but eager to claim credit for *Bahadur*. Uppal is very different from Surti in every way. Surti is more comfortable speaking Hindi or Gujarati, and a stereotypical absent-minded artist, often moving in conversation from child-like delight in a comics plot to philosophical musing. Uppal, on the other hand, speaks Oxbridge-enunciated English, chain-smokes imported cigarettes, and claims descent from India's former aristocracy. This personal interest in Indian history led to his first comics writing stint with *Amar Chitra Katha*. While Uppal is full of a particularly upper-class snobbery, he is unexpectedly and disarmingly affectionate about the characters in *Bahadur*, and seems to have genuinely enjoyed his ability to write stories based on current events and his own travels.

During Uppal's tenure at *Indrajal Comics*, Bahadur acquired super hero musculature, and a tight sweatshirt to replace the kurta (see Figure 2.7), to mirror Uppal's aesthetics ('those were the days you wore a kurta with jeans, most of the artists were wearing that. So I said, let him wear the jeans, no doubt, but let him wear a jersey … I didn't like long hair and all that, I said make him a gentleman' Uppal 1995). The action also moved from the Chambal Valley to more cosmopolitan surroundings. Bahadur himself seemed cosmopolitan, hunting down international smuggling rings on the high seas, or nabbing environmental terrorists. Bela acquired an overt sexiness missing in the earlier comics, and also began to function independently of Bahadur.

Uppal, along with his wife Kamini as a writing partner, also created another *Indrajal Comics* series, based on Dara, 'the Prince of Spies'. Of royal descent, educated in England, and fond of well-cut suits in his public life, Dara seems like an underemployed playboy, but he also has a secret identity: that of a member of an elite secret service. When called upon by his country, Dara hunts down terrorists in the Kashmir Valley, and helps out the heads of state of friendly foreign countries. However, Dara never acquired the popularity and status of Bahadur, and after attempting one more character, Aditya, the yogic super hero, *Indrajal Comics* closed shop.

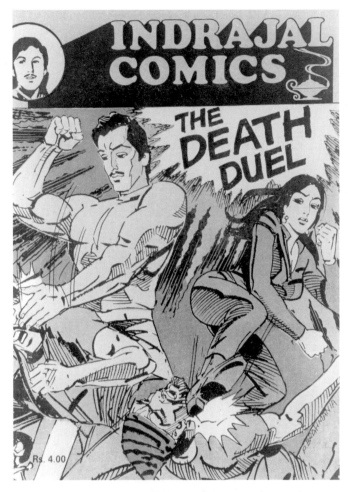

Figure 2.7 *The Death Duel, Indrajal Comics* (Courtesy of The Times of India Publishing Division).

By 1981, *Indrajal Comics* had monthly sales of nearly 5.8 lakh (580,000) copies (Singh 1982). However, the company was closed down in 1990. As in the case of *Amar Chitra Katha*, the reasons for ceasing publication are unclear. Reports in newspapers indicated that flagging sales forced *Indrajal Comics* to close down. At the time, it was noted that *Indrajal Comics* were being published only in Hindi and Bengali (North Indian languages). They had formerly been published in Marathi and English (languages marketable in the Bombay region) till the previous year, and three years before that, in the south in Tamil, Kannada, and Malayalam. The slow withdrawal from other language editions suggests that the series could no longer maintain the national appeal necessary to sustain sales. Other reasons were cited, namely the competition from television and video, as well as from small publishers who sprang up overnight with cheaper adventure comics. Another reason offered was that the context of the series became dated in the 1990s, as the dacoit gangs of the Chambal Valley had surrendered to police by then. However, Jagjit Uppal asserts that there were no external reasons to close the company, and that there was internal conflict within the management group.

> ... this was the idea of that person who was handling the management of *The Times of India*, who thought that because of the challenge of TV. Even the last issue was on sale, the order copies was the same, none of the distributors had reduced the number of copies. There was a tussle between the management, I had nothing to do with that. But the editor at the time told me, that it's surprising that our figures are maintaining, or rather it's increasing, why it had to be shut down. I don't know. (Uppal 1995).

Uppal believes that the publishing group changed its interests from comics to other media, and therefore decided to close the comics unit down.

The New Comics: super heroes to the rescue

At the time that the predominantly English-language, nationally oriented comics industry experienced a loss of audience due to creative or corporate differences, regional comics publishers took over the comics industry. The new comics emerged from Delhi, the capital city in North India, where the business and cultural climate is very different from cosmopolitan Bombay. The boom was led by a Delhi-based publisher, Diamond Comics. Their success spawned a series of similar ventures, leading to a frequently changing landscape of comics that seemingly appear overnight, and disappear just as fast. Most, like Diamond Comics, are offshoots of businesses that already publish Hindi language pulp fiction, and are based in Delhi and surrounding towns, such as Meerut.

Diamond Comics: designs for a media empire

Diamond Comics is a family-owned business, currently operated by Gulshan Rai and Narendra Kumar, brothers who inherited their parents' modest publishing company. Diamond Pocket Books was the original company, and specialized in Hindi pulp fiction and religious texts. That part of the business still exists, but the brothers have diversified into comics and magazines, and are now exploring the possibility of entering film or animation.

Diamond Comics publishes three kinds of comics. Of these, the most well known comics are *Pran's Features*, a series created by the cartoonist Pran Kumar Sharma, who prefers to go by his first name. These are primarily short gag cartoons compiled into comics format. *Pran's Features* mostly depict urban, middle-class family situations. The most popular of these characters is Chacha

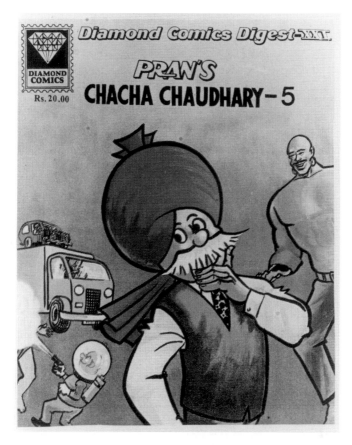

Figure 2.8 *Chacha Chandhary* (Courtesy of Diamond Comics).

(Uncle) Chaudhary, based on the exploits of an avuncular, turban wearing hero, sporting a giant handlebar mustache, who is accompanied by a gigantic alien sidekick from Jupiter called Sabu (see Figure 2.8). In a market survey (Diamond Comics Press Release) 10–13-year-olds ranked Chacha Chaudhary as their most recognizable character in comic books. He was also ranked as the third most recognizable character among teens and young adults. Pran (1995) explains the success of his creation in this way: 'Each family has its wise old man. He solved his problems with common sense, but with a touch of humor. Humor is the base of my cartoons'. Maneesh Kumar (1995), the son of Diamond Comics co-founder Narendra Kumar, suggests that Chacha Chaudhary was a familiar figure to the rural or less westernized middle-class:

> What we came out with was mass entertainment. Chacha Chaudhary was a mass kind of a character, which was basically a character of a village. An

old man full of wisdom. That is in a village. This is based on the fact that in the late 1970s, even till the early 1980s, the young generation was not given any importance in any field, maybe it was in business, or social life. So the old man in the house, or the head of the family was given more importance.

Other series from *Pran's Features* range from *Shrimatiji* (the Indian equivalent of addressing a woman as 'Mrs.'), about a wisecracking middle-class housewife, to *Pinki*, about a precocious young girl. Again, their popularity is attributed to the fact that readers can identify with them. Maneesh Kumar (1995) notes that 'Billoo, Shrimatiji are life-like characters. Because you see these things in everyday life. Shrimatiji you see in every household. Billoo you see in every household'. Pran believes it is his ability to tap into the humor of everyday details that attracts readers. He also asserts that his comics are 'message-oriented', a phrase that most comics creators believe is an indication of their moral strength. He says, 'First I make my readers laugh, when they open their mouth, I put the message in'. This kind of down-home moralizing is rampant in *Pran's Features*, and a point of honor in Diamond Comics rivalry with the other Delhi comics, Raj Comics and Manoj Comics, both of which specialize in horror and fantasy comics which have few claims to a 'message'.

The second area that Diamond Comics focuses on are feature length action-adventure comics, such as *Mahabali Shaka*, about a Tarzan-like hero, *Dynamite*, based on a brooding anti-hero reared in a circus, and *Agniputra Abhay*, about a boy who can summon up a super-human alter ego to fight crime. Of these, *Dynamite* is the series that Diamond Comics is most interested in promoting, and perhaps an indication of the direction they intend to go in. The series demonstrates the strong influence of Hindi film on both the creators and the readers of Diamond Comics. The protagonist is a brooding, social outcast prone to fits of violence, closely modeled on the popular anti-hero of the movie *Khalnayak*. Much of the success of the movie was attributed to the physical attributes of actor Sanjay Dutt, who set a precedent among his contemporaries for working out and acquiring a Hollywood-inspired body. Dynamite is drawn to resemble Dutt closely, down to the floppy rock-star hair. *Dynamite* can be described as an Indian appropriation of western pop culture icons such as Rambo.

Finally, Diamond Comics brings out *Film Chitrakatha*, a black and white photonovella series that summarizes the plots of newly released Hindi films. These comics feature bloody melodramas, sunny musicals, breast-beating tragedies, or a combination of all three. Their popularity is linked inextricably with the popularity of Hindi film.

Quantity, not quality

The process of producing Diamond Comics is managed like a factory that begins and ends with the editor, who is often a member of the family. The editor frequently produces a story concept and sends it to a writer, who writes a story and sends it to the illustrator. If the visuals are approved, another writer writes the dialogue, a group of illustrators draw the cover illustration, and others draw the rest of the comic. There are still other people hired as translators to rewrite the dialogue in the various languages in which the comics are eventually published. Most of these employees are freelancers and paid by the page.

This style of comics creation results in a colorful, wildly incoherent, and usually crude product. Despite this, the comics also convey an exuberant energy, suggesting that the people who make the comics are also the ones who read them. There is no talking down to the audience here; the language is colloquial and uncensored; there are hilariously off-center plots and plenty of violence. The influences on these comics are obviously American super hero comics and Hindi films. The overall impression is as if someone with little English read western comics, was impressed by the artwork, and frankly could make no sense of the story, and so decided to substitute his or her own plot onto the illustrations. Consequently, there are masked super heroes who go home to their parents at night, and villainesses seeking to blow up the universe because they cannot find a man to marry.

The stories are often almost dreamlike in their brevity, graphic violence, and improbable plots. These are obviously hastily put together comics, and cater to a very different audience from the English-speaking middle class children that *Tinkle* targets. These comics are often available in newsstands in train and bus stations, as well as street bookstalls in major urban areas, which are patronized by less affluent customers than the major bookstores. However, with no objective market studies conducted as yet, it is difficult to know just who the readers are. It has been speculated that they are the 'neo-literate' urban population, including working-class urbanites as well as recent migrants from rural areas (Subbarao 1995).

Marketing Diamond Comics: a free gift with every purchase!

The success of Diamond Comics is directly related to the decline of the Bombay comics industry, and to the company's own marketing skills. As the Bombay comics began to fold, a large number of seasoned comics illustrators and writers were suddenly available to work quickly and cheaply. The only serious competitor in comics was *Tinkle*, which was oriented towards a narrow, English-speaking, middle-class consumer base. An untapped audience, largely consisting of children as well as young, working class, neo-literate men in small towns, or recently arrived in metropolitan areas, was looking for the kind of inexpensive entertainment that comics could provide. To attract this reader, Diamond Comics jumped on a bandwagon increasingly common in Indian business – marketing partnerships. *Amar Chitra Katha*, *Tinkle*, and *Indrajal Comics* had always been a focus for advertising products aimed at children and teenagers, such as candy and soft drinks. Diamond Comics took this a step further by directly associating their comics with consumer products. For example, Diamond Comics created a new comics character called the Rasna Genie to market a soft drink concentrate called Rasna, and placed inserts featuring this character in their other popular comics. Rai (1995) describes this process as '...we are encouraging our advertiser to join hands with us, to reach to the distributor, or to the user, with their cooperation. Suppose, the bubble gum manufacturer wants to join with us, we distribute a bubble gum with our comic'. Rai ticks off an impressive list of corporations that he says are interested in tie-ins with his comics, including multinationals like Pepsi-Co, and giant national corporations like the textile manufacturer Vimal.

The emergence of Diamond Comics as the dominant comics publisher signals a significant change in the aims and attitudes of the comics industry. While Rai pays lip service to the idea of responsible publishing for children, perhaps mainly in an effort to denigrate his rivals, the bottom line is the main concern at Diamond. The sense of moral responsibility and ethical constraints that pervaded *Amar Chitra Katha*, and to a lesser extent *Indrajal Comics*, is no longer the primary concern of comics. Rai (1995) jokes that 'We always try to give the facts, but if somebody objects then we change it'. He also notes that, 'We have to live in the market, we have to live in the environment ... We had to change certain things according to the circumstances, *na*, otherwise we cannot do the business, you know, we are commercial people'. This pragmatism has allowed Diamond Comics to become the best selling comics in India.

Others in the fray

While Diamond Comics is clearly the leading comics publisher today, other comics are emerging in Delhi and surrounding areas that have achieved a fair amount of success. The two most prominent rivals are Raj Comics and Manoj Comics, who in a plot that could have come from the comics, are owned by estranged brothers. Both specialize in a blend of action, fantasy, and horror comics hard to categorize. Many of the comics illustrations and plots appear to be appropriated from western comics, but are also uniquely Indian in their incorporation of this influence. Additionally, the influences of *Amar Chitra Katha*, folk tales, and urban myths are also strong.

Raj Comics is owned by Maneesh Gupta, a young businessman who operates a production facility on the outskirts of Delhi. An uniformed guard and heavy gates protect the unit, perhaps an indication of the conflicts within the Delhi comics industry, where warehouses have been mysteriously set on fire in the recent past. Raj Comics is an offshoot of Raja Pocket Books, which publishes pulp fiction in Hindi. Much of this background is similar to Diamond Comics, but Raj Comics has not ventured into any market outside the Hindi-speaking north.

Raj Comics typically specializes in four kinds of comics: medieval fantasies, in which manufactured rural and urban legends are set in a vaguely delineated medieval past involving swords and sorcery; horror comics published in the *Thrill Horror Suspense* series, with stories involving mad scientists who turn into giant bats, or a man murdered by his own shadow; super hero comics, where a hero with a special ability or mutation battles villains, and comedies.

The fantasy comics surprisingly have a strong narrative, and even more surprisingly, showcase strong female protagonists. The stories are usually coherent, with a tone very similar to the ornate, melodramatic style of movie dialogue. There is a great deal of consistency in these comics, with the same writer's name appearing in many of the same kind of comics. Pratap Mullick, the former *Amar Chitra Katha* illustrator who now runs his own comics workshop, usually provides the richly detailed cover art. Most illustrators appear to have trained with *Amar Chitra Katha*, and are familiar with the 'historical' setting, costumes, and architectural details used to lend an air of authenticity to the comics.

Horror comics are very similar to the fantasies, albeit with a lot more blood and gore. Plots can be bizarre, such as *Jantar-Mantar-Chu*, in which a newborn infant is possessed by a demon and kills hospital personnel, or follow a conventional horror plot, such as the scientist who injects himself with an experimental drug and becomes a monster bat.

Raj Comics superhero comics are most strongly influenced by western comics. Stories often center on international criminals and super villains who are mutant hybrids of human and animal (Boss, a lion/man, and Elephanto, an elephant/man). In the *Bhedia* (Wolf) series, a wolf/man called Bhedia lives in the forest, protecting animal life from hunters. In each story, he finds himself the target of the humans or mutants who seek revenge for past defeats, or intend to use the forest for their own purposes. These comics are atypical in that they seem to have transcended the usual need to confine themselves to an Indian context. When Nagraj (see Figure 2.9) (with the powers of a king cobra) seeks out evil, he is as likely to go to Italy to bring Bam-Bam-Begelow to justice as to the Himalayas to trap Indian terrorists. Their internationalism may owe more to slavish imitation of foreign comics than any research on international crime, but it still indicates that Indian comics, especially super hero comics, may soon closely resemble western comics in many ways.

Raj Comics humor-based comics are very different from Diamond Comic's *Pran's Features* in content and treatment. Raj Comics publishes feature-length comics, only one of which is a recurring series, based on a character named Bankelal. The *Bankelal* comics are intended to be humorous, in that the characters are drawn in cartoon style, and Bankelal plays situations for laughs, but they also incorporate Raj Comics' trademark blend of fantasy and horror. Unlike the bloodless violence in *Pran's Features*, violence is depicted with plenty of detail. These comics are also set in the same medieval locale as the fantasy comics, so that elements of folk tales about pranksters and court jesters can be incorporated.

Indian Comics: past and present

The most prolific comics are currently published in Delhi. This signals a shift in both the production and consumption of comics. Bombay, where the previously

Figure 2.9 *Thodanda Ki mauth, Nagraj Series* (Courtesy of Raj Comics).

successful comics were based, is a cosmopolitan, westernized, liberal city, where most people have at least a smattering of English, and women have a large measure of social freedom. Delhi is a far more conservative society, where knowledge of Hindi is essential, and traditional social barriers are common. The comics produced in Bombay are intended for a national audience and are more or less free from regionalism, while the comics from Delhi are made for a localized, regional, Hindi-speaking market. The age groups for the two comics are also different, with the *Amar Chitra Katha* and *Tinkle* being intended for a preteen audience, while Diamond Comics and Raj Comics seem to be targeting an older, teenage audience.

Almost any subject seems to be appropriated into comics form. The superstar of Hindi films, Amitabh Bachchan, was mythologized in comic book form as Supremo, a costumed super hero on the lines of the Phantom, complete with a island paradise and a secret identity. After the assassination of Indira Gandhi, the former Prime Minister, comic books profiling her life were on sale outside Parliament as members filed in. India Book House and Diamond Comics both claim to be producing a comic based on the life of Rajiv Gandhi, the former Prime Minister.

While most comics are published in the major metropolitan areas of the north, and accordingly reflect that culture, there are comics that have emerged from other regions. *Sudden Muanga* is a comic published by the author, Lal Sang Zuala, a college teacher in the small town of Churachandpur in Mizoram (a state in the northeastern Himalayan region whose people are racially and culturally dissimilar to those in the central parts of the subcontinent). The surprisingly Americanized series deals with the adventures of a Mizo cowboy named Sudden Muanga and is based on current politics in Mizoram. The existence and local popularity of this comic book is a refreshing reminder of the sheer diversity of Indian comics, and the fact that there are probably many other publications of this nature that have not been exposed to a national audience.

The comics industry: an overview

An important aspect of the Indian comics industry is that management has enormous creative control over their product, usually far more than the writers and illustrators. For instance, Indrajal Comics' manager A.C. Shukla is credited with creating and conceptualizing Bahadur, while Abid Surti maintains that he created the character. Similarly, Anant Pai at India Book House retains control over the content of all comics, and actually wrote some of the early *Amar Chitra Kathas* himself. As indicated earlier, most illustrators and writers tend to be freelancers with no loyalty to any one series, or even to the comics medium. For example, the writer for *Bahadur*, Jagjit Uppal, is also an astrologer and fortuneteller, and novelist. Abid Surti, who also wrote for *Bahadur*, describes himself as an artist who used comics to pay for his canvasses. Ram Waeerkar and V. B. Halbe, two of the best-known comics illustrators today, refuse to identify themselves as comics artists, as illustrators tend to work with a wide range of businesses that require cartoon style art, such as advertising or magazine illustration. In fact, thinking of themselves as primarily comics illustrators lowers their status in the larger business world.

A fact mentioned by people in the Bombay industry is the lack of new talent attracted to comics. Many of those who work for the comics see their jobs as a stepping stone to other, better-paid jobs. Middle-class Indian parents are notoriously intolerant of their children choosing any career path that is off the beaten track, and almost all bright young people are channeled into medicine and engineering, the two most widely respected professions. As a result, the same people who entered the comics industry in the 1970s and 1980s, such as Subbarao and Luis Fernandes, are those who are still creating comics in Bombay.

The Delhi comics employ writers who are less educated and poorly paid, and have little commitment to a long-term career in comics, where priority is given to illustrators, who, again have no stake in the comics. A new feature in the industry is the comics workshop created by Pratap Mullick, a veteran illustrator, to produce illustrations for the industry and train comics illustrators. The workshop produces most of the illustrations used in comics today. This consolidation of talent may result in higher standards for comics illustration. Additionally, the move towards a greater emphasis on visuals in comics has changed the text-based orientation of Indian comics. As India becomes part of the global marketplace through the process of economic change, the influence of western comics on content and style is greater than it was in the 1980s and early 1990s.

The smaller publishers without a national audience, like Raj Comics, and the Meerut based Manoj Comics may not be able to sustain long-term growth. Diamond Comics, which dominates the comics industry currently, has started reaching outwards to a larger South Asian market in the neighboring countries of Bangladesh and Sri Lanka. This international readership indicates that comics may expand beyond Indian borders, and find a larger audience.

Notes

1 Govind Bhramania, illustrator for *Indrajal Comics*, loaned me his entire collection of out-of-print comics, and Abid Surti, writer for *Indrajal Comics*, gifted his collection for research.

2 Enid Blyton, with various series set in English boarding schools and villages, is the most popular author for Indian pre-teens.

3 Rama is one of the central gods in the Hindu pantheon, and the central figure of the *Ramayana*, one of the two epic poems of India.

4 Krishna, enormously popular as a child-god all over India, is the figure who lays out the tenets of Hinduism in the *Bhagavad Gita*, now one of the central texts of Hinduism. *Shakuntala* is a classical Sanskrit play, and the Pandava brothers are the central characters of the *Mahabharata*, one of the two major Hindu epic poems.

5 India has a myriad of languages and dialects, many with their own distinctive scripts. Hindi is the most common (spoken by 30 per cent of the population) followed by major languages like Tamil, Gujarati, Bengali, Telugu, Kannada, Malayalam, Marathi, Oriya, and Punjabi.

6 Waeerkar illustrated the first *Amar Chitra Katha, Krishna*, and is one of the most respected figures in comics today. Waeerkar's son Sanjiv is now a comics illustrator and is training to be an animator. His style is far more influenced by the western Disney style than that of his father.

7 The 'Uncle Pai' persona has generated a series of reader response columns in another India Book House publication, *Tinkle*, which was conceived as a magazine that combines both entertainment and education. Pai's staff answer questions ranging from how to do school science projects, to raising self-esteem.

8 No one suggests that the name has a relevant meaning. Pai merely says he liked the sound of the word. It is similar to the sometimes anglicized names that Indians give

their children, which range from Goldie in the north to Baby in the south. There is a tradition within all Indian languages of giving children similarly affectionate pet names, while official names are reserved for formal use.

9 Jawaharlal Nehru was India's first Prime Minister, and a popular, charismatic politician of great intellectual stature. His liberal English education, socialism, and the struggle for independence profoundly influenced him. He believed that India could progress only through investment in industrial, economic, and scientific advances.

10 Gandhi advocated an economy based on agriculture and a localized cottage industry. While other nationalist leaders, including Nehru, had little faith in this model of economic development, they respected his spiritual leadership and the profound attachment that Indians had for him as the 'Father of the Nation'. Gandhi was assassinated by a Hindu fanatic just before independence.

11 The term 'sati' refers to the mythological story of Sati, the wife of the god Shiva, who chose to immolate herself to protest against an insult to her husband. Studies of this horrifying practice (Mani 1992) have suggested that even when it was common, it was rarely voluntary. Widows were coerced by relatives, and sometimes drugged and placed on the pyre, or even thrown in despite their struggles. The practice of sati disappeared for most of this century, but made a rare reappearance in 1987, when a woman named Roop Kanwar drew crowds to watch her burn alive on her husband's funeral pyre. After her death, she was venerated as a saint, and a shrine was built in her honor. Most modern Indians would be opposed to the practice of sati. However, there is a cultural undercurrent of respect for the 'virtuous' woman.

12 A southern city with a large and well-established Muslim population.

13 All Hindu names.

14 One of the most famous films of the 1970s was *Sholay*, which borrowed heavily from the western film genre. It deals with the exploits of two friends on the run from police who ride into a town in the Chambal Valley, and rescue the town from the bandits who terrorize it.

3

SHAPING A CULTURAL IDENTITY: THE PICTURE BOOK AND CARTOONS IN TAIWAN, 1945–1980*

Shu-chu Wei

Taiwan returned to Chinese rule in 1945 after 50 years of Japanese colonization. In 1949, Chiang Kai-shek lost his battle to the Communists in the civil war and retreated to Taiwan. His government launched a Chinese educational system on the island. Indigenous school children began to learn the new official language, Mandarin Chinese, without the usual guidance from their parents, who were themselves struggling to cope with the linguistic changes. Under Japanese colonization, Taiwanese residents were educated to speak and read Japanese at school but at home spoke their local Chinese dialects, the major ones being Southern Min and Hakka. Written words in Chinese were the same, but pronunciations for the same word varied, sometimes drastically, in different dialects. Oral communication between speakers of Mandarin and local dialects was extremely difficult, if not impossible. For the Taiwanese educated to read Japanese, knowledge of the Chinese words used in Japanese helped only slightly in the change of official languages. Thus, in its post-colonial era, indigenous Taiwanese culture was 'silenced' again, 'in so far as its voice ceased to be heard in the arenas of power, and its values ceased to be privileged or even recognized in the new hierarchy of control' (Griffiths 1995:166). The new settlers from mainland China became, in a sense, the new colonizers to the indigenous islanders, although the majority of both groups belong to the same Han Chinese race.

This power imbalance consisting of 15 per cent new settlers and 85 per cent indigenous dwellers would continue for decades until the younger indigenous generation learned to express themselves in the official language and until the mainlanders learned to appreciate the local culture from their indigenous friends, classmates, and neighbors. Picture books in Chinese with Mandarin pronunciations marked next to the words in a phonetic system called *zhuyin fuhao* were created as a way to help educate children. While children of both groups studied together traditional Chinese values from adult mainlanders, they also absorbed residues of the Japanese culture passed on to them by their elders whose only education had come from their previous colonizers. Cartoons, an art form already existent during the Japanese occupation, were made available either in

Chinese translation from the Japanese or in new Chinese publications. They became popular reading materials for children, probably because the use of pictures as a medium is more direct and powerful than that of written words, especially at a time of linguistic change.

Picture books and cartoons went through several states of evolution from the 1950s to the 1980s, mirroring the linguistic, pictorial, cultural, economic, political, and national interactions that took place on the island. During these changes, writers and illustrators looked everywhere for inspiration. By the end of the 1970s, picture books and cartoons began to appear in unique forms – blending cultural elements of traditional China, modern Taiwan, Japan, and the west. New and old residents on the island worked together to establish a new cultural identity through the making of picture books and cartoons.

Because of the complexity of the issues shaping these Taiwanese genres, a complete historical survey is beyond the scope of this chapter. But to provide an overview for readers unfamiliar with thematic and formal developments of picture books and cartoons in Taiwan, I will examine the most important and representative texts in chronological order. Colonial and post-colonial concerns presented in this chapter are applications of ideas from Edward Said (1978), Homi K. Bhabha (1994), Bruce King (1996), Gareth Griffiths (1996), and others, although some of them are not directly quoted. For the analysis of illustrations and their interactions with the text, I make use of ideas and methodology presented by Barbara Bader (1976), Molly Bang (1991), and William Moebius (1986). As Bader reminds us:

> A picturebook is text, illustrations, total design; an item of manufacture and a commercial product; a social, cultural, historical document; and, foremost, an experience for a child.
>
> As an art form it hinges on the interdependence of pictures and words, on the simultaneous display of two facing pages, and on the drama of the turning of the page.
>
> On its own terms its possibilities are limitless.
>
> (Bader 1976:1)

Bader's idea of a picture book works equally well for cartoons. The two genres share many similar qualifications and characteristics, which probably explains why children embrace both of them with enthusiasm.

1945–1965

At the beginning of Chiang Kai-shek's rule on Taiwan, the Ministry of Education barely had time or funding for textbooks, let alone bedtime stories for children. In the first two decades after 1945, a time of financial difficulties for most families, private publishers filled the vacuum with anything that could be produced inexpensively. The Eastern Publishing Co. (Dongfang Chubanshe) was established in 1945. Its *Dongfang Shaonian*, (Eastern Youth) a monthly

65

magazine for children, was published in 1954 and terminated in 1961. Another monthly magazine for children, *Xueyou* (Learning Companion), put out by the Learning Companion Publishing Co., lasted from 1953 to 1959. Both magazines reflect Japanese influence and contain a large proportion of comic strips that include both indigenous productions and translations from Japan (Hong 1994: 25–26).

Cartoons and comic books

These publishers found cartoons and comic books easiest to produce and most popular. In the late 1950s, approximately six or seven publishers entered the comic-books market. Comic strips first appeared in weekly or monthly magazines for children. The most successful ones would then be published in single volumes. These books, mostly printed in black and white or blue and white, were inexpensive, simple, creative, and entertaining.

One of these pioneers was Chen Dingguo (born 1922). He started his 'Journey to the West' (Sanzang Qujing) serial in *Learning Companion* in the 1950s. This serial continued for more than three years and sold well. He was famous for illustrating historical stories of popular heroines such as Lu Siniang, Meng Jiangnu, and Fan Lihua (Lin 1979:9). However, his portrayal of Monkey King in 'Journey to the West' and Little Sister Hua (Hua Xiaomei) proved more engaging than that of the historical heroines to the young readers. Both characters were innocent, mischievous, and lively, in many ways similar to Curious George and Pippi Longstocking in the west. Chen contributed a link to the Chinese legends to the readership on the post-Japanese-colonial island.

In 1951, Li Feimeng (born 1925), by the pen name of Niu Ge, started his trademark cartoon character Uncle Niu (Niu Bobo) in the *Zhongyang Ribao* (Central Daily News). Although the Uncle Niu stories, especially those of him in combat, were anti-communist in essence, they were unlike the blatant and clumsy propaganda produced by the military. Instead, they were satirical and funny. The characterization of Uncle Niu – meaning Uncle Ox, indicating his being stubborn and slow in learning – as a misfit in the new metropolitan society won him both sympathy and laughter. Uncle Niu's trademark features of his large bald head with three hairs growing like weeds and two conspicuous, protruding teeth became immediately recognizable (Lin 1979:17). This comic relief in the portrayal of Uncle Niu probably made the young readers feel closer to the civil war veterans from mainland China, most of whom were poorly educated and financially deprived. These veterans had become underdogs not only from the point of view of the neo-colonizers but also in the society of the colonized.

In the heyday of comic books publications between 1956 and 1966, many children, including those in the remote countryside, would wait impatiently for the new serial to be published. One of the most popular cartoonists of this period was Ye Hongjia (1924–1990). Having graduated from junior high school, Ye went to Japan to study fine arts for two years. After returning to Taiwan, he first illustrated pictures for friends' books, then he decided to draw his own cartoons. He started the adventures of 'Zhuge Silang' comic strips in 1958 and earned immediate success. In 1961, around the time of the Chinese Lunar New Year, one of his 'Silang' stories was made into a film in the Southern Min dialect. Children swarmed to see it (Lin 1979:12–13). The 'Silang' serial depicted two heroes' fights against evil forces with a lot of spying, captures, and rescue missions. This story line seemed to go well with the government's propaganda about the Chinese communists as evildoers, regardless of whether the author so intended it or not. In an episode from *Zhuge Silang Dadou Shuangjiamian* (Zhuge Silang Fights against the Two Masks) in which Silang and his friend Zhenping fight against Crying Iron Mask (see Figure 3.1), we see an example of Ye's skills in story-telling and illustration. Having encountered the evildoers alone, Silang is engaged in a dangerous battle with Crying Iron Mask and his attendants. Silang's sword is being dragged away by Crying Iron Mask's chain and he is perspiring in his struggle. He is depicted as very tiny and cornered to the lower left side of the column, indicating that he is in a disadvantageous position, yet there is a possibility of an escape off the page[1]. He is also out-numbered by the archers positioned high on the roof top. Just before he is ambushed by the archers, however, Zhenping comes to his rescue on horseback. Together, they are able to get even with their foes, whose identity remains a mystery until the very end. Ye's intriguing use of suspense attracted children back to the bookstores for new serials. Due to his educational background, Ye exhibited traces of Japanese influence, notably in his portrayal of the characters and his drawings of the buildings.

Another cartoonist of the best sellers is Liu Xingqin, who graduated from Taipei Teachers' College majoring in Fine Arts. According to his recollection, his interest in drawing cartoons was inspired by a propaganda comic strip dropped from one of the US airplanes during the Pacific War. An elementary school student at that time, he enjoyed a hearty laugh reading the ugly depiction of the Japanese officers in the cartoon (Lin 1979:24). His most popular cartoon characters, Brother Asan (Asan Ge) and Great Auntie (Da Shenpo) first appeared in 1956 in a magazine called *Mofan Shaonian* (Model Youth). In his busiest period illustrating stories of these characters, he drew 20 pages per day, which would bring him NT$500 per day, compared with a NT$480 monthly payment as a teacher (Lin 1979:25). His *Asan Ge Da Shenpo You Taibei* (Brother Asan and Great Auntie Visit Taipei), as well as stories about their visits to other places in Taiwan, is of special significance in the history of Taiwanese cartoons, as it details lifestyles and activities of local residents during that time period.

Liu's characterization of Brother and Auntie (see Figure 3.2), two country folks experiencing the big city for the first time, reflects stereotypical presentation of comic or farcical figures in antithesis. While Brother Asan is as skinny as a bean sprout, Great Auntie is round like a ball. Brother's hair protrudes to the front; Auntie has a bun sticking to the back of her head. Brother

Figure 3.1 *Zhuge Silang Fights against the Two Monks*, (Ye 1990:38).

has a hair dangling backward from the top of his head; Auntie has one arching forward from her forehead. Brother has long and pointed lips; Auntie's lips are round and hawk-shaped when she is angry or in distress. Putting these two figures together generates an atmosphere similar to that created by Laurel and Hardy or Popeye and Olive. They are designed to be funny, as are duets in all comic art. Indeed, the serial of Brother and Auntie reveals meaningful and often hilarious differences between the perspectives of urbanites and country folk at a time when travel even within the island was a great event.

After these years of development and prosperity, quality domestic cartoons declined to a state of stagnation in the following two decades[2]. The market was

Figure 3.2 *Brother Asan and Great Auntie Visit Taipei*, (Liu 1992:67).

taken by domestic cartoons of poor quality and pirated Japanese ones, both of which could be produced by the publishers without much investment. This is another sign indicating how Japanese economic and cultural colonialism persisted on the post-colonial island. Worse yet, the government started to regulate the publication of comic books in 1966 as a response to parents' criticism of cartoons. Some parents, even teachers, found cartoons convenient targets for children's academic failures. The censorship allowed little space for creative minds to prevail. Consequently, prominent cartoonists who started in the 1950s stopped drawing and turned to other professions. The government's censor system, in some ways still puzzling to critics and historians today, opened the market to pirated Japanese cartoons, which, including those with sex and violence, have dominated Taiwan's cartoon sales ever since (Lin 1979:3–5; Hong 1994:38–40). To find a new crop of quality domestic cartoons, we have to wait until the late 1970s and early 1980s[3], especially after the martial law, imposed on Taiwan by Chiang Kai-shek in 1949, was lifted in 1987 by the first Taiwanese president.

Historical stories

Another group of picture books, Chinese historical stories, was also widely available, but these were less creative than the comic books. Most of these stories depict brave heroes and diligent children greatly rewarded. Didacticism has always been an important part of Chinese education; however, some stories teaching the virtue of filial piety went overboard. For example, several publishers seemed to favor a classical anthology called *Ershisi Xiao* (Twenty-four Tales of Filial Piety) and made the tales into picture books. One of the tales introduces a small boy, Wang Xiang, who, on hearing that his sick stepmother would like to eat a carp in deep winter, goes to a frozen pond, takes off his coat, and tries to melt the ice with the warmth of his body. Heaven is moved by his filial piety and makes a carp jump from the pond. Parents and educators raised objections to tales like this, which gradually disappeared from the picture book shelves. Passing traditions on to the new generation was an important task. In their struggle to modernize, however, the residents on Taiwan decided that they could discard that part of tradition that did not fit into the modern concept of education.

Folktales

Chinese and foreign folktales were also available. China has many traditional folktales; they should have served as a rich source for picture books, but were somewhat neglected by the publishers. Most anthologies of Chinese folktales were published without illustrations or phonetic marks, being intended for more mature readers than children. Some were published with poor, dull illustrations, perhaps due to a lack of funding for qualified illustrators. Taiwanese folktales were either absent from most anthologies published in this period or limited to several 'approved' tales. It is possible that this circumstance is the result of official censorship of Taiwanese local culture for political reasons; for example, students were not allowed to speak their dialects at school. This regulation can be viewed as a drive to popularize the official language and an attempt to silence the indigenous voice.

In contrast, European folktales, mostly from the collections of the Grimms and Hans Christian Andersen, were numerous and appeared in beautifully printed formats with fancy illustrations in color. I suspect the publishers simply copied the illustrations from the west, since at that time, Taiwan did not recognize international copyright. As a result, Taiwanese children of many generations grew up more familiar with 'Snow White', 'Cinderella', 'Tom Thumb', and the 'Three Little Pigs' than with Chinese folk heroes and heroines. Such a reading list did not help the government in its effort to establish a Chinese identity on the island. Despite some residents' concerns that the children were being too exposed to western culture, however, western folktales gave the children an opportunity to widen their scope of imagination and to increase their access to the world outside the isolated island.

UNICEF Books of the Late 1960s

The 1960s saw the first large-scale, systematic official publications of picture books in Taiwan. These were published by the Ministry of Education through funding from UNICEF. An editorial board, organized by the government in 1964, took charge of the selection of writers and illustrators, many of whom were nationally famous. The United Nations also sent American experts to

Taiwan to supervise this project (Hong 1994: 26). Most of the books were well written and illustrated in splendid colors. They were indeed high-quality reading matter for children, much better than the books of historical stories and folktales mentioned above. In this case, western funding and professional supervision produced positive results, which would benefit the future development of children's books.

Initially the UNICEF books were not for sale, but were sent from the Ministry of Education directly to the elementary schools, which before Taiwan's economic boom had inadequate facilities and equipment[4]. Books sent to schools without libraries were locked in bookcases in the Teachers' Office (a large office for the faculty) for safekeeping. Teachers took turns taking care of these books – that is, keeping the key and circulation records. These books, under the general heading of *Zhonghua Ertong Congshu* (Chinese Children's Books), are now available in the bookstores. Some of these books are worthy of individual attention.

Collections of nursery rhymes

One of the earlier attempts in Taiwan to put together nursery rhymes from all over China in their different dialects was *Jier Wowoti* (The Rooster Crows, 1967), edited by Zhu Jiefan and illustrated by Huang Changhui. Although the written words are understandable to all educated Chinese, these rhymes should be read in their dialects to achieve the local flavor and rhythms. There is a Taiwanese nonsense rhyme in the collection, probably the first Taiwanese nursery rhyme in print[5]. Another collection, *Keren Dao* (Here Comes the Guest), edited by Xia Shude, appeared in 1969. This volume does not indicate the origins of the rhymes, but most of them appear to be from northern China, judging from the language and rhyming patterns. That different artists illustrate the different rhymes enhances their diversity. Unfortunately, however, Taiwanese rhymes are excluded.

Science information books

The most interesting book in this group is *Caihong Jie* (Rainbow Street, 1971) written by Lin Liang and illustrated by Wang Shi. The science of color combinations is introduced by having three creatures – Little Yellow, Little Blue, and Little Red – visit an artist's studio. When Little Yellow and Little Blue dance together, they turn green; and Little Yellow and Little Red join hands to create orange. The story is imaginative and the illustrations are vivid and lovely, but the presentation of the artist as a man who looks more western (possibly a Parisian?) than Chinese is both amusing and puzzling (see Figure 3.3). Does it indicate that science comes only from the west, or that a western artist is more appealing? The book reflects the confusion being experienced by post-colonial Taiwanese facing a blurring line between modernization and westernization.

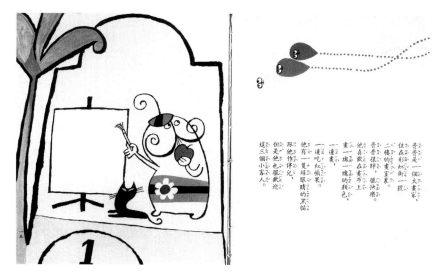

Figure 3.3 From *Rainbow Street* (Lin and Wang 1971:14–15)

Adaptations of western stories

None of these books indicates the sources of the stories, but they read like European tales, and the illustrations are definitely in European styles. The books are of good quality. The only flaw is the negligence in reporting the sources.

One book serves as a good example: *Dongtian li de Bailingniao* (A Singing Bird in Winter, 1969), written by Zheng Rui and illustrated by Zhao Guozong. This is a didactic story about a singing bird whose feathers turn to gold when he is sprinkled by the spring water on Mount Youth. Having unique feathers has made him a snob and estranged him from all his friends, but he accepts good counsel from an ant in time to rebuild his friendships and starts to help the needy with his golden feathers. In particular, he frequently gives them to a poor sick boy, singing in his happiness at being able to help. By the time winter comes, he is almost naked; in the bitter cold, he sings to lift his spirits. The sick boy hears his familiar songs, seeks him out, and takes him in: good deeds are rewarded. The excellent woodcuts are rich and heavy in color, complementing the magical elements in the story. They depict the buildings and the characters' features, clothes, and gestures in obvious European styles.

Presentations of Chinese legends

Two books stand out for their efforts to present old tales in new and creative ways. *Maoqi de Yuanbao* (The Steaming Silver Nuggets, 1968), written by Tang Yitao and illustrated by Cao Junyan, tells an imaginative legend of how Chinese dumplings came into being. The theme involves traditional values of filial piety and loyalty to the emperor. Instead of serious moral teachings, however, both the text and the illustrations are full of humorous elements. *Xiao Gushou* (The Little Drummer, 1968), written by He Linken and illustrated by Gao Shanlan, is a combination of historical events, legends, and some traditional activities of the Dragon Boat Festival, all wrapped up in a boy's effort to become the best drummer in a dragon boat competition. As literature, this book has too many subplots. It is exemplary, however, as a cultural display, enhanced by the illustrator's colored paper collages and black-and-white drawings.

New stories

In this category we see the most exciting of the UNICEF books. The stories discussed above are more or less old tales retold, but the books in this group are fresh. Their success encouraged a climate in which picture books could flourish in Taiwan. Two books are worthy of more detailed consideration for their originality.

The first is *Laoxiejiang yu Gou* (The Old Cobbler and the Dog, 1969), written by Pan Qijun and illustrated by Zhou Chunjiang. In this story, Chen Fu, a homeless old cobbler, sets up an awning against an apartment wall in an alley and starts his shoe repair 'shop'. An orphan boy collects garbage on the streets in this area. He has recently been adopted by a janitor of a nearby apartment. One day, the boy comes to the cobbler with a pair of boots he has scavenged from a garbage can. He receives free repairs and the cobbler's promise to take nightly care of a stray dog, which the boy has adopted off the street but has not been allowed to keep in his new father's residence, the basement of the apartment. Soon, the cobbler, the boy, and the dog become good friends. The cobbler decides to persuade the boy's father to send the boy to school. It turns out that the father is already planning to do so. The thankful father eventually invites the kind-hearted cobbler to share their basement and complete their family.

The story depicts the warmth of human compassion, especially among the have-nots. The two single men are typical veterans who left family members in mainland China and followed Chiang Kai-shek to Taiwan, although the author does not directly state this fact. Their presentation in a positive light by concerned writers is itself an encouraging sign for future social developments on the island. The central character seems to be the old cobbler, an unusual feature in picture books when a child character is also involved. The illustrator, however, gives the boy more space and more conspicuous positions than the old cobbler and portrays the boy as a charming darling whom everyone would love. This shift of focus in the pictures makes the book more like a book for children. Another notable aspect of the illustration is that every detail reveals careful observation, faithfully representing contemporary Taiwan.

A second book that reflects the same novel spirit is the 1968 title *Xiaolanqiu Dada* (Little Basketball Dada), written by Chen Yuewen and illustrated by

Lin Yulou. Dada, an animated basketball, has a famous father – also a basketball – who gives him very strict training. Tired of the training and unwilling to be tossed about, Dada runs away from home, a bit uncertain and fearful at the beginning but gradually becoming wild and adventurous. After several unpleasant experiences, Dada realizes that chimneys have their work and flowers have their roles to play, and that they are happy doing what they are supposed to do. So he returns home to take part in the basketball game.

Personification of the basketball is not limited to its verbal manifestations. Dada is illustrated as a child who has a large, round head with standard basketball lines and simple yet distinctive human features. In comparison with the huge head, the tiny body indicates that the head is the major qualification and the body is there just to help with movements and gestures. The bouncy and rolling nature of the basketball is also made obvious in more than half of the illustrations. Although the story line follows the traditional didactic pattern that directs the youngsters to obey their parents and to work hard, the Dada character and the illustrations demonstrate considerable imagination.

1970–1980

In the late 1970s and early 1980s, picture books in Taiwan followed two trends. One was the continuity of the old formats, as discussed above; the other indicates new directions. The most noticeable continuity of the old trend was the prevalence of Grimm and Andersen tales for small children and Chinese tales for older children. Japanese comic books also continued to be translated and published in large quantities. But a renaissance of quality domestic cartoons was on its way. Other changes were occurring too. Creative writing for preschoolers was not available until this time, when simple and interesting books were finally published by the Xinyi Foundation, a private body devoted to the well-being of children. Another innovation was the 1982 publication of *Zhongguo Tonghua* (Chinese Folktales), a twelve-volume collection of Chinese myths, folktales, historical legends, and holiday celebrations by the Echo Publishing Company (Hansheng Chubanshe). The books have Chinese texts with phonetic marks and colorful illustrations, making them the first picture books of Chinese tales for children of all age groups. Discussions below will reveal that these books were of great importance in the development of the picture book and cartoons in Taiwan.

Signs of a revival for cartoons

Shortly before the lifting of decades-long martial law and censorship of publications there was a period of loose political control. This space allowed the silenced people to find their voices. In 1979, a scholarly journal, *Shuping Shumu* (Book Reviews and Bibliography), devoted two issues (75 and 76) to discussing Taiwan's publication of comic books, not without some harsh criticism of the government's system. Some daring cartoonists started to challenge the authority by publishing comic strips of political satire and social commentary in newspapers and magazines. This new trend of political and social cartooning would fully develop in the next decade. Some other cartoonists would soon find a receptive market, which had become relatively prosperous by this time, for their modernized comic books of classical literature and philosophy. One outstanding figure in this group, Tsai Chih-chung, is exemplified in the discussion of his works in Chapter 8.

The Xinyi Foundation books

The overall design of the books published by the Xinyi Foundation demonstrates that the editors, authors, and illustrators have a fine understanding of the intellectual development of early childhood. All the books use simple language in large print with phonetic marks. The pages are thick and glossy. The illustrations are drawn in clear, neat lines and vivid colors. The stories are animated and imaginative. A good example is *Dongwu de Ge* (Songs of Animals, 1979, 1981) with text by Xie Wuzhang and illustrations by Zhang Zhengcheng. Instead of collecting existing nursery rhymes, Xie wrote eleven new rhymes about animals. They are simple and funny. Children can recite them out loud and play with the words, which may lead them to create their own rhymes.

Family life, especially a child's immediate family, is an important theme in the Xinyi books. *Mama* (text by Lin Liang, illustration by Zhao Guozong, 1978) is a charming book. The first half of the book introduces the readers to animal mothers and their children. The second half describes activities between a little girl and her mother. The last page unites the animal and human worlds by having the little girl reach out to the little animals, exclaiming, 'Little puppy, kitty, chick and duckling! Look, this is my mama!'

The colors used in this book are bright and warm – yellow, pink, green, and blue. Yellow is the most important color, linking the little girl to her mother and to the baby animals. The little girl has yellow hair, which is tied to the color of her mother's hairpin and necklace. The mother is depicted as a typical Chinese woman with black hair. The daughter's yellow hair does not present her as a western blonde but rather, as a Chinese phrase for little girls goes, as 'a yellow-haired girl' (*huangmao yatou*), or young child. The idea of little girls having yellow hair is strengthened on the last page, on which we see all the baby animals colored yellow. The full, steady lines in bold black encircling every creature and object give a sense of security to family life (see Figure 3.4).

The same writer and illustrator completed the pair with *Papa* (1980), stylistically and emotionally similar to its predecessor. Socially, *Papa* is conservative; the male creators of this book depict a traditional family in which the father is the head and goes out to earn the rice and the mother stays home to take care of the children. The father answers the son's questions, solves his

Figure 3.4 From *Mama* (Lin and Zhao 1978:31).

problems, and provides a loving, all-powerful image. The book does not reflect social reality in modern Taiwan; for example, today many mothers work.

The best of the Xinyi books are the tales adapted from classical Chinese literature. It is hard to imagine anyone trying to turn such a complex and difficult literature into picture books for today's small children, but the author and illustrator Xi Song has done so. Two books of his are outstanding: *San ge Huaidongxi* (Three Bad Creatures, 1979) and *Taohua Yuan* (Peach Blossom Spring, 1979). The first book is based on a historical legend about a street bully named Zhou Chu who eliminates three destructive creatures in the village. In Xi Song's version for children, the bully encounters a little girl crying because her family has to move away to avoid three bad creatures. Zhou Chu, being a bully fond of 'heroic' deeds, volunteers to destroy the three bad creatures to stop her tears. After he kills the tiger in the mountains and the huge snake in the river, he realizes that the third bad creature is none other than himself. The bad things that Zhou Chu does in this book include stealing from the orchard, killing the farmers' chickens for a barbecue, and destroying a wheat field in his pursuit of the chickens, all of which are deeds of violence miniaturized so as to be acceptable in this context, yet bad enough for children to recognize as unacceptable. The little girl, now convinced that he is a true hero, encourages him to serve the community with his courage and strength. As a result, he sets about correcting his own mistakes by helping to harvest in the orchard and the wheat field, an ingenious simplification of the complex process of self-discipline in the original story.

The illustrations, too, are striking. They are both classical, in the style of certain traditional Chinese paintings, and modern, according to the western

76

standards for a good picture book as posited by Bader (1976), Bang (1991), and Moebius (1986). Xi Song uses solid colors and brush pen outlines to create a mixture of classical Chinese figure paintings and woodcut prints, resulting in a sense of certainty without blocking the flow of movement. Xi Song is obviously very much concerned with the flow of movement and interactions between text and pictures. As he states in the epilogue, 'Some Words to Parents', 'Several illustrations in the book, having possessed a flow of movement in themselves, are self-explanatory; therefore, no text is added to them' (Xi 1979a:24).

On pages 12 and 13, there is a good example of how the illustrator depicts movement (see Figure 3.5). On page 12, we see a picture without text. Zhou Chu is riding on top of the tiger, one hand grabbing the tiger and the other raised high, exactly at the highest, central point of the page, with a powerful fist ready to pounce on the tiger. The tiger bends his body in pain and looks toward the left for an escape off the page. But on the next page, the text says, 'Zhou Chu carried the dead tiger to see the little girl'. The tiger has not had a chance to escape, after all. On the top right-hand corner of the page, the child watches Zhou Chu carrying the tiger on his back with an expression of admiration and awe, her left hand covering her mouth. The movement that connects the events here is her right hand pointing to the water at the bottom left corner, its waves lapping leftward, indicating more activities related to water on the next page. The text tells us that the girl is talking about the second bad creature, the snake in the river. Thus the illustrations and the text work together to present a smooth flow of events and to demand the turn of the page in order to satisfy the reader's curiosity.

Peach Blossom Spring is a simplification and revision of Tao Yuanming's utopia[6]. The illustration on the first page shows a happy fisherman in his traditional costume, netting fish and looking up to the left where the turning of the page is expected. We see a clear and steady horizontal line to show stability and definite location. The next picture (see Figure 3.6) presents the fisherman

Figure 3.5 *Three Bad Creatures* (Xi 1979a:12–13).

Figure 3.6 From *Peach Blossom Spring* (Xi 1979b:5).

traveling to a place he has never visited. With his back to the readers, the fisherman rows upward to a cave among mysterious-looking mountains. Readers are directed to follow the fisherman into the white cave in the upper-middle position, which serves as a vanishing point suggesting mysteries, adventures, and opportunities. The cave is so high up in the mountains and so near the two auspicious-looking clouds that it connotes heavenly elements. On the next two-page spread, we share the heavenly view of the Peach Blossom Spring with the surprised, speechless fisherman. When he decides to leave the upwelling spring, he carries a branch of peach blossom as a token. The cave that leads him to the mysterious, happy land is still visible in the upper-right corner, safe and sacred. The blossoming branch in the fisherman's hand is positioned almost at the center of the picture to signify its importance. Its conspicuous pink flower, symbolizing warmth, glamor, and hope, looks as if it were waving goodbye to the cave and following the fisherman and the river toward the left into a new world.

Tao Yuanming's fisherman does not pluck a peach blossom branch from the Spring, and the utopia is forever lost to the fisherman, his friends, and to us. But Xi Song does not want his young readers to view a happy land as unreachable. He creates new lands and new hopes for the children by making his fisherman plant the withering branch in his own village. The result of diligent watering and tender care is a small peach tree with new leaves, illustrated on the extreme left of the page, indicating new blossoms on the turning of the page. Another Peach Blossom Spring is created in the fisherman's own world, not somewhere in the remote mountains beyond a mysterious cave or in a mysterious historical past. What Xi Song has done is 'to construct a usable cultural past' (King 1996:25) while providing modern concepts for children.

Echo's Chinese Folktales

Xi Song's influence is also evident in Echo's *Chinese Folktales*, as he is one of the executive editors. (The set received a government award for Best Publications of the Year.) The editors, lamenting that Taiwanese children know more about European tales and Japanese comics than about Chinese tradition and culture, vowed to fill this 'serious gap' (1982:preface). They also recognized that techniques commonly used at the time for illustrating children's books lagged behind those of western nations. Determined not to copy the westerners, the editors and illustrators looked back to historical materials and folk arts for inspiration. They found rich resources in festival and wall paintings, paper cuttings, embroideries, and pottery decoration. They used Chinese brush and rice-paper techniques to illustrate the pictures, paying close attention to historical changes in buildings and costumes.

The outcome of their effort is a collection of tales that represents the diverse eras and regions of China, including, notably, many local Taiwanese and aboriginal tales long neglected. The texts, though accessible to young readers, are in excellent prose. The attractive illustrations use the traditional Chinese colors of primary red, yellow, and blue, plus black. Local and ethnic differences are presented with clarity and respect. Central unity on a page seems to be the major illustration technique, reflecting a traditional Chinese tendency in folk art and painting. Yet the illustrators have also paid attention to movement and the drama created by the turning of the page (see Figure 3.7).

Conclusion

Xinyi Foundation's picture books, Echo's *Chinese Folktales,* and comic books appearing in the late 1970s and early 1980s mark the culmination of decades of development of children's books in Taiwan. They have pointed the way to a new direction for picture books and cartoons, which will influence many later publications. The books will be treasured as a happy combination of the identities of modern Taiwan, traditional China, Japan, and the west, serving as 'a social, cultural, historical document' (Bader 1976:1). Both the indigenous residents and the new settlers on the island worked together to make this possible by carefully sorting through the old and the new as well as the domestic and the foreign. This new establishment of a cultural identity in post-Japanese-colonial and post-Chinese-neo-colonial Taiwan is 'the result of fusion' (Griffiths 1996:169) and worthy of celebration.

Figure 3.7 *Chinese Folktales*, (1982:84–85). The illustration depicts a legend of the Sun pursuing the Moon.

Notes

* This chapter is an expanded version of 'Shaping a cultural tradition: the picture book in Taiwan, 1945–1980', p. 116–121 in *Children's Literature Association Quarterly* 20 (3). The author would like to thank the editors for permission to use parts of the original article here.

1 One reads a Taiwanese picture book by opening the book at what western readers think of as the 'back' and reading the right-hand page and then the left, so that the far left side of the book is the 'page turn' side.

2 The quantity of comic books published during this period was still greater than that of other books for children, according to Hong's estimation (1994:25, 38–40).

3 The category of comic books was added to the list of Hong Jianquan Children's Literature Awards in 1979 until its last offerings in 1990 (Hong 1994:63–4).

4 Although some scholars mark 1964 as the year the Taiwanese economy started its steady rise, residents did not have much buying power until after the mid-1970s. The establishment of libraries in the elementary schools reflects this pattern of economic development. In 1979, fewer than ten per cent of the 2400+ elementary schools contained a library. By 1985, the percentage had increased to more than 70 (Hong 1994:2–3).

5 The written words are marked with the *zhuyin fuhao* phonetics in Mandarin pronunciation, which do not reflect the proper rhyming scheme in its Southern Min dialect. Local terms for two kinds of fruit mentioned in the rhyme are written in Chinese words bearing Mandarin pronunciations similar to the dialect and are explained in a footnote.

6 Tao Yuanming (AD 365–427) was a famous poet, whose description of an ideal world has long been a favorite topic for Chinese scholars.

4

CARTOONING IN SRI LANKA

John A. Lent

In a country torn asunder by civil war and a number of political assassinations, one might not expect much humor and frivolity; yet, comic art continues to prosper in Sri Lanka. It is visible in the mainstream press, the mini[1] and comic papers, advertisements, and galleries, but also as decorative fixtures of trishaws, street lights, and Buddhist temples.

Comic art in Sri Lanka is traceable to at least the fourth century, evident in 'very humorous figures' of temple relief sculptures and in mural paintings (Dharmasiri 1993). Even today, according to comics scholar Leonard Rifas (1995:114), 'entering Sri Lankan Buddhist temples is like being encompassed by a walk-through, holy comic book'. The brightly colored paintings function as panels in a graphic narrative, retelling the tales of Buddha built around ten virtues contained in the *Jathaka Katha*. Each mural is a combination of

Figure 4.1 Early Sri Lankan caricature in Sigirya Frescoes, 5th Century A.D.

81

illustrations and verses, and, according to the Venerable Nayaka Thera Piyadassi (1993), noted author and head of a Sri Lankan monastery, both the visual and textual components of these temple murals, some dating 300 to 1000 years ago, contain 'innocent humor'.

Western-style cartooning, characterized by their appearance in printed media, appeared after the British conquest in the early nineteenth century, but the history of Sri Lankan cartoonists, for the most part, dates to the 1930s–1940s. Bevis Vawa contributed cartoon humor in story format to the *Daily News* and *Observer* at that time. With national independence in 1947, other local cartoonists emerged. Most notable was Aubrey Collette (1920–1992), who drew political and strip cartoons for the *Times of Ceylon* and then the *Ceylon Observer*, 1947–1964. Collette came into cartooning, propelled by a swift boot. He had been teaching at Royal College (Colombo) until one day, he tried to enliven his history class by drawing caricatures of government officials on the blackboard. As fate would have it, the education minister dropped in on the class at the moment Collette was executing a particularly unflattering caricature of him (Collette 1970). After joining the *Times of Ceylon* in 1947, Collette's cartoons were very quickly acclaimed the paper's most popular feature. Collette left Sri Lanka in the 1960s. From then on, he attained fame throughout Asia with his laid-back strip character 'Sun Tan', created for *The Asia Magazine* in 1964.

Close on the heels of Collette were G. S. Fernando (*Observer*), W. R. Wijesoma (*Times of Ceylon*), and Susil Premaratna (*Lankadipa*). All were primarily political cartoonists, except for Premaratna, credited with doing the first strip, a copy of an English cartoon. Fernando was a very important figure in Sri Lankan cartooning, especially hard hitting during the Kothalawala government. Wijesoma has had the longest career, spanning nearly 50 years.

Wijesoma joined the *Times of Ceylon* as a proofreader in December 1947; five years later, he started drawing 'What a Life', which he claims was the first pocket cartoon[2] in the country. It appeared in both the *Times* and *Lankadipa*. After that, he drew a pocket 'Tikiri-Tokka' (Tiny Nook), for the Sinhalese-language *Lankadipa*, and invented a new style strip, four frames on four separate news events, which he called 'Sittarapati'. Wijesoma (1993) described it as having a 'cinema effect with perforated edges'. Two other major moves occurred, first to the Lake House Group (later called Associated Newspapers) in 1968, and Upali in 1981. At Lake House, he drew cartoons for the dailies, *Observer*, *Daily News*, and *Janatha*, and the Sunday *Silumina*, and continued through the government confiscation of the company in 1973. He switched to *The Island* and *Divaina* when Upali Wijewardene started his media group Upali in 1981–1982.

Discussing differences in cartooning between the 1950s and 1990s, Wijesoma said that, today, there are more cartoonists and that the audience is larger, more diverse, and more sophisticated, the latter lessening the need for insertion of news items or other language cues within cartoons. On the other hand, complete

Figure 4.2 Political cartoonist S. C. Opatha usually uses a sledgehammer approach to cartooning, with strong messages, a heavy bold stroke, and exaggerated characterization. 'Silva' has been his common man character. Courtesy S. C. Opatha.

freedom existed in the 1950s as the leaders came from the educated class and were more tolerant, he said.

Other cartoonists who advanced the profession came out of the 1960s; among them were S. C. Opatha, Jiffry Yoonoos, W. P. Wickramanayake, and Camillus Perera, whose first name is used as his signature and the name of his company.

First attached to the *Ceylon Daily Mirror* as a political cartoonist, Opatha was known for his hard-hitting drawings, especially in the relatively free atmosphere of the 1960s. His stock as an oppositionist force against the government was bolstered in 1977 when he and another cartoonist, Chanrandran, drew a booklet of cartoons denigrating the Bandaranaike administration. Published by the opposition in time for the national elections, the 30-page work sold about 100,000 copies and has been credited by other cartoonists as having hurt Bandaranaike's image and campaign (Wickramanayake 1993; Hettigoda 1993). Opatha (1993) agreed 'I believe the booklet did big damage to her campaign as everyone was carrying it'. Mrs. Bandaranaike tried to have Opatha and Chanrandran arrested but, according to Opatha, the 'gods saved us'. Since 1977, it has been usual for two or three booklets of mudslinging cartoons to be issued by political parties during campaigns (Hettigoda 1993).

Yoonoos began his political cartooning with the Tamil-language daily, *Thinakaran*, part of the Lake House Group. He remembered only three or four political cartoonists, all pro-government, drawing then. After 16 years at Lake

House/Associated, Yoonoos moved to the then-Communist Party daily, *Aththa*. A longtime foe of government, he has often been the victim of official harassment. He left Associated because of the sycophant role the group's newspapers played towards the authorities:

> I did not like working there as the work was boring, always supportive of government. I was put on the market research desk. I drew maps of the various electorates, putting in police stations, hospitals, and bridges. I realized the government wanted that information so they could blow up bridges, etc. to keep people from voting. I went to my Lake House superior to complain and after that, the government was gunning for me. I was forced to resign.
>
> (Yoonoos 1993)

Wickramanayake and Camillus played significant roles in the development of strips and comic papers. Upon joining Independent Newspapers in 1965, Wickramanayake drew strips for the daily *Dawasa* and for *Tikiri* (Children's). He moved to Lake House in 1968, where he became one of the first cartoonists to work for *Sathuta*, Sri Lanka's pioneer comic paper. With the government takeover of Lake House in 1973, Wickramanayake joined Wijeya Publishers, which had obtained *Sathuta* by court action. His forte was the love story; one such strip 'Chaturika', was carried in the Sunday newspaper *Silumina* for a considerable time. After *Sathuta's* closing in 1992, Wickramanayake contributed 'Attakaka Pipimal' (a serialized ghost story) to *Lankadipa*. In his view, strips have deteriorated since the 1960s because of the influences of television upon the public's pace and desires. Wickramanayake (1993) said, 'Because of social changes, strip language is more slang-like and drawings have deteriorated, using more violence demanded by television-viewing audiences'.

The largest comic paper publisher in Sri Lanka, Camillus Perera, started freelancing humor strips to major newspapers in 1966, and within two years, had developed characters for *Observer* and one called 'Dekkoth Pathmawathi' for Lake House's film magazine. He played key roles in the starting of the first comic papers, *Sathuta* and *Sittara*, and later *Sathsiri* and *Rasika*, and created Sri Lanka's most enduring strip characters.

Contemporary Status of the Profession

Large publishing houses in Sri Lanka are well endowed with cartoonists, Upali especially so with nine full-time cartoonists/artists working on its two dailies and women's, science fiction, and children's magazines. The difficulty lies in the smallness of Sri Lanka, which can support few publishing houses and dailies, all located in Colombo. Thus, the number of cartoonists supported by comic papers and daily/Sunday strip drawing is about 25; five times that number exist if 'marginal' (meaning freelance) cartoonists are counted (Ratnayake 1993). As might be expected, breaking into fulltime cartooning can be a long, laborious process.

Established cartoonists have no difficulty making a living from drawing even on a freelance basis, according to longtime cartoonist W. P. Wickramanayake (1993). Among ten to fifteen popular cartoonists who work as freelancers, Wickramanayake finds most of his work with newspapers which pay him a piece rate. Freelancers on comic papers usually make Rs 1000 (exchange rate of Rs 48 to US$1) per page of art; some earn exorbitant sums of Rs. 10,000 to 30,000 per month. Freelance story writers are paid Rs. 1000 for four installments of a story (Perera 1993).

Fulltime cartoonists in publishing houses carry hefty work-loads as they are expected to draw cartoons and illustrations for their publisher's various dailies and magazines. Famous cartoonist Janaka Ratnayake, for instance, draws a weekly strip, detailed sketches to accompany Sunday edition stories, color artwork for the science fiction weekly, and a picture story each for *Divaina* and *Nawaliya*, the women's weekly. For the three sketches and two picture stories per week, Ratnayake is paid the comfortable salary of Rs. 15,000 monthly.

Other remuneration is possible but on a limited basis. About fifteen comics stories have been turned into movies over the years, for which their creators received one-off sums of Rs. 20,000 to 30,000. Three comics each by Ratnayake and Wickramanayake were adapted for the screen, and both said the process was very easy for them as the film directors did not deviate far from their original stories (Ratnayake 1993; Wickramanayake 1993). Television advertising also offers opportunities as a number of commercials, especially for milk and baby foods, cosmetics, and sweets, are done in a cartoon style. One cartoonist, S. C. Opatha, offsets his meager income from cartoons by operating his own advertising agency, Pack Ads. Started in 1990, the agency is staffed by ten artists (Opatha 1993). Income for some cartoonists comes from the sale of paintings and/or from exhibition fees.

Political and strip cartoonist Winnie Hettigoda is particularly adept at organizing exhibitions, the proceeds from which he uses to support various causes. For example, his first exhibition, 'Sketches of Reality', was given free to universities whose student organizers charged an entrance fee and used the proceeds to purchase equipment or establish scholarships. Between 1991 and 1993, Hettigoda amassed Rs. 25,000 from exhibiting his works, which he banked and used the Rs. 339 monthly interest to support handicapped and poor students (Hettigoda 1993). His most successful exhibitions were staged throughout Sri Lanka in 1993, after he and the entire staff of the tabloid, *Lakdiva*, resigned because of the publisher's editorial interference. Determined to start what they called a 'people's' newspaper, the resigned staff organized film and theatre festivals and sold paintings donated by sympathetic artists. Hettigoda mounted an exhibition of his political cartoons, called 'Siddhi' (Incidences), first in Colombo and then in 24 other locations. As he explained, 'No tickets were needed for admission. We say, "Just give us money if you think it is right to start a new paper; otherwise, see the exhibition free".' After five days, the donations in Colombo grew to a stack of money 'four feet high' (Hettigoda 1993);

Figure 4.3 Mini papers, such as this 1993 example of *Kinihira* are full of caricatures, humorous drawings, and political cartoons, affording some cartoonists a publication outlet.

altogether, the exhibition garnered Rs 1,200,000 (US$25,000) and the tabloid *Hiru* (Sun) came out on 26 September 1993.

Other problems besides limited outlets that Sri Lankan cartoonists face include lack of training, outmoded equipment, insufficient and usually poor quality supplies, and a feeling of professional isolation.

Training is a priority for most Sri Lankan cartoonists. Some complain that individuals unstudied in art come to cartooning with notions that damage the profession, such as that a cartoon is an incomplete illustration (Hettigoda 1993); others claim that 'cartoonists are talented as artists but not adept at writing stories' (Ratnayake 1993), or the obverse, that 'cartoonists here have good ideas, but they are not artists' (Hettigoda 1993). Siriwardena (1993) said he could not understand why formal training exists for journalists and photographers, but not for cartoonists.

The lack of up-to-date equipment and high-grade drawing materials results from government controls and the demise of specialty shops for artists. Lamenting that only four web offset machines (all in the largest newspaper plants) and three color separation facilities exist in Sri Lanka, Hettigoda (1993) blamed the regime of the late President Premadasa, when there was 'no chance to import newsprint and printing equipment; at the same time, there was no chance to import weapons and poison'. Wickramanayake (1993) and Wijesoma (1993) agreed that better brushes, papers, and inks were available 30 years earlier when there were a few shops that catered to artists' needs. 'Not today', Wickramanayake (1993) said, 'when every Tom, Dick and Harry now imports anything, and they bring in poor stuff and sell it at high prices'. The result, Wickramanayake said, is 'I put my brush in India ink and it comes out like a broom'. Wijesoma added cartooning books to the list of items in short supply.

Professional activities are limited by the cartoonists' isolation from the rest of the cartoon world and from one another. As Hettigoda (1993) explained: 'We know there are a lot of cartoon competitions in the world, but we don't know the details as we are isolated here. If one knows of foreign competitions, and enters them, he becomes the best cartoonist in Sri Lanka'. An attempt to tie cartoonists together in a formal organization was attempted, but, according to Wijesoma (1993), it failed for lack of 'motivation' and because 'the low pay of cartoonists does not make for [support] a club'. Since 1989, an organization started by Givantha Artasad, an artist working for television, has recognized cartoonists as part of their media awards ceremony each October.

Comic Strips and Comic Papers

Comic strips and comic papers are distinct genres – the former usually appearing in daily and Sunday newspapers and an occasional magazine and consisting of three or four panels; the latter published as a separate, 16-page weekly periodical, each page a different story. They blend as strips have a tendency to shift from mainstream dailies to comic papers and comic strips and comic papers have common favorite themes of love and romance[3].

Sri Lanka comic strips are much like those elsewhere, with one exception – a peculiar type of social satire cartoon made up of one panel, in which a number of people answer a question or comment on a current issue. For example, one person in the panel might ask, 'Have you heard...?' to which the other half dozen each respond in a humorous way while making a point. Dating to at least the 1950s, when Henry Tennekoon[4] mastered the form in *Lankadipa*, these cartoons use the same setting or locale each time, only varying the discussion topic and responses to it. For example, Hettigoda's 'Halt' is built around a bus stand where seven people discuss a current issue.

Locally-created strips are confined to the Sinhalese-language press, since English-language dailies prefer American or British comics. The rationales for this preference are that foreign strips are less expensive to obtain through syndication, and there are so few English-speaking cartoonists willing to do a local strip. A check of dailies in mid-1993 found that the English-language *The Island* had three US strips, while the Sinhalese *Lankadipa*, *Dinamina*, and *Divayana* had three, two, and one local strips, respectively. The distinction is even more noticeable with Sunday editions: On 18 July 1993, *The Island* carried a full page of US color strips; *Sunday Times* four US strips in black and white, and *Sunday Observer*, two US strips in color. The Sinhalese Sunday newspapers, *Silumina*, *Divaina*, and *Lankadipa*, each had two local strips in color.

Common characteristics of locally-drawn strips are their rather large format, compared to eye-squinting American strips, their concentration on love and romance, and their serialized nature. Some romance strips are more daring in portraying the dress and actions of female characters than those in the US and elsewhere[5].

Comic papers commenced in 1972, reached their peak in numbers (thirteen) and combined circulation (450,000) in 1987, and began a steady descent in the 1990s, the reasons for which are discussed later. Printed on 8½ × 11 inch newsprint and in color, they appear weekly in sixteen-page editions that sell for Rs. 6 (US 12 cents) per copy. Rifas (1995:109) described the characteristics of comic papers as:

> The predominant theme is romance, and the usual format, a thin anthology of continuing serials, each progressing by one multi-paneled page per weekly installment. Most of the pictures show one or two people, usually talking, sometimes waving guns or slapping each other around. The differences between titles tend to be either very subtle or found in those inscrutable balloons.

Camillus Perera (1993), involved with comic papers from their beginning, said that longevity characterized the stories which 'last at least two years; one has continued since 1986. If a story is very popular, we add episodes and keep it going; the readers don't want us to stop them.' Although most deal with love and romance, Camillus said story types keep varying with the appearance of an occasional jungle tale or a legend set in an ancient royal court. An unusual trait is the brevity (one page) of each serialized story, meaning that a comic paper will carry fourteen or fifteen stories, often by as many artists. Occasionally, comic papers use other features, such as a pen-pal page.

Figure 4.4 'Samaja Samayan' is one of the popular 'commentary' cartoons. It was started by Henry Tennekoon in the 1950s, and revived by Daya Rajapaksa for *Lankadipa* more recently.

In the only known survey of comic paper readers, Karunanayake (1990) found that 57 per cent were purchasers, 51 per cent borrowers, and that nine per cent read comic papers in the public library, and five per cent in the office or at school. Historical/legendary stories were favored by 66 per cent, 59 per cent love, 52 per cent thrillers, and 66 per cent legends. As for motivations for reading the comics, 57 per cent said for entertainment/leisure, 41 per cent out of curiosity, 36 per cent as fantasy fulfillment, 34 per cent out of habit, 22 per cent as an escape, and five per cent to 'while away the time'.

The first comic paper, *Sathuta*, was launched 29 August 1972, by Lake House, which was interested in comics from the 1960s, when it recognized the popularity of the expensive and scarce foreign comic books among Sri Lankans. Wijesoma (1993), an advisor to *Sathuta*, recalled that he recommended the target audience should be eight to thirteen year-olds, 'but it ended up being three to 80'. Most stories in *Sathuta* were copies of foreign comics, although Wickramanayake and Camillus made local contributions. Camillus's 'Gajaman', one of the country's longest-lived characters, was born in that first number of *Sathuta*. When the government took over the Lake House Group the following year, Wijeya Publishers went to court and won the right to retain *Sathuta*; thereupon, Lake House (by then Associated Newspapers) started another comic paper, *Madura* (Ratnayake 1993).

Multi-Packs, a packaging and printing firm, launched a third paper, *Sittara*, on 20 October 1975. According to Camillus (Perera:1993), who was at the helm of *Sittara* from its start until 1986, a director of Multi-Packs had been attached to *Sathuta*, where he became well aware of the profits to be made with comic papers.

One of the most ambitious comic paper ventures was *Chithra Mithra* (Picture Friend), the brainchild of Sri Lanka's only multinational entrepreneur at the time, Upali Wijewardene. Within months after it began in February 1981, the weekly *Chithra Mithra* attained a circulation of 200,000, eclipsing both *Sittara* (100,000) and *Sathuta* (75,000). Its formula, according to *Media* (1981:11), was a mixture of 'romance, booze, money, travel, dreams, adventure, wild women', crammed into 16 pages. Very shortly, *Chithra Mithra* expanded to 32 pages, every page a different story. Editor Janaka Ratnayake said the paper had 'many topics – romance, detective, sci-fi, heroes, two pages built around movie stars, and almost a page of pen pal' (Ratnayake 1993). All episodes were serialized and in black and white with a spot of one color.

Wijewardene entered comics because the medium offered the largest market for a new publication aiming to support itself without advertising, and because it provided an opportunity to try out the company's new printing presses. Publication of *Chithra Mithra* was an experiment – the first step toward Wijewardene's goal of bringing out a picture story daily (Ratnayake 1993). But, that dream and others died in 1983, when the publisher was killed in a plane crash. *Chithra Mithra* lasted until 1986 when its circulation was down to a dismal 15,000. Ratnayake (1993) said Wijewardene's premature death was one of the contributing factors, as was the paper's substandard printing quality attributed to unskilled mechanics, and the keen competition provided by about a dozen or more other comic papers[6].

By 1993, only eight comic papers published by six companies were still in existence. They were Camillus Publications (*Sathsiri* and *Rasika*), Prahbath (*Sathwaruna* and *Hithawatha*), Multi-Packs (*Sittara*) Associated Newspapers (*Madura*), Himeshan (*Sadawasana*), and Four Line (*Chithra Katha*)[7]. The leaders in circulation were *Sathsiri* (about 100,000) and *Sittara* (about 90,000); all others were in the less than 20,000 circulation range. In 1993, Camillus saw a bleak future for all comic papers except for *Sathsiri* and *Sittara*. He predicted that *Rasika* would survive, 'not to make money' but to provide its sister *Sathsiri* a set of backup artists[8], while *Madura* would last, primarily because of its government sponsorship.

Camillus Publications

Camillus Perera has figured prominently in many stages of comic art growth in Sri Lanka; his strip characters are the country's oldest, his comic paper, *Sathsiri*, the largest.

Camillus Publications is one of the largest publishing houses in the country, producing eight magazines – *Sathsiri* and *Rasika*, comics; *Punchi* (Small),

Figure 4.5 A one-page serialized story in a Camillus comic paper of 1993. Courtesy of Camillus Perera.

educational to grade two level; *Hapana*, grades three to five; *Samatha*, grades six to eight; *Sammana*, grades nine to eleven; *Sivu Desa*, a general public monthly for literary conscious and educated classes, and *Asiri*, a Roman Catholic periodical.

All full-time staff members of Camillus Publications, except for one each chief artist and editor, are in administration (20), production (25), or sales (28). Artists and storywriters are hired on a regular freelance basis. Camillus (Perera 1993) explained that some story ideas emanate from the artists and the few storywriters used, but most are conceived by him.

The largest proportion (44 per cent) of the Camillus Publications budget is reserved for production, while 23 per cent goes to the government in the form of a business turnover tax, 20 per cent to distribution, and ten per cent to labor. The company operates its own distribution system. Promotion is mainly through television, which consumes 90 per cent of the Camillus advertising outlay (Perera 1993).

After about 20 years of drawing for dailies and the pioneering comic papers, during which time he also headed *Sittara* for a decade, Camillus stepped out on his own beginning in 1984, with three special collections of his famous characters in magazine format. They were published by different companies commissioned by Camillus. The first magazine in April 1984 was *Camillusge Gajaman*[9], which spotlighted the humorous title character in a Sri Lankan new year atmosphere. A sale of 200,000 copies prompted Camillus to bring out a second magazine, *Camillusge Samayan*, that December, and *Camillusge Gajaman #2* a year later, and on the strength of these successes (each sold 200,000–300,000 copies), Camillus Publications was established. The explanation Camillus (Perera:1993) gave for incorporating was that,

> Publishers had seen my magazines' and characters' popularity and they tried to finagle my copyrights from me. A court case pending about *Gajaman* has been dragging since 1988. Because of this, I had to form my own company; I also registered all fifteen of my characters with the Department of Registry and Patents.

Camillusge Gajaman Samaga Sathsiri (literally *Camillusge Gajaman* along with *Sathsiri*, shortened to *Sathsiri*) appeared in 1986 as the first comic paper under the new corporate name. The first issue sold 150,000 and, within six months, circulation jumped to 200,000. The second magazine, *Camillusge Don Sethan Samaga Rasika* (shortened to *Rasika*) was based on the day-to-day problems of the family of Don Sethan, the country's oldest character, created by Camillus, 1 May 1966, for the daily *Janatha*. By Camillus' own admission, *Sathsiri* and *Rasika* are rather similar, the major difference being they are drawn by separate teams of artists.

In the 1990s, Camillus had other plans, such as the development of other periodicals, including a weekly cartoon joke magazine, and breaking into the offshore animation industry.

Prahbath and Multi-Packs

Besides publishing the comic papers *Hithawatha* and *Sathwaruna*, Prahbath was involved in an array of other business activities – publishing the daily *Lakdiwa*, *Thiratharu* (Screen and Star), *Kendare* (Horoscope), *Senehasa*, *Kiripani* and the children's magazine *Kakulu* and producing films, operating one of the leading advertising agencies, and importing/exporting goods such as glassware, cosmetics, paper, and so forth. The company started in 1988 as an outgrowth of the ad agency, itself begun in 1984 (see Rifas 1995)[10], and folded in the mid-1990s.

A budget breakdown for Prahbath showed that 70 per cent of revenue went to the publisher/printer and ten per cent each to agents, subagents, and the shops.

Accounts had one week credit to pay for the comics they ordered. Freelancers were paid according to 'the artist and artwork,' not circulation of comic paper, and their income ranged from Rs. 450 to 1500 monthly (Rifas 1995).

Multi-Packs continues to publish *Sittara*, as well as books and magazines; however, like other comic papers, the company has faced cutbacks in recent years. In the late 1980s, Multi-Pack's comic papers circulation was 240,000; today, *Sittara* does not reach 100,000 (Rifas 1995).

Among reasons cited for the precarious state of comic papers, the impact of television looms largest. Rupavahini, the national television service, has become a serious competitor of the comic papers, providing its viewers one to two hours of animated American (and a few Russian) cartoons every afternoon; since 1987/1988, they have been dubbed into Sinhalese, enlarging their audience even further. The public prefers television cartoons because they provide complete stories with action and color, unlike serialized comic paper episodes with their limited number of frames (Wijesoma 1993, and Ratnayake 1993). Comic papers and other print media face the added challenge of expanded television schedules, which take away Sri Lankans' time to read. A second problem relates to the competence of cartoonists and the quality of product provided their audiences. In the 1980s, and even earlier, comic paper readers got a bargain as they paid the low price of Rs 1 (about two cents US) to enjoy the fruits of the best artists the country offered. 'Now there are only a few good fellows in some of these papers', according to Ratnayake (1993), who added, 'A lot of the new fellows are teenagers without experience in life'. Thus, most comic papers contain only one or two well-developed stories; the rest feature the same old cliche love stories, recycled week after week.

Even a more serious concern in the view of Camillus (Perera:1993) is that the schools discourage reading comics, relegating them to the category of 'smut'. Instead, the authorities want children to read educational magazines, he added, thus explaining the boom in children's papers publishing, especially at Upali and Camillus. In 1993, eight weekly children's papers[11] were published with a combined circulation of 200,000. Although they all include many elements of comic art, text dominates and the cartoons used are designed for an eight-year-old or younger audience (Dayananda 1993).

Other factors affecting comic papers are the mushrooming of tabloid magazines and mini papers that have gnawed away at their circulations; the high cost of materials, particularly newsprint; the small Sri Lankan market, easily saturated and lacking potential for further growth, and some competition from imported US comic books or their pirated versions (see Rifas 1995; also, Wickramanayake 1993).

Political Cartoons

Not many political cartoonists operate in Sri Lanka because of the few dailies, but those who do exist have made their presence known. They have contributed to the development of other genres such as strips; nurtured new cartoon formats such as investigative and the aforementioned group commentary cartoons; exploited the exhibition circuit to promote humanitarian and democratic causes, and, most importantly, taken editorial stands that have incurred the wrath of governmental and other political forces.

For unexplained reasons, Sinhalese dailies generally use more political cartoons than those in English. Most Sinhalese newspapers use both an inside-page political and a front-page pocket cartoon every day (Wijesoma 1993). The English-language *The Island* has a daily political cartoon by Wijesoma and the *Daily News*, a pocket, 'Laugh It Off', by Opatha; the *Observer* does not carry a daily cartoon, although the *Sunday Observer* has a full page, entitled, 'Through the Eyes of the Cartoonist' (Opatha 1993). Wijesoma's cartoon is translated daily and recycled in the company's Sinhalese paper. Siriwardena also contributes cartoons to newspapers in both languages, doing five political panels per week for the daily *Lankadipa* and one small front page cartoon, 'Times Smiles', for the *Sunday Times*. As has been the tradition, probably born out of financial necessity, some political cartoonists draw strips as well; Opatha's 'Silva', the exploits of a problem-plagued family man, appeared three times weekly in the *Observer*[12], before he switched to the new *Sunday Leader* in 1994.

An unusual approach to doing political cartoons was developed by Siriwardena in 1993. Asked by *Times* editors to do investigative cartoons on at least three occasions that year, Siriwardena went to the site of an important news happening, drew sketches, questioned police, and researched photographs and backgrounds of individuals involved. From that information, he would draw four instructive panels that explained how a particular news event unraveled (Siriwardena 1993a, 1993b).

The political cartoonists expectantly espouse different political and social viewpoints. Hettigoda (1993) believes Marxism/Leninism is the system of the majority; Yoonoos (1993) and Opatha (1993) think it is vital to look out for the interests of the impoverished. Yoonoos' (1993) contention is, 'The man in the street – if he can eat, drink, have clothing and a roof over his head and employment to meet his qualifications, then that is all there is. I'm not asking that people get everything that they want, just the bare necessities is all I'm asking for'. Opatha (1993) who comes from a predestination belief system, said 'We have a short period [on earth]. We have to do good things while we are here. God gave me a talent and I should use it to help the poor people'.

Perhaps imitative of some Indian colleagues, most Sri Lankan political cartoonists employ a 'common man' character in their work; such a regular figure acts as a connector, providing continuity from day to day. Hettigoda has such a regular character called 'Maraputhra', Opatha has 'Silva', Yoonoos, 'Appu Hamy', and Wijesoma, 'Punchisinglo'. The latter was described by a reviewer as a character 'with a forlorn face, expressionless and without a way [sic] of hope, his tattered clothes, the broken umbrella and the worn-out

Figure 4.6 Launched in 1975, *Sittara* is one of the longest-lived and largest-circulated comic papers of Sri Lanka.

shopping bag symbolizes the common man to whom nothing matters except his never-ending fight for survival' (Dorakumbure 1990:6). Hettigoda's character differs from the others. He is young with a degree but without a job. He is with the people and against the government and participates in pickets and strikes with the common people. He is fully bearded and always wears a black shirt. As Hettigoda (1997) said, he wanted an active, not pensioned, common man.

Political cartoonists in Sri Lanka work in a precarious atmosphere, subjected to both physical and verbal attacks from governmental and other political forces, and self-censoring guidelines and actions from their own editors. The situation worsened during the Premadasa regime in the early 1990s. Cartoonists and other journalists were bombarded with acts of violence, death threats, and harassing

Figure 4.7 Wijesoma's 'common man', 'Punchisinglo.' Courtesy W. R. Wijesoma.

incidents believed to have emanated from the president's dreaded goon squads, the 'Lawrence Mafia'.

Perhaps the most harrowing experience was that of Yoonoos, cartoonist for *Aththa*. Although Premadasa had arranged for his housing earlier, Yoonoos continued to draw what he himself termed 'very harsh' cartoons against the president. At first, the government reacted by offering Yoonoos a cushy job on the state owned newspaper, but the cartoonist turned it down, saying he could not 'sell my soul for that price'. After a hard-hitting cartoon directed at the housing minister in 1992, the government's repressive actions against Yoonoos intensified, as he explained:

> One day in August, three cars full of about twenty of Premadasa's goons came to my house. A minister's bodyguard shoved a pistol into my mouth, broke a tooth, and then put the gun next to my head. He threatened to kill me in front of my wife if I did more cartoons against his excellency. The next day, they returned, smashed up my furniture, and stabbed me. I required sixteen stitches.

> (Yoonoos 1993)

When I interviewed Yoonoos about a year later he was homeless, living in one small room of the *Aththa* office. His wife, who lived elsewhere for safety, brought his meals to him daily.

Hettigoda's life has also been made difficult because of the stands he has taken, and like Yoonoos and Wijesoma, he has received death threats[13]. In 1993,

Figure 4.8 Hettigoda used his 'commentary' cartoon, 'Halt', to ridicule governmental and social practices, which often got him into trouble. His 'common man', 'Maraputhra', is shown on the right. Courtesy Winnie Hettigoda.

after Hettigoda wrote and illustrated an article detailing how a senior politician had been killed, he was tracked by the goon squad, and saved, he said, by the assassination of Premadasa a week later. In 1996, Hettigoda was charged with libel by the Minister of Industrial Development, who felt he could be identified in a cartoon where some common folks at the bus stand discuss the drunken antics of an unidentified person of authority. The minister was awarded a Rs. 50 million judgment (Hettigoda 1996).

The temerity of the newspapers and the general public in the face of oppressive governments has adversely affected some cartoonists. In July–August 1991, Hettigoda lost his job at *The Island* after press reports about pro-government students attacking his exhibition at the Colombo campus. He said, '*The Island* saw the story and thought it was damaging to them; they were scared of the repercussions' (Hettigoda 1993; see Rifas 1995). When I interviewed him in 1993, Hettigoda was forced to move from his rented quarters by a landlord frightened of possible government actions. 'No one wants to rent to me', he said (Hettigoda 1993).

Compounding the difficulties of the political cartoonists are their low wages and insecure tenures. Many cartoonists must take other jobs to support themselves, and because there is room for only about a half dozen political cartoonists in the media, those who do have positions must do what it takes to retain them. As Yoonoos (1993) said, 'If I get sacked from one paper, no one else will take me as they have their cartoonists already'.

Given the plight of Sri Lankan cartooning, especially political, Opatha's reincarnation prayer makes sense: 'I pray to God every day that in my rebirth, I will be a cartoonist in any part of the world, but not in Sri Lanka' (Opatha 1993).

Notes

1 Mini papers are the size of tabloids folded in half and feature political news and just 'about anything else, including poor cartoons' (Hettigoda 1993). They date to 1993, when *Colama* (Column) appeared, followed by about a dozen others (e.g. *Kaputa* (the sound of a crow), *Thrisule* (Trident), *Thoppiya* (Hat), *Kinihira*, etc.).

2 A pocket cartoon is one column wide, about two to three inches deep, and appears on the front page. Usually, it deals with a social or political event in the news.

3 One strip cartoonist explained Sri Lankans' fondness for love and romance, thus: 'Basically we are a romantic people. Love stories are popular particularly among young people who have not yet experienced love and therefore get a vicarious feeling from reading these comics' (Wickramanayake 1993). Other themes have been gaining popularity as well, such as ghost, family feuds, humor, and historical fiction. Ratnayake draws a strip for the Sunday *Divaina* about divorced parents fighting for the custody of their child, and Wickramanayake does one in *Lankadipa* that is set in the past. He explained its popularity: 'People are changing; they want a simpler life and escape into my comic strips which are mostly based in the old days and use old dress, period furniture, and bullock carts' (Wickramanayake 1993).

4 Tennekoon's popular strip appeared in *Lankadipa* under the title 'Samaja Samayan' (Societal Nonsense). It was revived in the new *Lankadipa* and drawn by Daya Rajapaksa.

5 A notable controversy about sex in the strips occurred in 1980, when the *Sun* carried on its sports page the British strip 'Axa', featuring a nude heroine. The newspaper received many letters complaining about the nudity, including one from a minister who said he would skip the sports page until 'Axa' was removed (*Asiaweek* 1980:84).

6 Comic papers were in abundance, Ratnayake (1993) said, because they were inexpensive and easy to start: 'One only needed five cartoonists who get Rs. 25,000 in total salary, plus Rs 25,000 for printing, to make Rs. 35,000 in profits'.

7 Camillus (Perera:1993) said there were also a couple of Tamil-language comic papers, *Kopaleikarak* and *Kapalam*. *Jathaka Katha* which faced serious problems in 1993 when the publisher, Hettigoda Industries, manufacturers of Ayurvedic balm, toothpaste, lozenges, and herbal drinks, planned to phase it out. A Sinhalese monthly, *Jathaka Katha*, taught morals through stories of Buddha's previous incarnations; it was distributed mainly through Buddhist Sunday schools and temples (Medagama 1993; see Rifas 1995).

8 Camillus Publications is known for its team of excellent cartoonists (Ratnayake 1993).

9 Camillusge prefixes all comic titles of the company to identify the works as those of Camillus Perera and to protect copyright.

10 Rifas (1995) is the source for all information on Prahbath. My many attempts to locate the company headquarters and then to interview personnel, met with futility. A co-editor, Kusal Perera, whom I did meet, was both evasive and uncooperative. He failed to show up for a scheduled interview.

11 *Bindu* (Upali), *Punchi* and *Hapana* (Camillus), *Kakulu* (Prahbath), *Mihira* (Associated), *Athuru Mithuru*, *Viwjaya*, and *Piyawara*. The oldest is *Mihira*, the largest, *Punchi* (Dayananda 1993).

12 Two other political cartoonists were mentioned: Piyal Samarawera, who draws a pocket and a political cartoon for the Sunday *Lankadipa*, and Chandrika (a female name), who does a political cartoon for the Sunday *Divaina* (Siriwardena 1993a).

13 Another artist, Dhammika Bandara of *Vinivida* (Spectrum) *Magazine*, was kidnapped by Premadasa's 'Black Cats' in 1989, never to be heard from again.

5

LIANHUANHUA AND *MANHUA* – PICTURE BOOKS AND COMICS IN OLD SHANGHAI

Kuiyi Shen

In the early twentieth century, one form of commercial art, *lianhuanhua* (illustrated story book), became very popular in Shanghai, along with the development of publishing industry. Although lithographic illustrations appeared in the late nineteenth century, two distinctive genres of serial illustration, illustrated story books and comics, developed quickly in Shanghai during the 1920s and 1930s. The contents, styles, production methods and distribution systems of these two genres reflect the different tastes of contemporary social groups in China's major metropolis, Shanghai.

The embryonic form of *lianhuan tuhua* did not appear until the late nineteenth century, after lithographic printing was introduced to Shanghai from the west, although some scholars claim that the origin of the form lianhuanhua may be traced back to much earlier periods (A 1982:1–12; Huang and Wang 1993:17–18). The technique brought new possibilities to the Chinese illustration press which saw diminished costs, along with simplified and increased production.

From the 1880s, therefore, many magazines, such as *Dianshizhai Pictorial*, showed an interest in exploring the potential of this technique. The public especially appreciated illustrations of popular novels and scenes of the time, both in print series, which could be considered the direct predecessor of the lianhuanhua. Ten illustrations to accompany a narrative about the Korean rebellion published in the 1884 *Dianshizhai Pictorial* may be the earliest example (Bai *et al*. 1989:77–81). In 1899, Wenyi Book Company in Shanghai published the illustrated lithograph, *The Story of the Three Kingdoms,* drawn by Zhu Zhixuan, which became a great success. It was called *huihui tu* (chapter pictures), because it had one illustration for each chapter, *hui*. By putting the text and picture into a single composition, huihui tu is close in format to the later lianhuanhua.

On the dawn of the revolution of 1911, the new popular literature, in the form of newspapers, magazines, and booklets continued to emerge. In 1916, *Caobao* newspaper bound their single-piece pictorial into the format of an album, which was much like the format used for later lianhuanhua (Huang and Wang

1993:17–18). Because a newspaper bound in this format was much easier to carry, and its contents of texts mixed with pictures attracted more middle and lower class readers, it quickly became very popular in Shanghai. Many small publishers, especially those previously publishing only the librettos of operas, vied with one another to find painters to prepare pictures and to issue this kind of picture-text mixed album. Although the contents of these albums were mostly news and current events mixed with pictures, and not illustrated stories, the prototype for the format lianhuanhua was then established in Shanghai.

After lithography, new processes of printing used in Europe and the United States appeared successively in Shanghai and then in other large cities of the country, beginning in the early twentieth century. These gave way to the spread of a pictorial literature that became a cultural product more and more sought by the public. Certain narratives were almost cartoon strips, the lianhuanhua. But the term 'lianhuanhua' was not used until 1927. At that time, this kind of book was called different names in different regions: *xiaoshu* (little book) or *tuhuashu* (picture book) in Shanghai, *gongzaishu* (kid's book) in Guangzhou, *yaya shu* (children's book) in Wuhan, or *xiaorenshu* (kid's book) in the north.

In 1918, a famous Peking opera serial, *Limao huan taizi* (Exchange the Prince for a Leopard Cat), successfully played in Shanghai for several months, and became a hot topic in the city. Many small publishers saw an opportunity to make money, so immediately asked painters to draw illustrated story books based on the script of the opera. Compared to the previous *xiaoshu* which focused on news and current events, the contents of these illustrated opera stories were more common and less exotic, and the story continuity made them much easier for people to comprehend. But most of these books were drawn quite coarsely. The backgrounds in the paintings were simply copied from the stage sets, and images of the figures were also exact copies of the opera, keeping all the traditional symbolism of the objects, gestures, and make-up. The reason for this might be because a major concern of these small publishers was time. They tried to keep the publications following the schedules of the performances, so the cartoonists they commissioned were asked to draw at least ten pieces every day. It is not surprising, therefore, that these drawings were done in such a rough and slipshod way. This type of literature, however, reproduced rapidly and became very popular.

Later, the themes of illustrated story books were expanded to novels and current social events. The earliest example might be *Xue Rengui zhengdong* (Xue Rengui Going on an Eastern Expedition) (see Figure 5.1), which was painted by Liu Boliang, and based on the novel of the same title published by Youwen Book Company in 1920. The format used by Liu Boliang in this book was followed by most lianhuanhua painters in the next decade.

At the center of this abundant production, the lianhuanhua illustrated by Zhu Runzhai was among the most successful and popular. Zhu (1890–1936), a native of Yancheng in Jiangsu, was one of the earliest painters drawing illustrated story books. He was educated in an old-style private school and learned traditional

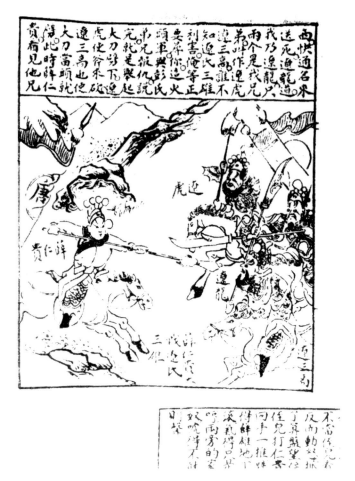

Figure 5.1 Liu Boliang, *Xue Renui zhengdong* (Xue Rengui Going on an Eastern Expedition), 1920, published by Youwei Book Company of Shanghai.

painting from local painters. In 1912, he went to Shanghai to pursue his career. After failing to sell paintings for a living, he started to draw illustrations for small publishers, where he got to know two cartoonists, Liu Boliang and Li Shuchen. Encouraged by Liu and Li, Zhu turned his talents to drawing lianhuanhua. The themes of his drawings were mostly adopted from novels and historical romances. By the 1930s, he asserted himself as one of the principal cartoonists in Shanghai. In his work, the influence of the stage background was eliminated, and the postures of figures were also more vivid. Although he died early, at 46, he completed more than 30 comic serials, which included *Sanguo yanyi* (Historical Romance of Three Kingdom), *Tianbaotu* (Heavenly Treasures), and *Dibaotu* (Earthly Treasures) (see Figure 5.2). His works were very popular

Figure 5.2 Zhu Runzhai, *Dibaotu* (Earthly Treasures), 1933, published by Wende Book Company of Shanghai.

and influential among the lower class people; there was a common saying at the time that 'If you read the *Tianbaotu*, you won't feel hungry' (Bai *et al.* 1989:84).

The popular market also attracted some big publishers. In 1927, World Book Company (*Shijie shuju*), which was established in 1921 in Shanghai, published *Sanguo zhi* (History of Three Kingdoms), one of the most popular novels in China. It was painted by Chen Danxu, and entitled *Lianhuan tuhua sanguo zhi* (Illustrated History of Three Kingdoms) (see Figure 5.3). This was the first time the term 'lianhuan tuhua' was applied to xiaoshu, the illustrated story book. Since then, *lianhuan tuhua* has become a special term indicating this kind of picture book. Later people even omitted the character '*tu*', and simply called them lianhuanhua (Chen 1979:66–9; Huang and Wang 1993:18; Bai et al. 1989:78).

The popularity of this kind of picture book at the time should perhaps be partly attributed to its unique distribution system. Because themes of xiaoshu were mostly plays, wild anecdotes, and legendary stories, xiaoshu was considered vulgar and low taste by intellectuals, and most bookstores did not want to sell them[1]. However, they attracted readers from certain groups of society, mostly children and lower class people. A unique distribution network, therefore, appeared in Shanghai during the time, that is, the small publishers sold xiaoshu to street bookstall owners, instead of going through the bookstores. The street book stalls, in most cases, did not sell these books, but rented them out to

Figure 5.3 Chen Danxu, *Lianhuan tuhua sanguo zhi* (Illustrated Story of Three Kingdoms), 1927, published by World Book Company of Shanghai.

those people who did not have enough money to buy books or just wanted to spend 'nickels and dimes' to read more books (Lu 1981:51–52) (see Figure 5.4).

During the 1920s and early 1930s, most small publishers who produced lianhuanhua were located on a street called Beigongyili in the Zhabei district of Shanghai. Every night, the owners of book stalls would come to these small publishers to buy newly published and popular comic serials. At that time, there were two new volumes of each comic serial going on the market nightly, most issued in quantities of more than 2,000 copies. Usually after 24 volumes of the serial were issued, publishers bound them together and put them into a box, making them look like old-style books (Huang and Wang 1993:18–19). This distribution network developed very quickly and to coordinate it, street book stall owners and publishers established the 'Shanghai Lianhuan tuhua Promotion Society' at Taoyuanli in southern Shanghai in 1935 (Huang and Wang 1993:115–119). It actually became a comic book exchange. Later, the center of comic publishing was moved from Zhabei to the new place. Every afternoon at two o'clock, publishers brought newly published comics there, and then at about six o'clock, the new comics appeared in the street bookstalls (Huang and Wang 1989:115–119; He 1996; Wang Yiqiu 1995).

This distribution network also required a unique production system. During the late 1920s and the beginning of the 1930s, besides the World Book Company and a few other big publishers involved in this business for a short time, there

104

Figure 5.4 A street bookstall in 1930s Shanghai. (*Shanghai:150 Years,* Deng Ming, ed., Shanghai People's Fine Arts Publishing House, 1992, p. 97)

were about 20 small publishers which published comic serials, and no more than ten professional cartoonists worked for them. Each small publisher usually had a couple of commissioned cartoonists. The work, however, was not done by a single cartoonist but by a kind of traditional workshop. Each cartoonist usually had several disciples working for him. This master–disciple system continued in cartoonists' circles until the beginning of the 1950s. Because of the requirements of the special market and distribution system, speed of production was crucial to publishers. They usually required commissioned cartoonists to hand in finished works every day. When cartoonists received a commission from the publishers, the master would determine the compositions and draw the main images, and then let his disciples draw the rest. Each student would be in charge of different details, such as architecture, rocks and trees, animals and flowers, and even the patterns and motifs of the clothes. Some students, after several years of training, received commissions independently and accepted their own students. Others worked in the workshop for several years without ever having a chance to draw figures. If the cartoonist became famous, however, he might choose the themes and publisher himself (Wang Yiqiu 1995; He 1996).

Besides Zhu Runzhai, three other younger cartoonists, Zhou Yunfang, Shen Manyun, and Zhao Hongben, were quite famous in the lianhuanhua field during the 1930s. They were even called 'Four Famous Female Roles' (*Sida mingdan*) of lianhuanhua following the tradition of Peking opera (Ling 1981; Zhu

Guangzheng 1982:51–58; Huang and Wang 1993:1–20; Wang Yiqiu 1995; He 1996).

Zhou Yunfang learned to draw cartoons at fifteen. He was not only good at drawing ancient topics but also modern themes, because he had learned western art styles. He attracted many young followers, who even formed a Zhou Style of comics to compete with the followers of Zhu Runzai. In the 1940s, he adapted the major characters from the famous comic serial of 1930s' Shanghai, *Wang xiansheng*, which was drawn by Ye Qianyu, to make a comic book called *Wang xiansheng chushi* (The Birth of Mr. Wang) (see Figure 5.5). His death at 29 was attributed to smoking opium.

Shen Manyun (1911–1978), a native of Shanghai, was from a merchant family. When he was in elementary school, he collected cigarette cards, from which he copied paintings, bringing him numerous compliments from his teachers and classmates. Later, when he worked in a pharmacy after his parents died, he still didn't give up hope of becoming a painter. In 1926, he left his hometown and went to Shanghai to seek a career. By good fortune, the place he stayed was Beigongyili, the center of the production and distribution of lianhuanhua. There he got to know the well-known cartoonist Liu Boliang, and became his pupil. His first picture book, *Jigong zhuan* (Tale of Jigong), was published by Guangji Book Company on the recommendation of Liu. Shen Manyun was good at drawing opera themes and legendary stories (see Figure 5.6). He regularly attended opera performances and movie screenings to find new topics for his work (Ling 1981:82–88; Huang and Wang 1993:19). Zhao Hongben (b.1915), a native of

Figure 5.5 Zhou Yunfang, *Wang xiansheng chushi* (The Birth of Mr. Wang), 1946, published by Jiuyi Book Company.

Figure 5.6 Shen Manyun, *Huozuo Yizhilan* (Capturing Yizhilan Alive), Gangwen Book Company, 1946.

Jiangsu, was also a self-trained painter, learning drawing by copying elder cartoonists' work. He went to Shanghai and began his career in 1931, working in a small press. At the beginning, he followed Zhu Runzhai's style and drew narratives based on traditional novels of fantasy and chivalry. During World War II, having remained in Shanghai, Zhao Hongben adapted to cartoon strips progressive literary works such as *Sunrise* or *The Storm*, by Cao Yu, as well as his version of *The Story of Ah Q* (Zhao 1978:55–62). In other illustrated stories, he exalted the patriotism of national heroes, Shi Kefa and Zheng Chenggong, who fiercely resisted the Manchurian invasions of the seventeenth century. The composition and perspective applied in his work are believed to have brought a new appearance to lianhuanhua. His famous later work, *Monkey King Beats the White-bonded Demon*, showed such mastery (see Figure 5.7).

Adaptation of knightly novels to the cartoon format was often preceded by a movie version. Close to 20 movies in a series under the title *Huoshao Honglian-si* (Burning the Temple of the Red Lotus), were realized between 1928 and 1931. Hu Die (Butterfly Hu), one of the most famous Chinese actresses, played the main character in these movies. The films were such successes that they were immediately made into comic strips, unfortunately, with a rapidity that jeopardized drawing quality. From this point on, film became one of the main sources, along with theater, of lianhuanhua. The public in the big cities had the opportunity to read and view repeatedly the achievements of its favorite heroes. For those who did not yet have access to movies, lianhuanhua became the means of knowing about the popular stories.

Figure 5.7 Zhao Hongben, *Sanda Bagujing* (Monkey King Beats the White-boned Demon), 1959, published by Shanghai People's Fine Art Publishing House.

By the end of the 1940s, there were more than 30 professional lianhuanhua cartoonists in Shanghai. A younger generation appeared, which included Qian Xiaodai (1912–1964), Chen Guangyi (b.1918), and Yan Meihua (b.1927), some of whom were commercial designers in their earlier careers. The number of lianhuanhua publishers reached more than 100, and there were more than 2,000 street book stalls in Shanghai. They even expanded their distribution network farther to Hong Kong, Singapore, and Indonesia (Lu 1981:51–53).

At almost the same time as the professional cartoonists were developing this distinctive genre, picture book, or lianhuanhua, with its special distribution network, and thereby creating a new market for commercial art among the lower-class consumers of Shanghai, another group of commercial artists began contributing comic strips to magazines and newspapers, and later developed professional cartoon magazines. The appearance of these comic strips, along with the newspapers and magazines in which they were published, was greatly stimulated by the development of the printing industry, but more importantly they catered to the needs of a quickly rising middle-class of consumers in Shanghai. Because consumers of these journals and newspapers were usually educated people and distinct from those of picture books, the contents of the comic strips were different. These satirical drawings denounced the seizure of Chinese territory by foreign imperialism and evils of society, such as the use of opium or gambling. Other works shed a humorous light on the particularities of everyday life in China and abroad. These were shown more often in one frame, rather than series format. Because most of the authors of these comic strips were better educated commercial artists, some of whom had received training abroad, the styles of their work emulated western comics and cartoons.

One of the well-known early comic draftsmen was Qian Binghe (1874–1944), a native of Zhejiang, who early on was good at traditional Chinese painting. He worked for the daily pictorial, *Minquan huabao* (Civil Rights Pictorial) but his comics were published also in *Minguo ribao* (Republic Daily), *Minli ribao* (Minli Daily) and *Shen bao* (Shanghai Daily) (Bi and Huang 1986:37–38). One of his most famous comic strips entitled 'A Hundred Appearances of the Old Gibbon' was published in *Civil Rights Pictorial* and *Minguo xinwen* (Republic News) for a year in 1913. The gibbon (*yuan* in Chinese) was a rebus for Yuan Shikai, who tried to restore the monarchy after he became the president of the republic. The cartoon series illustrated Yuan's activities of restoration and Sun Yat-sen's 'Second Revolution' (Zheng 1979:3).

Shanghai Puck (see Figure 5.8) may be the earliest comic magazine in China. Published in 1918 by Shen Bochen (1889–1920), it was also called *Bochen huaji huabao* (Bochen's Comic Pictorial). Shen learned traditional painting from a minor artist, Pan Yasheng, but was known as a cartoonist, in fact, the most influential and representative cartoonist of the May Fourth Movement, a period of highbrow political and cultural ferment that began in 1919. More than 1,000 of his cartoons were published in *Shanghai Daily, Shenzhou huabao* (Shenzhou Pictorial), *Civil Rights Pictorial, Da gonghe ribao* (Great Republic Daily), *Shishi xinbao* (Current News) and other Shanghai newspapers and pictorials during the 1910s (Ding 1928; Bi and Huang 1986:48). After a short visit to Japan and Beijing in 1917, he established *Shanghai Puck*, a bilingual comic monthly. According to the statement he wrote in the first issue, the magazine had three responsibilities: first, to give advice and warning to both governments of the south and north, and spur them to work in concerted efforts to create a unified government; second, to let westerners understand Chinese culture and customs, and thus, raise the position of China in the world; and third, to promote the new morality and practices and discard the old (Shen 1918:2; Bi and Huang 1986:51–52). Besides Shen Bochen himself, other painters, such as Chen Baoyi and Wang Dungeng, also contributed their comics to the magazine. *Shanghai Daily* reported that the first issue of the bilingual comic monthly issued more

Figure 5.8 The cover of the first issue of *Shanghai Puck* (1 September, 1918), edited and published by Shen Bochen.

than 10,000 copies in the lower Yangtze River region (Bi and Huang 1986:56). Because it was published in the May Fourth period, most cartoons were directly related to the then-current political issues. However, the magazine published only four issues and stopped publication after Shen Bochen died in 1919.

Manhua, the term used to indicate comics and cartoons in China, was borrowed from the Japanese word *manga* (comics). Zheng Zhenduo was the first to use this term in 1925, referring to Feng Zikai's painting, which he published in *Wenxue zhoubao* (Literature Weekly). In 1926, Feng's comic book, entitled

110

Zikai manhua (Comics by Zikai) was published. Since then, this term has been used for comics and cartoons. Feng Zikai (1898–1975), then, is also considered one of the founders of Chinese comics.

Feng started his art career when he was a student at the Zhejiang First Normal School, where he was strongly influenced by his two teachers, the artist Li Shutong and writer Xia Mianzun (Bi and Huang 1986:71). In 1921, he went to Japan to study art and music. The style of the Japanese painter Takehisa Yumeji (1884–1934) strongly influenced his later painting. He began his cartoon drawing in 1923 and his first published comic strip appeared a year later in the *Women de qiyue* (Our July), a magazine published by two famous writers, Zhu Ziqing and Yu Pingbo, in Shanghai (Wang et al. 1994). Feng's comics also attracted the attention of the scholar Zheng Zhenduo, who was the editor-in-chief of *Literature Weekly* at the time. In 1925, Zheng set up a column, 'Zikai Manhua', to run Feng's cartoons in his weekly newspaper, *Literature Weekly*. After that, Feng's simple and naive, funny and humorous comics became very popular in Shanghai (Zhu 1980:25). The style of Feng's comics was obviously influenced by Takehisa Yumeji and the Chinese painter Chen Shizeng (1876–1923), whose poetic flavor may also be found in Feng's drawings (Zhu 1980:25). During the Anti-Japanese war, he sent his editor a manhua version of Lu Xun's novel, *Ah Q Zhengzhuan,* which was followed by several series based on other works by the same author (see Figure 5.9). But most of his works were single-piece cartoons depicting people's everyday life (see Figure 5.10).

The earliest manhua group, Shanghai Comic and Cartoon Society (*Shanghai manhuahui*), was organized by a group of young cartoonists in 1927. Its major members included Ding Su (1891–?), Wang Dunqing (1899–?), Zhang Guangyu (1900–1964), Huang Wennong (?–1934), Ye Qianyu (1907–95), Lu Shaofei (b.1903), Zhang Zhengyu (1904–76), and others (Bi and Huang 1986:82–83). The major activity of the group was to publish a weekly journal, *Shanghai manhua* (Shanghai Sketch), which featured not only comics, but also photography, paintings, and essays. It sold about 3,000 copies each issue in Shanghai and other areas through the newspaper network (Bi and Huang 1986:86). In the foreword of the periodical, the editors (*Shanghai Manhua* 128:2) stated that:

> We don't want to be a guard-dog of the old morality in order to curse evil, and don't have interest in praising vanity fair either. The irregular changes of the world, however, must be the natural phenomena of the mixture of lives.
>
> Our effort is to express our feelings about the great and colorful life in Shanghai.

Shanghai Sketch, therefore, was less political. With only a couple of political cartoons included in each issue; most works were comic strips of social life, the most famous being *Wang xiansheng* (Mr. Wang), drawn by Ye Qianyu.

Ye, whose real name was Ye Lunqi, a native of Tonglu, Zhejiang, loved painting when he was in middle school, but never received formal training. In

Figure 5.9 Feng Zikai, *Manhua Ah Q zhengzhuan* (Comic Ah Q), 1938. Reprinted in *Feng Zikai*, Hebei Educational Publishers, 1994, p. 116.

1925, he went to Shanghai and worked in a fabric company, where he learned to sell cloth every morning and paint advertisements for the company in the afternoon (Xie 1991:33–43). During the 1920s, many foreign newspapers and magazines were issued in Shanghai, but, as we have seen, various Chinese periodicals and newspapers also were published. The cartoons and comics in the latter were always the favorites of Shanghai people. Ye started to draw comics in 1926, and his first publication was in *Sanri huakan* (Three Day Pictorial), which was published by cartoonists brothers, Zhang Guangyu and Zhang Zhengyu. In 1927, when the Zhangs and Ding Su organized the Shanghai Comic and Cartoon

Figure 5.10 Feng Zikai, *Chengfengliang* (Relaxing in a Cool Place), 1940s. Reprinted in *Feng Zikai*, Hebei Educational Publishers, 1994, p. 128.

Society, Ye naturally became a major member (Bi and Huang 1986:82–86). He and Wang Dunqing were also in charge of the editorial work for *Shanghai Sketch*.

The comic series, *Mr. Wang* (see Figure 5.11), was published in *Shanghai Sketch* beginning in its first issue. The image of Mr. Wang embodied different social classes of Shanghai and exhibited societal problems, such as sharp conformism, hunger for social success, and lack of education and culture. This funny and satiric cartoon also described the humble people of Shanghai, making fun of their breadth and their immodest taste for gambling, particularly *mah joong*. On the whole, the strip clearly depicted these people justly, often showing unmanageable creditors and brutal police officers. Ye exhibited an indisputable sense of characterization: Mr. Wang is a character type, a true comic strip hero, the first and one of the most original of this kind in China. This funny image, therefore, very quickly became a favorite figure in Shanghai. Later, when *Shanghai Sketch* stopped publication in 1930, the *Mr. Wang* series was continued

Figure 5.11 Ye Qianyu, 'Who will buy this coffin?' in *Wang xiansheng* (Mr. Wang), 1936, in *Shidai huabao.*

in *Shidai huabao* (Modern Miscellany), which Ye himself edited. After 1932, Ye Qianyu painted another series of Mr. Wang, called *Wang xiansheng biezhuan* (Another Story of Mr. Wang), for *Tuhua chenbao* (Picture Morning News). This time Mr. Wang wore a hat, which was fashionable in Shanghai at the time. The hundreds of stories of Mr.Wang were a true portrayal of life, and through the depiction of the lives of two major characters, Mr. Wang and Little Chen (Xiao Chen) dealt with the everyday life of the middle and lower classes of Shanghai; the corruption and incompetence of officials; sympathy for the poor, and the humorous and funny things of life. *Mr. Wang* was not a favorite just in Shanghai for Ye also painted *Wang xiansheng nanzhuan* (Story of Mr. Wang in the South) for Guangzhou and *Wang xiansheng beizhuan* (Story of Mr. Wang in the North) for Tientsin. The comic series was even made into a Shanghai movie in 1934. *Picture Morning News* continued to publish *Mr. Wang* for 182 issues (Xie 1991:88).

Besides Ye, other cartoonists also did comics for *Shanghai Sketch* and *Shidai manhua* (Modern Sketch) such as Lu Shaofei's *Daxiaozi* (Big Boy) and the many short stories of Liao Bingxiong (b.1915) (see Figure 5.12).

The mid-1930s was the golden era for the publication of comics and cartoons in China. In Shanghai alone, nineteen comic and cartoon magazines were

Figure 5.12 Liao Bingxiong, *Yijia* (Bargain), 1934. Reprinted in *Liao Bingxiong*, Hebei Educational Publishers, 1994, p. 64.

published, including *Modern Sketch* (1934–37), *Manhua shenghuo* (Comics and Life) (1934–35), *Duli manhua* (Oriental Puck) (1935–36), and *Manhuajie* (Comic Circle) (1936). Among them, *Modern Sketch* edited by Lu Shaofei, was most representative. It was considered the best quality comic magazine of the time, because every issue included several color pages and the cartoon pages were printed in zincography. The first issue published more than 10,000 copies (Wang 1935:3). During three years of publication, more than 100 cartoonists contributed their works to the magazine. Its major contributors were former members of the Shanghai Comic and Cartoon Society of the 1920s.

Another important cartoonist, Zhang Leping (1910–1992), was born in Haiyan, Zhejiang. His mother, said to be good at embroidery and papercuts, might have been his first art teacher. He went to Shanghai in 1926, entered a painting studio to learn the craft of painting female beauties, then popular in tobacco advertising, and later, worked in several printing companies painting commercial ads. In 1928, he replaced Ye Qianyu as an employee at the Sanyou company after Ye left to edit *Shanghai Cartoons*; the following year, he started to paint comics and submit them to *Modern Sketch, Oriental Puck,* and other comic magazines. His famous character, 'Three hairs' (Sanmao), was first published in Shanghai's *Xiaochenbao* (Little Morning News) in 1935. The tragic story of the poor but lovable Sanmao immediately became a favorite of both children and adults in Shanghai. During World War II, Zhang participated in the Anti-Japanese Cartoonists Brigade, working in Wuhan and Chongqing. He went back to Shanghai after the war and resumed drawing Sanmao. The layout was the same as the original that had appeared in 1935–1936, and the character kept his cunning nature, but the tone changed so that Sanmao became the victim of a materialist world consumed by money, where people indulged themselves with greed. A movie based on this story produced in 1948–1949 only partially captured the bitter sweet emotion. He drew *Sanmao Joins the Army* for *Shanghai Daily,* then in 1947, started his most famous *Sanmao liulang ji* (Adventures of Sanmao the Orphan) for *Dagong Newspaper* (see Figure 5.13).

Shanghai was besieged in August 1937, a few weeks after China's official entrance into war with Japan. Shanghai cartoonists immediately organized the Shanghai Cartoonists Association for National Salvation, and published a journal *Jiuwang manhua* (Cartoons for National Salvation) in September (see Figure 5.14). Many cartoonists contributed their works to this journal, including

Figure 5.13 Zhang Leping, 'Jianjia jingmai' (A Price War), in *Sanmao liulang ji* (Adventures of Sanmao the Orphan), 1947. Reprinted, Joint Publishing Co. (Hongkong Branch), 1981.

Figure 5.14 The cover of the first issue of *Jiuwang Manhua* (Cartoons for National Salvation), 20 Sept., 1937.

Ye Qianyu, Zhang Guangyu, Shen Yiqian (1908–1944?), Cai Ruohong (b.1910), Liao Bingxiong, Huang Miaozi (b.1913), and others. *Cartoons for National Salvation* published twelve issues before the fall of Shanghai in December 1937, and was even issued in Hankou, Guangzhou, and Hong Kong (Bi and Huang 1986:152–157). By the end of the year, great numbers of illustrators and cartoonists fled toward Canton and Hong Kong, where they regularly used their art to struggle against the invaders.

In August 1937, Ye Qianyu and Zhang Leping founded a Cartoon Propaganda Team in Shanghai, which included Te Wei (b.1915), Hu Kao (b.1912), and other cartoonists. For almost three years, this group followed the itinerary of retreat towards the southwest by governmental forces after the fall of Nanking, the capital, in December 1937; they moved from Wuhan to Changsha, Guilin, and finally Chongqing. Becoming a division of the political department for the governmental and communist armies united in combat against the Japanese, the group organized exhibitions of posters, caricatures, and satirical comic strips along the way (Xuan 1980:34). These exhibitions, held in parks or on the streets, expanded to the east (Jiangxi and Zhejiang) and the south (Canton and south of Guangxi). The cartoonists propagandized about atrocities committed by Japanese soldiers, opposed the Japanese occupation of China, and sought financial contributions to support the struggle for national salvation. These themes were reiterated in bound booklets, small newspapers, and big pages of comic strips and caricatures that were printed in these regions with whatever means available, often pitted woods. These cartoonists also published a cartoon magazine, *Kangzhan manhua* (Cartoons of the Anti-Japanese War) (see Figure 5.15), which appeared in fifteen issues, twelve of which were issued in Wuhan and three in Chongqing. More than 30 cartoonists contributed their works, with those of Zhang Leping, Liang Baibo, Liao Bingxiong, and Ye Qianyu the most popular. The magazine not only published its members' works, but some anti-fascist cartoons by European and American cartoonists (Xuan 1980:34). In 1940, because all means of support were ceased by the government, the group stopped their activities. Individually, however, the members stayed active and found themselves allied with those who rallied in Chongqing after the siege of Canton at the end of 1938, and Hong Kong in December 1941. Liao Bingxiong, Zhang Guangyu, Ye Qianyu, and Ding Cong are the most well-known among the group.

Conclusion

Between the political and social chaos of the 1920s and the Japanese invasion of 1937, Shanghai, the most modern metropolis in China, enjoyed a short, peaceful break. After the metropolis had developed for 70 years, a well-educated middle-class was solidly established. Even lower-class people had an opportunity to experience the life of the modern city, although it was not necessarily peaceful and happy.

Besides the booming economy, cultural activities also took place on an unprecedented scale. Many public and private colleges and professional schools were established; various cultural, art, and literature groups and societies were founded; various shows and exhibitions were held daily, and a variety of magazines and newspapers dazzled people's eyes. To count only art magazines, there were more than 70 published in Shanghai from 1928 to 1936, not including art supplements of newspapers (Xu 1992). The response to modernity in Shanghai was extremely exciting but complicated. New and old, avant-garde and

图 二〇二 《抗战漫画》创刊号封面 (1938) 叶浅予

Figure 5.15 The cover of the first issue of *Kangzhan manhua* (Cartoons of the Anti-Japanese War), 1938.

conservative, wholesale westernizing and more conservative national essence – a great variety of ideas, styles, and practices coexisted in the city. The short, peaceful break created a fantasy for the Shanghainese, that they might have unlimited opportunity to do whatever they wanted. But behind this, there was a general trend to seek a peaceful, fair, and well-to-do life that was fundamental to most Shanghai people. In comics, the middle-class could get their complaints about corrupt officials, dissatisfaction with unfairness, and disgust about bad habits off their chests with a relaxed laugh. Xiaoshu, on the other hand, by using a new vehicle to convey the old style culture, let people more easily comprehend novels, operas, and movies, in which they could find their idealized heroes and a fair society. Therefore, the development of comics and lianhuanhua alike catered to the needs of the middle and lower-class people.

Note

1 The attitude to these xiaoshu raised a debate in literature circles during the 1930s. Many writers and scholars were involved in the debate, including Lu Xun, Mao Dun (Shen Yanbing), Hu Qiuyuan, and Du Heng. See Zhao Jiabi 1981.

6

THE CORPOREALITY OF EROTIC IMAGINATION: A STUDY OF PICTORIALS AND CARTOONS IN REPUBLICAN CHINA

Yingjin Zhang

The present study is part of a larger project that aims to sort out the complex relationship between film and print cultures in Republican China (1910s–1940s). The first move I undertook was to extend the perimeter of print culture to include these previously marginalized urban publications – pictorials (*huabao*), cartoons (*manhua*), and fan magazines. After examining selected texts from these publications, I have come to realize that erotic imagination remained a central theme in the Republican period, and the precedents of such erotic representation could be located in several late Qing publications.

Inasmuch as print culture is concerned, one might speculate that the consistent inclusion of nude photos in *Liangyou* (The Young Companion) and *Beiyang Huabao* (The Pei-yang Pictorial News) in the late 1920s served basically the same function of luring the male readership as the photos of courtesans did in contemporary butterfly magazines, such as *Xiaoshuo Daguan* (The Grand Magazine) and *Banyue* (The Half-Moon Journal). In the butterfly magazines, literati's calligraphy and red seals were inscribed on the margins of the courtesans' photos, as if with such inscriptions and touch-ups, these 'beauty photos' – a relatively new kind of cultural product at the time – would become authentic art works as respectable and collectible as pieces of traditional Chinese calligraphy and painting. Around the mid-1930s, the first few issues of *Qingqing Dianying* (The Chin-Chin Screen) not only printed nude photos but also advertised the photographic books of nude study produced by the editor Yan Ciping and his associates. The modern artistic taste displayed in this fan magazine, however, marks itself off from its butterfly forerunners. By juxtaposing nude photos with the photos of movie stars, *The Chin-Chin Screen* alluded to the central position the female body occupied in the erotic imagination of its male readers.

The erotic pleasures were further intensified in numerous illustrations in contemporary cartoon magazines and pictorials, such as *Duli Manhua* (Oriental Puck) *Shidai Manhua* (Modern Sketch) and *Manhua Jie* (Modern Puck). Printed between illustrative texts and advertisements of cigarettes, facial powders, and toothpastes, erotic pictures formed a circuit of desire in Republican China that discursively linked everyday practice to artistic representation. Short articles on sensuality, sexuality, and pornography in pictorials and fan magazines added spice to visual treats, which were stylishly executed by promising young cartoonists such as Cao Hanmei, Ding Cong (b. 1916), Hu Kao (b. 1912), Hua Junwu (b. 1915), Huang Miaozi (b. 1913), Xiao Jianqing, Ye Qianyu (1907–95), Zhang Guangyu (1900–65), Zhang Leping (1910–92), Zhang Yingchao, and Zhang Zhengyu (1904–76)[1]. Indeed, their cartoons in popular magazines and pictorials functioned as an imaginary site of visual and psychological compensation where erotic poses and sexy dialogues that would not have been permissible on the Chinese screen were printed in graphical detail and were circulated for mass consumption at a price as cheap as a nickle or a dime per issue.

As is evident in the above brief sketch, this study will move intertextually among cartoons, illustrations, photos, captions, and articles. In what follows, I shall first identify some historical precedents for the narrative function and visual style of cartoons and pictorials, and then focus on certain recurring motifs (for example, prostitution and modeling) and discursive modes (such as condemnation and condonation, or fetishism and voyeurism). It is through these motifs and modes that a number of seemingly unrelated photos, pictures, texts, cartoonists, writers, editors, readers, and publishers are connected to one another, and together they endow a kind of corporeality to the otherwise intangible and intractable erotic imagination in Republican China.

Courtesan Culture and the Fin-de-Siècle Ethos

The publication of *The Dianshizhai Pictorial* (*Dianshizhai Huabao*) in 1884 as a complimentary supplement to the subscribers of *Shen Bao* (Shanghai News), a leading Shanghai newspaper, marks a threshold across which works of visual arts entered the age of mass production in late Qing China. Thanks to the newly imported rotary lithographic presses from the west, Chinese readers began to enjoy 'pictorial news' in the familiar form of traditional book illustration (*xiuxiang* or *huitu*), a form which nonetheless conveyed current events as well as overseas wonders. A brain child of Ernest and Frederick Majors, the owners of the *Shen Bao* and the Dianshizhai Publishing House, *The Dianshizhai Pictorial* was issued every ten days from May 1884 to December 1898, and exerted considerable influence on emerging Chinese urban culture (Lu 1980:129; Wu Xiangzhu 1958:1–3; Ye 1990). As the master artist of the pictorial, Wu Youru (1850–93) drew on his expertise in traditional Chinese painting and recreated vividly and imaginatively the everyday life of the denizens of varied social strata and nationalities in the fast-changing treaty port of Shanghai. His pictures from *The Dianshizhai Pictorial* and later from his own publication, *Feiyingge Huabao* (The Feiyingge Pictorial), were posthumously collected in 1908 in *Wu Youru Huabao* (A Treasury of Wu Youru's Illustrations) a multi-volume set that includes, in terms of subject matter, 'tales of moral edification drawn from the demi-monde, reports of the latest western scientific inventions ... portrayals of freaks, frauds, fashions and family feuds', as well as 'fictional anecdotes [and] artistic renderings of famous beauties and boudoir scenes' (Cohn 1987:2–3).

A close look at three of Wu's illustrations of the demi-monde will suffice as evidence for the popular appeal his lithographs held for the contemporary readers. 'A Flower-Eating Insect' focuses on a stealthy moment when a playboy vents his anger against an 'unfaithful' Suzhou courtesan by clipping a lock of her hair during her sleep (Wu Youru [1908] 1983:v. 11, pt. 2, no. 9). The decor of the courtesan's boudoir, intentionally catered to visual feasting, spotlights its high-cultural ambience: on the wall are hung a Chinese banjo and a scroll of figure painting flanked by two calligraphic couplets; suspended from the ceiling are four lanterns with pretty pictures and a large oil lantern with a tassel streaming down from its bottom; on the floor are a set of traditional-style square table, stool, chairs, and a huge decorated bed, on which the courtesan sleeps behind a half-drawn curtain with her back toward the playboy (and the viewer as well). The only modern objects in the boudoir are two small frames of photos and a huge mirror, which reflects the playboy hiding the courtesan's hair lock inside his coat. The commentary written across the top margin of the illustration laments the courtesan's despoiled beauty and condemns the playboy's disregard of the accepted rule of the sexual game.

The same motifs of banjo and oil lantern find their way into the second illustration, 'Whoring with a Harlot'. Don Cohn's translation captures the original flavor of Wu's anecdote:

A certain young gentleman named Wang ... was frequently seen traveling around the famous beauty spots of China in the company of his concubine. This young lady, a noted beauty, would from time to time shed her normal attire and put on men's clothing, so that when she went riding with him it was impossible to determine her true gender ... One day Wang went for a stroll through the district of ill repute where he was delighted to discover a number of women with faces as fresh as lotuses in springtime and the exquisite physiques of immortals ... Wang and his consort arrived in the Banjo Lanes, and before long found themselves in the company of a twittering flock of elegant young maidens, who lavished on them the greatest cordiality and plied them with wine and song, making their stay a thoroughly joyous occasion. From then on, the couple visited the flowery quarter at least once every two or three days ... One evening, Wang's concubine was being entertained by a small band of girls who, after urging her to drink beyond her normal capacity, proceeded to dally with her. As their playful struggles intensified, she grew more and more inebriated, until her tiny lotus feet were revealed, setting off a great shock among all those present.

(Cohn 1987:100)

In terms of visual effects, however, Wu's picture renders this revelation of gender identity a moment not so much of shock as of amazement or even amusement, for the cross-dressing concubine – who is not exactly a 'harlot' as named in Cohn's translation but rather a pleasure-seeking subject on her own – intensifies the experience of erotic pleasure in this illustration. What is more, her pleasure is one that has altogether eluded her husband Wang, who is presumably the proportionately tiny figure sleeping in the next room on the left margin, nearly blocked by a waiter serving food and drinks.

A similar, though less decorative, room setting of the pleasure house, with a sleeping couch, a giant mirror, and a table full of foods, is presented in the third illustration, 'No Room for Intercourse'. In contrast to an atmosphere of gentility in the other two illustrations, this picture dramatizes a scene of fighting between 'two European gentlemen with blue eyes and purple beards and moustaches' and a group of Chinese 'maidenly denizens of the night' terrified at the prospect of a 'proverbial death struggle' with the two 'towering monsters' from the west (Cohn 1987:54). The foreigners visited the pleasure houses in the British and the German Concessions but failed to get the sexual service they demanded. Aroused and desperate, they grabbed two elderly women and refused to leave until the local constabulary came and threatened them with arrest.

The sensational news as depicted in these three illustrations by Wu Youru would surely become hot items for tabloid journalism in the late Republican era, but one must remember that courtesan culture had been as much part of pictorial representation as of literary representation in the late Qing period, and together these two types of representation had enhanced the fin-de-siècle ethos of print culture in China (Wang 1997:53–116). In the realm of fiction writing, *Haishang Hua Liezhuan* (Profiles of Blossoms in Shanghai, 1892), a celebrated novel by Han Bangqing (Han Ziyun, 1856–94), not only offered detailed pictures of courtesan culture but was written and edited mostly in the pleasure houses Han had frequented (Ts'un-yan Liu 1984:11–18; Wu Zuxiang et al. 1991:1–43). Most interestingly, Chapter 20 of *Profiles of Blossoms in Shanghai* depicts a courtesan's nightmare similar to the one illustrated in Wu Youru's 'No Room for Intercourse': she dreams of two foreigners dragging her out and wakes up in cold sweat (Wu Zuxiang *et al.* 1991:front illustration pages). From the 1890s to the 1910s, many urban novels either elaborated on or alluded to courtesan culture, so much so that prostitution seemed to have been conceptualized as an indispensable way to experiencing and understanding the turn-of-the century Chinese city (Y. Zhang 1996:62–66, 118–126). As literary counterparts to Wu Youru's lithographic illustrations, many of these late Qing novels 'tend to give a positive image of courtesans as witty ladies with great conversational skills and sufficient talent to compete with literati in improvising poetry, writing calligraphy, etc'. (Henriot 1994:35).

Similarly, in the realm of journalism, courtesan culture was highly commended in the late Qing, and the readers would eagerly follow the latest news on such public events as crowning the 'queens' of the flowery world (Xu

1994:37–38). Just as notable figures of late Qing literati like Han Bangqing and Wang Tao (1828–97) had played a crucial role in promoting courtesan culture by directly addressing the reading public, in the early Republican era, many butterfly writers, including Bao Tianxiao (1876–1973) and Zhou Shoujuan (1895–1968), were instrumental in making the demi-mondes once again the central focus of visual imagination. Instead of the lithographic press, butterfly magazines such as *The Grand Magazine* and *The Half-Moon Journal* relied on the recently available copperplate press and published the photos of famous courtesans in their frontal illustration pages.

As Bao recalled in his memoirs, it was actually Di Pingzi (Di Baoxian, style Chuqing, 1872–1940), the editor of the influential *Shi Bao* (Eastern Times) and owner of Youzheng Bookstore, who first urged Bao Tianxiao to publish beauty photos in their *Xiaoshuo Shibao* (Fiction Times) as added attraction, along with other regular, but admittedly less engaging, features of scenic spots around the world and items of classical Chinese painting and calligraphy. Since maidens from respected families would not display their figures publicly, Di came up with an ingenious idea; he would host 'flower banquets' in his newly opened photography shop on Nanjing Road and take pictures of famed courtesans while they were there. In addition, Di suggested distributing coupons to the pleasure quarters and invited the demi-mondes to sit for photographic study free of charge. As a result, popular journals connected with the *Shi Bao* had a surplus of 'fashion photos', some of which were published with the calligraphic captions and seals of their collectors. This practice was so successful that Youzheng Bookstore issued a separate photo album named *Jinghong Yanying* (Gorgeous Beauties) which sold extremely well (Bao Tianxiao 1971:359–361).

Intertextually, the practice of inviting courtesans to the photography shop described in Bao's memoirs had already been anticipated by one of Wu Youru's lithographs. In 'Pitiable Self-Perception', two Shanghai ladies in traditional costumes, one sitting by a round table and the other standing by with her hand on a potted plant, are being photographed against the background of a painted canvas of western-style balcony. What merits special attention in this illustration is the ladies' demure expression, which seems to convey an uneasiness (if not quite anxiety) as they are simultaneously fascinated and threatened by the presence of western civilization, symbolized here by the camera and the painted backdrop (Wu Youru [1908] 1983:v. 3, pt. 1, no. 16). The emotional and self-conscious state of mind in Wu's two ladies becomes striking if we contrast this lithograph to the majority of cover photos that display the flirtatious, coquettish movie stars from the late 1920s onward (see Figure 6.1).

Historically, the uneasy or even slightly vulnerable positioning of the Chinese ladies in front of western technology in Wu's 'Pitiable Self-Perception' perceptively foreshadowed the eventual replacement of the lithographic press by the copperplate and the photographic plate in the early Republican era. In modern Chinese publishing business, high-quality copperplate prints, like those collected in the photo album *Gorgeous Beauties* and in the frontal illustrations of

Figure 6.1 Wu Youru, 'Pitiable Self-Perception'.

many butterfly magazines, soon won over the market previously held by lithographic pictorials. In a short span of 50 years, the predominant technology of Shanghai pictorial production had undergone four phases of change: from first, the engraved plate of the 1870s and second, the lithographic press of the 1880s–1900s, to third, the copperplate press of the 1910s, and fourth, the photographic plate by the mid-1920s[2]. Yet, as will be demonstrated in the next section, in spite of all these technological changes, a fundamental fascination with the sexualized female body remained intact, and erotic imagination concealed and displaced in Wu Youru's lithographs was given fullest expression in two newly emerging forms of visual representation – photography and cartoon.

Fetishistic Icons and Male Connoisseurship

In July 1928, *The Pei-yang Pictorial News* published a photo display bearing an original English title 'The 15-Beauty-Points of a Woman'. On the one hand, what immediately sets this photo display off from Wu Youru's highly decorative illustrations of traditional Chinese ladies is its self-conscious attempt to present the female body both with an anatomical precision and in a sexually provocative pose. The result is a series of extreme close-up shots – to borrow from film language – of 15 specific beauty points in a female body: hair, eyebrows, eyes, nose, teeth, lips, ears, neck, shoulders, arms, hands, thighs, feet, waist, and breasts, all stripped bare of any covering except for the make-up, earrings, and a

126

beaded necklace. On the other hand, however, what connects this photo display with Wu's depiction of late Qing courtesan culture is the language of its captions that is completely immersed in the age-long literati tradition. Consider these poetic lines that accompany the individual photos: for the eyes, 'An intense gaze yielded to a smile of profound meaning'; for the nose, 'A piece of jade flanked by two autumn pools'; for the lips, 'A taste of cherry, a bite of red velvet'; for the ears, 'A soft whisper delivered to the depth of night'; for the hands, 'Gently massage the tender heart in spring sickness'; and so on (*BYHB* 7 July, 1928:7). This kind of lyrical language reminded the contemporary pictorial readers of an aesthetic tradition in Chinese literature, whereby a literatus would improvise poetic lines exalting a courtesan's physical beauty and her extraordinary talents. Indeed, in its textual evocation of eroticism, these captions functioned very much like 'rhetorical fetishism' Emily Apter identifies in the nineteenth-century French novel – 'the taste for epithet, mannered syntax, and tropes of hyperbole and accumulation used ... to render the codes of *féminitié*' (Apter 1991:68). It is feminine beauty associated with specific, erotic parts of the female body that is graphically presented and aesthetically described in the Chinese photo display.

Still, the fact that *The Pei-yang Pictorial News* regularly published photos of naked female bodies in the late 1920s bespeaks its metropolitan taste and its liberal editorial policy. In the cover of the same issue where the above-mentioned photo display is printed, a work of classical western painting, Regnault's 'Les Trois Graces' (printed in the original French), was featured inside a rectangle frame at the center with a Chinese caption – 'Zhen Shan Mei' (Truth, Humanity, Beauty). With its rich visual associations, the three full-bodied western 'Goddesses' in Regnault's painting expose themselves with complete self-confidence to Chinese viewers, thereby establishing an intertextual linkage to the Chinese beauties displayed inside the front cover and reinforcing the pictorial's commitment articulated in these eye-catching lines: 'spread current news, promote arts, and provide common knowledge' (*BYHB* 7 July, 1928:front cover).

Packaging 'Les Trois Graces' as part and parcel of a common knowledge of western arts confirms Stephen MacKinnon's observations that since the 1920s 'the Chinese press had developed a symbiotic relationship with the western press in content and format' and that 'the major editors and publishers of the 1930s were entrepreneurs who published to please an audience, expand circulation, and turn a profit' (MacKinnon 1997:7–8). Two effective strategies of pleasing the audience had been adopted in the Chinese press during the 1920s–30s: first, a consistent display of the naked female body (in photography, painting, and drawing) was aimed to fix the male gaze and intensify the viewer's pleasures through voyeurism and fetishism; second, intermittent prize competitions were organized to encourage readers' participation and sustain their interest in the periodicals.

The best example of the second strategy is a prize competition organized by *The Pei-yang Pictorial News* in 1927, in which readers were required firstly to match the drawings of ten different hairstyles to the missing faces of the film actresses who 'owned' these styles, and secondly to estimate the number of people who would participate in the competition. A total of 1,081 people, most of them male, participated in the competition, and the winner of the first place, who got all answers right, was awarded a Kodak pocket camera in addition to a free subscription of 50 issues of the pictorial. The second to the fifth places each won a five-color copperplate print of a French beauty plus a picture frame, and the sixth to the fifteenth places were each awarded a book of biographies of movie stars (*BYHB* 30 March, 1927). The popularity of such prize competitions revealed the fascination of the general readership with women's latest hairstyles and fashions. To satisfy the audience's needs, pictorials in the 1920s–30s would publish discussions of women's underwear (*BYHB* May–June 1927) as well as fashion drawings done by artists like Ye Qianyu (*LY* March 1927:34; April 1928:31). Invariably, fashions of coiffure and clothing were soon transformed into fetishistic signs for both male and female readers.

Nevertheless, in the actual page setup of the pictorials of the early Republican period, fashion drawings and photos would certainly pale against the prominent space given to the pictures of naked women, most of them western figures identified in English captions such as 'An Occidental Beauty', 'A Naked Dancer on a Paris Stage', and 'A Study of Pose for Model' (*BYHB* 6 July, 1927; 10 December, 1927; 26 May, 1928). As the first strategy of pleasing the audience and expand the circulation mentioned above, the consistent display of voluptuous western beauties who return the male gaze in an 'unabashed' manner would no doubt arouse the curiosity and desire of Chinese readers (hence, the recurring features of nude photos in *The Pei-yang Pictorial News* from 1926 to at least around 1933).

As if the full-bodied, completely naked woman might somehow prove too exotic – if not too offensive – to the traditional Chinese 'aesthetic' taste, several Chinese pictorials and fan magazines would rather present images of women whose bodies were concealed behind layers of clothing and thus leave ample room for erotic imagination. Two quintessential objects of male fetishism captured most attention in visual representations: women's breasts and lips. 'The Female Stars Wearing Brassieres of Various Shapes and Types', a two-page spread of composite photos (of the faces) and cartoons (of the bodies) in *The Chin-Chin Screen*, pokes fun at the actresses who wore brassieres presumably because they believed that the rounded breasts were a sign of the advancement of civilization. Unfortunately, sometimes they dropped their brassieres in public, or their brassieres were misplaced on to their shoulders or their waist while they danced with their partners in the ballroom (*QQDY* 5 November, 1935). Another article in the same magazine delineates in fairly vulgar detail the body shape of a 'romantic' actress and judges her to be number one among all Chinese actresses by the large size of her hips and breasts (*QQDY* 5 May, 1937).

It is ostensible that by the late 1930s many verbal descriptions found in *The Chin-Chin Screen* had helplessly degraded into a kind of textual eroticism and had lost much of the lyrical charm that had once prevailed in the early Republican period. On one occasion the magazine tried to provide some 'intellectual' excitement by reading the enigmatic shapes of the actresses' lips. In a two-page photo spread, the enlarged details of the actresses' lips are taken from the photos of their smiling faces and given arbitrary interpretations with regard to their personalities and 'fates' (*QQDY* 5 April, 1937). Admittedly, fetishistic descriptions of women's lips had already occurred in contemporary literary works, such as Ye Lingfeng's (1904–75) two urban novels, *Shidai Guniang* (The Girl of the Modern Era, 1932) and *Weiwan de Chanhui Lu* (The Unfinished Confession, 1934), but the photographic enlargement of the sensuous lips that belonged to the coveted female stars would undoubtedly provide readers with a psychologically reassuring and visually enticing icon of one of the most fetishized objects of male desire (Y. Zhang 1996:207–222).

From the female breasts concealed by the misplaced brassieres to the sensuous lips exposed by photographic enlargement, from the shiny skins of the Occidental beauties to the rounded hips of a Chinese actress, and indeed, literally from top to feet – starting with the fashionable coiffure and the alluring eyes to the slim waist and the thin legs – an impressive catalog of the reader's localized fixations on the eroticized female body parts had been produced and reproduced both visually and verbally in Chinese pictorials and fan magazines in the Republican period. Originally delivered for male connoisseurship, these sexually charged images have become certain symbolic concentrates in the visual field of fetishistic presentation, and therefore possess an undeniable significance to our understanding of print culture and its multiple functions at the time.

Cartoon Magazines and Voyeuristic Pleasure

It is a cliché to state that beauty lies in the eyes of the beholder, but the editor of *The Chin-Chin Screen* was resourceful in trying out new ways by which his readers could behold feminine beauty. In the front covers of the first two issues of this Shanghai fan magazine were printed the photos of actresses such as 'Tiny Bird' Chen Yanyan (smiling happily to the viewer) and 'Snake-like' Tan Ying (glancing upward with her enigmatic look). On the back covers, the photos of Chinese nudes – rarely found in *The Pei-yang Pictorial News* and *The Young Companion* – were featured as visual attraction: one girl submissively kneeling sideways on a sofa with her head bowed, and another girl looking up in a frontal pose holding a banjo against a flower-patterned backdrop (*QQDY* 15 April and 15 May, 1934). Upon closer scrutiny, the kneeing nude in the first photo may become a perfect embodiment of the ancient form of the Chinese written character *nü* (woman), which visually suggests 'a submissive, kneeling figure with arms clasped at the wrists' (Hucker 1975:8), while the banjo in the second nude photo at once links the modern-day nude to the late Qing courtesan and foregrounds the instrument as a fully 'embraced' phallic symbol. In such a visually provocative way, the juxtaposition of two types of feminine beauty encouraged the reader to view the film actress as a sexual object as desirable as the nude girl in photographic study. Yet, in a conservative society, full-page nude photos of nameless models seemed both outlandish and outrageous. Probably under external pressures[3], *The Chin-Chin Screen* soon abandoned nude photos, as did other leading pictorials in China.

As shown in the earlier discussion of a picture ridiculing the actresses' mishandling of their brassieres in public, *The Chin-Chin Screen* relied on both photography and cartoons as two principal means of visual representation, and numerous other contemporary pictorials and magazines did likewise at the time. As a point of fact, by the mid-1930s, cartoons had gained such popularity that many cartoonists established their own cartoon magazines and issued collections of their cartoons. With their trademark integration of social criticism and erotic titillation, cartoon magazines tended to replace older pictorials in the function of circulating erotic images among general readers. Partly for this reason, their numbers increased dramatically: there were seventeen different cartoon magazines between 1934 and 1937 (Bi 1982:64–66).

A closer examination of cartoons as a particular type of modern Chinese graphic art is warranted here. Although some scholars would like to trace the origins of cartoons in China all the way to the Dunhuang murals and the Southern Song portraiture, the term manhua itself (as pointed out by Kuiyi Shen in the previous chapter) is a translation of the Japanese manga and was believed to be imported from Japan by Feng Zikai (1898–1975) in the mid-1920s. Since then the manhua has been widely used as an umbrella term for several types of Chinese cartoons, such as *fengci hua* (satire), *huaji hua* (comic), *xiehua* (humor), *yuyi hua* (allegory), *shishi hua* (current events), *fengsu hua* (folk customs), and others (Bi 1982:1; Zheng 1992:5–9), and by the 1940s there appeared to be a consensus with regard to general ingredients of the manhua (Hung 1994:28–29). According to Wang Dunqing (b. 1899), if one excludes *The Dianshizhai Pictorial*, the oldest Shanghai cartoon magazine would be *Raoshe Zazhi* (The Raffle) issued by Kelly and Walsh in 1895, with H. W. G. Hayter in charge of cartoon drawings (*DLMH* 10 October, 1935). Yet, in terms of their fascination with feminine beauty, their interest in quotidian life, and their combination of pictorial and literary texts, cartoon magazines of the 1930s undeniably owed a great deal to previous lithographs such as those from *The Dianshizhai Pictorial*.

Take *Oriental Puck* for example: its cartoons and texts often reinforced each other in exposing social and sexual evils that ran rampant in the modern city of Shanghai. During 1935–36, three articles by Zeng Die elaborated the issues related to pornography, sensuality, and feminine beauty. To prove the 'innocence of being sensual', Zeng contrasted several local governments' attempts to ban 'outlandish clothing' with such social or anthropological evidence: in north-western China many poor girls over the age of sixteen did not have their own pants to wear, while Mongolian women would work in summer days naked from the waist up. Indeed, Zeng argued, to ban outlandish clothing was a pretext to ban women from exposing their legs and elbows in public, which would lead ultimately to a ban of the public display or representation of female sensuality (*DLMH* 10 October, 1935). After a brief speculation on pornographic books in China and the west (*DLMH* 10 December, 1935), Zeng discussed an essential experience of voyeuristic pleasure – 'gazing at women.' According to Zeng, a Parisian artist once boasted that, seeing with his 'erotic eye' (*yinyan*), a completely naked woman would fail to arouse his sexual desire as did a dead body wrapped in layers of clothing. The erotic eye, Zeng explained, must refer to the artist's ability to 'see through' women's clothing and appreciate the innermost (i.e. fleshly or corporeal) beauty of the female body. But Zeng was perceptive to point out that this kind of the erotic eye is as much Parisian as it is Chinese in origin, for Ximen Qing apparently had long before accomplished a similar feat of seeing through women's clothing in *Jin Ping Mei* (The Golden Lotus), a classic Chinese 'pornographic' novel (*DLMH* 15 January, 1936). In the novel's own historical context, its illustrations were related, however partially, to a 'tradition of erotic prints that had developed in the flourishing urbanity of the sixteenth and seventeenth centuries' (Hay 1994:53)[4].

The Chinese and the Parisian traditions of the erotic eye Zeng identified in his article were fully represented in the pages of *Oriental Puck* as well as other contemporary cartoon magazines, such as *Modern Sketch* and *Modern Puck*. The serial illustrations of Ximen Qing's sexual adventures with Pan Jinlian and Li Ping'er were done by Cao Hanmei and were published in each issue of *Oriental Puck*, alongside a selected passage from *The Golden Lotus*. In addition to the Chinese literary source, folk custom also provided legitimacy for erotic drawings in the 1930s. As editor of *Oriental Puck*, Zhang Guangyu published his own serial drawings, 'Folk Love Songs', which include romantic and at times highly erotic scenes, and advertised a collection of his cartoons bearing the same title. In order to exhibit the naked female body in his drawings, Zhang chose those love songs narrated from the woman's point of view. In one example, 'My man groped his way to my room in darkness, / And I led him by the hand to my bed' – with a picture showing a naked woman covering her lower body with a semi-transparent silk skirt (*DLMH* 10 December, 1935). In another example, 'I lie down first in a lioness position, / And my man roll up on me like an embroidered ball' – with a picture of the naked woman lying on her elbows and knees, eagerly waiting for her man who is yet absent from the picture (*DLMH* 15 January, 1936). In terms of decorative visual style, Zhang's cartoons resemble *nianhua*, a type of popular Chinese new year's pictures, and convey certain folk-cultural taste remote from cosmopolitan Shanghai experience.

The Parisian tradition, on the other hand, was manifested in the works of several Chinese cartoonists, all concentrated on the subject of nude modeling. It should be borne in mind that, historically, nude modeling was an extremely sensitive and controversial issue. 'The most notorious art world event of the 1920s was Liu Haisu's battle with the government over the acceptability of employing nude models for life drawing' (Andrews 1994:53). A co-founder of the Shanghai Academy of Arts at the age of sixteen, Liu Haisu (1896–?) eventually won the legal case and subsequently journeyed to France for advanced training himself. Two contemporary photos demonstrate Liu's remarkable achievements: one is a group photo of Liu's art students (male and female) surrounding the nude model at the center, who turns her face sideways but keeps her naked semi-frontal pose; the other is a session of life drawing, with the model's naked legs stretching out in the middle-ground, while six male students are standing or sitting by their easels and fixing their gaze on her (Tang 1993:202–203).

Historical controversies aside, the popularity of cartoons on the subject of nude modeling in the 1930s testifies to the persistent act of seeing with the erotic eye in the Chinese art world. In Xiao Jianqing's cartoon, 'A Model', an easel holding a nude painting occupies the central background, and beside the draperies lies a pile of nude pictures. In the foreground, a nude model leans back on her two stretching hands, which support her upper body in a upward position. With her legs spread far apart, she exposes herself to an artist with long hair (a sign of bourgeois decadence), who directs his camera ridiculously close at her private parts. As if totally unaware of the artist, the model turns her face sideways and smiles mysteriously to the viewer (Xiao 1936b:10). The titillating pose of Xiao's modern nude model forms a sharp contrast to the two demure ladies in Wu Youru's 'Pitiable Self-Perception', in which the potentially threatening presence of the photographer and his camera is relegated to the bottom right corner. In Xiao's picture, the artist intrudes into the picture from the middle right frame and seeks metaphorically to 'capture' his sexual prey with a camera. Instead of feeling vulnerable or threatened (as do Wu's traditional ladies gracefully dressed in their costumes), Xiao's nude model is represented here as fully conscious of the power of her newly revealed sexuality, and she confirms that 'naked' power by confronting and returning the viewer's – more than the artist's – 'erotic' gaze.

While treating the same motif of nude modeling, two pictures from the cartoon magazine *Oriental Puck* achieve a humorous effect. In a four-panel strip about a popular cartoon figure Niu Bizi (literally, the 'Buffalo's Nose'), Huang Miaozi shows the increasing embarrassment a self-acclaimed 'artist' experiences while his model takes off her clothes. By the time she is completely naked, Niu Bizi has thrown off his brush (his entrance key to the art world) and has covered his face in great shame. Ironically, his rare display of emotions greatly puzzles the model (*DLMH* 25 September, 1935). What is interesting in Huang's cartoon is that precisely at the moment of naked revelation, the pitiable 'artist' seems totally unprepared for the erotic encounter and is terrified out of his wits at the 'castratory' power of female sexuality. In another four-panel cartoon about the famous orphan boy Sanmao (literally, 'Three Hairs'), Zhang Leping shows how Sanmao is pushed out of a studio by an artist, peeks at the modeling scene through a key hole, goes out to find a small girl, and in blind imitation starts to draw a picture of her buttocks (*DLMH* 25 December, 1935) (see Figure 6.2). In a

Figure 6.2 Zhang Leping, 'Three Hairs' (Sanmao) Blind Imitation, 1935.

simple but effective way, Zhang Leping captures a kind of ironic peek-a-boo eroticism that simultaneously highlights Sanmao's innocence and ridicules the corrupted and corrupting social morals of the time.

Cartoons of the 1930s seem to suggest that the nude modeling provided the artists with a legitimate space for erotic experience, a space denied to laymen such as Niu Bizi and Sanmao. For most laymen, the best they could do was peek through a keyhole – a typical kind of voyeurism that reveals the viewer's subterranean longings for the naked female body. As an effective discursive means of projecting private fantasy, voyeurism was manifest in a couple of cartoons in the 1930s. In 'Besieged From All Corners', Chen Haoxiong dramatizes a scene where the naked body of a bathing woman is being 'consumed' by covetous peeping Toms from all conceivable places – the ceiling, the crack-hole in the wall, and the balcony from across her open window (*DLMH* 25 September, 1935; rpt. Y. Zhang 1996:254). In a cartoon of the similar theme, 'The Miss's Boudoir', Xiao Jianqing gathers a crowd outside a young miss' boudoir, peeking through her windows with their mouths wide open. A tiny figure on the balcony across the street even uses his binoculars. Completely unaware of the intrusion of these hungry eyes in her sleep, the young miss seems to engage in a kind of autoeroticism, her left breast exposed under the loosened brassiere, her right hand delicately balanced between her naked thighs, and her face turned toward a photo of her boyfriend – a tiny figure in a picture frame beside her pillow (Xiao 1936a) (see Figure 6.3). The presence of this tiny photo

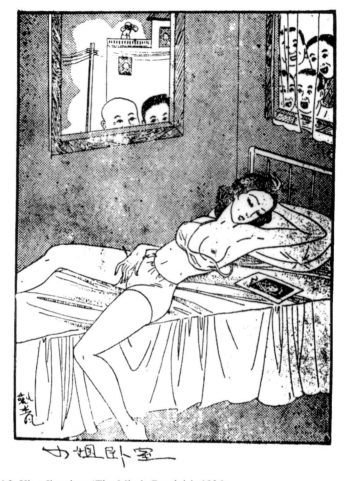

Figure 6.3 Xiao Jianqing, 'The Miss's Boudoir', 1936.

is crucial to the mechanism of voyeuristic identification in Xiao's cartoon, for the male voyeur is encouraged to fantasize that his object of desire (the sleeping beauty) is desiring someone like himself in return.

Conclusion: the corporeality of erotic imagination

To conclude this brief survey of pictorials, cartoons, and fan magazines in Republican China, it must be evident by now that, in spite of the didactic tone some urban publications assumed in their condemnation of social evils and their warnings against dangers of decadent urban life, many pictorials and fan magazines in the 1920s–40s continued to print nude or semi-nude photos, erotic or titillating cartoons, and racy or ravishing stories that both satisfied their readers' craving for a fetishistic presentation of the female body and returned the voyeuristic gaze with soothing, mesmerizing pleasures. Together with other popular urban institutions such as 'mosquito newspapers' (*xiaobao*), dance halls, night clubs, cinemas, theaters, as well as opera houses and amusement parks, pictorials and fan magazines might have contributed to the formation of an alternative public space where, among other things, erotic imagination was given a corporeal form in the metropolis of Shanghai.

Two interrelated observations follow in this concluding section. First, it is true that many pictorials and cartoon magazines were initially established for an educational purpose and devoted much of their space to covering sociopolitical issues. For instance, in *The Pei-yang Pictorial News* and *The Young Companion*, current events usually took up main sections, and pictures of political and social dignitaries frequently appeared in their pages. In cartoon magazines, the Japanese invasion of Northeastern China constituted a major theme during the 1930s. Indeed, the cartoon's efficacy as a vehicle for promoting patriotism or nationalism would fully materialize during the war (Hung 1994:93–150). Precisely due to their direct visual appeal to the masses, cartoons were regarded by serious cultural critics like Lu Xun (1881–1936) as 'extremely powerful'; consequently, 'erotic cartoons' as a 'deviant form' of this popular graphic art became an alarming sign for many artists who wanted to defend the moral integrity of the art (Hung 1994:31–35).

The morality issue leads to the second observation: in view of an absence of explicit nude scenes in the Chinese screen, erotic cartoons and nude photos in popular pictorials, cartoon collections, and fan magazines of the Republican era might have served a double function: psychologically, they provided a compensatory mechanism whereby the audience's unreleased libidinal energy could be spent or expended; economically, they constituted a promotional scheme whereby the publishers sought to increase mass circulation of their books and magazines. When the market economy prevailed in Shanghai during the Republican era, financial concerns negotiated with and often overrode moral issues. Instead of glossing over the existence of popular urban publications and dismissing their functions as inconsequential or insignificant in a cultural history, it would do little harm if we reopen a chapter of print culture that would promise a fuller picture of the psycho-social dimension of urban life in Republican China.

Notes

1 Zhang Guangyu, Cao Hanmei, and Zhang Zhengyu were brothers. For biographic notes on many of these cartoonists, see Bi (1982:67–94, 122–126); Zheng (1992:65–86).
2 In a recent Chinese study (Zhang Zhongli 1990:1067–1072), the following Shanghai pictorials (the year following a title indicating the year of its first issue) are cited as

representatives of each of the four phases of technological changes in the modern Chinese press: first, *Xiaohai Yuebao* (Children's Monthly, 1875), *Yinghuan Huabao* (Global Pictorial, 1877), and *Tuhua Xinbao* (New Illustrated Pictorial, 1880), all three owned by foreign sojourners; second, *The Dianshizhai Pictorial* (1884) and *The Feiyingge Pictorial* (1890); third, *Zhenxiang Huabao* (True-View Pictorial, 1912) established by Gao Qifeng; and fourth, *The Young Companion* (1926), the longest-lasting and the most comprehensive of all Shanghai pictorials. Pictorials from other major Chinese cities include *Qimeng Huabao* (Enlightenment Pictorial) in Beijing and *Liangri Huabao* (Two-Day Pictorial) in Tianjin, both published during the 1900s, as well as *The Pei-yang Pictorial* in the 1920s–30s.

3 Government censorship posed a real threat to the publishers of the 1930s. 'In February 1934 the Guomingdan banned 149 books in Shanghai and forbade the circulation of seventy-six magazines' (Wakeman 1995:33).

4 It is interesting to juxtapose erotic cartoons of the 1930s to what John Hay notes: 'Beyond even the special case of "the nude", a comparison between the pictorial arts of East Asian and the west might suggest a more general absence of the body' (Hay 1994:43). For issues related to the body in Chinese art and culture, see also Elvin (1989); Hershatter (1994); Wu Hung (1996).

7

RED COMIC BOOKS:
THE ORIGINS OF MODERN
JAPANESE *MANGA*

*Shimizu Isao**

Japan's modern[1] story cartoons began with those of a few frames. First was the six-frame cartoon drawn by Honda Kinkichiro in the 27 July 1881 issue of the weekly satire magazine *Kibidango* (1877–83) A six-frame cartoon[2] (see Figure 7.1) drawn by Taguchi Beisaku appeared as a three-part serial, starting from the 21 March 1896 issue of the weekly magazine *Marumaru Chinbun* (1877–1907).

From the late 1890s, right after the Sino-Japanese War of 1894–1895[3], through the beginning of the twentieth century, many cartoon books were published. They were called *ponchi* books (see Figure 7.2) because the word ponchi was in their titles. Ponchi derived from the title of Britisher Charles Wirgman's satire magazine, the *Japan Punch*, founded in Yokohama in 1862. These books carried story comics that were a few frames or even 20 to 30 frames long. In periods of war, woodblock prints (*ukiyo-e*) on war themes sold well. Entering the modern period, ukiyo-e lost their market share to lithographic genre pictures, but were revitalized by the time of the Sino-Japanese War.

Out of work when the war ended, ukiyo-e artists turned to publishing ponchi books for survival. Since the content of these comics for the masses was vulgar and nonsensical, their publishing boom was over by about 1905, the year the Russo-Japanese War[4] ended, although they apparently remained popular among children. One famous cartoonist, Tagawa Suiho[5], had vivid memories of reading ponchi books as a boy, sparking him to want to become a cartoonist when he grew up[6]. Also, in *Meiji no Tōkyō Seikatsu* (Tokyo Life in the Meiji Period), by Kobayashi Shigeyoshi, a book introducing the diary of Kobayashi's mother who died aged 33 in 1906, there are two mentions that in 1898, relatives bought a ponchi book for Kobayashi's elder brother, who at the time was eight years old. The ponchi books were sold to the general public but there were also ones that catered to children.

Japan's first full-fledged comic strip was *Eiga Shōsetsu: Onna Hyakumensō* (Cinematic Novel: The Woman with One Hundred Faces) by Okamoto Ippei[7], that appeared serially in *Fujokai* (Women's World) in 1917. As the title suggests, this work (see Figure 7.3) was influenced by the motion pictures, applying frames that resembled film and captions that carried the tone of a film

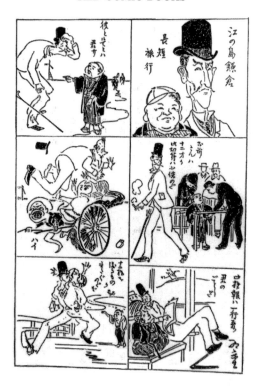

Figure 7.1 Taguchi Beisaku, *Enoshima – Kamakura Chotan Ryoko* (*Marumaru Chinbun*, 21 March, 1896 issue). Japan's first serialized frame-comic strip.

Figure 7.2 Artist unknown, *Haikara Ponchi* (1902). First comic book for mass audience in Japan's modern period.

Figure 7.3 *Saishoku-shugi no Neko* (The Vegetarian Cat), by Okamoto Ippei, appearing in *Eiga Shōsetsu Onna Hyakumensō*, 1917. The comic-strip artist produced a high quality comic strip with a story.

interpreter. The sharp wit of the captions in characterizing human nature made this comic strip popular. That same year, Okamoto produced a comic strip, *Chinsuke Emonogatari* (The Illustrated Story of Chinsuke) (see Figure 7.4) as a serial in a children's magazine, *Ryoyu* (Good Friend). This work marked the birth of the full-scale comic strip for children. Okamoto also created a comic strip adaptation of one designed for children by German artist Wilhelm Busch. Overall, Okamoto's major contribution was the introduction of a novel-like style of describing human nature to cartooning.

From the late 1920s to the 1930s, comics for children spawned a number of popular characters and bestsellers, examples of which were *Shōchan no Boken* (The Adventures of Shōchan)[8], *Nagagutsu no Sanjūshi* (The Three Musketeers in High Boots)[9], *Norakuro* (Blackie the Stray)[10], *Tankutankuro*[11], and others.

Figure 7.4 *Chinsuke Emonogatari*, by Okamoto Ippei, appearing in *Ryoyu*, 1917. This work was the start of high quality story comics for children.

Oyaji Kyōiku (originally 'Bringing up Father' by George McManus and serialized in *Asahigurafu* in 1923) influenced Japanese comics, particularly *Nonki na Tōsan* (Easy-going Daddy)[12] by Aso Yutaka. The use of four frames and balloons came from the influence of *Oyaji Kyōiku*. A major difference was that whereas *Oyaji Kyōiku* had a rich man as its main character, *Nonki na Tōsan* was about a man who was broke and perennially unemployed. *Nonki na Tōsan* is considered a masterpiece in modern Japanese cartoon history for its humorous depiction of the pathos of life; it surpassed *Oyaji Kyōiku* in terms of ideas and description of the human condition.

The excellent nonsensical and farcical comics that appeared in Japan in the 1930s undoubtedly received their impetus from Okamoto Ippei's works and foreign nonsense comics, introduced in such magazines as *Shinseinen*, *Asahigurafu*, and *Mangaman*.

As indicated earlier, Japanese comic books for children are found among booklets and ponchi books that appeared in the 1890s made by woodblock print and lithography. Entering the Taisho Era (1912–1926), these *ponchi* books grew in size (to B5, or one-half the size of a magazine page), published chiefly by Enomoto Hōreikan in Osaka. In the mid-1930s, publication began in Tokyo and Osaka of 20-page comic books with rounded spines and covers made of thick paper. *Nakamura Shoten*, founded in Tokyo during this time, began by publishing comic books of this type.

These were called 'red comic books', because many had covers of a gaudy red color. After World War II, these red comic books were immediately revived in Osaka.

Birth of Red Comic Books

Red comic books of the post-war period were published in Matsuyachō, Osaka's wholesale toy district, from 1947[13] to about 1956. Usually, they did not go through regular sales channels such as bookstores but were sold in places such as candy stores, night stalls, and stands at shrine or temple festivals. Inexpensive, they were priced generally from ten to about 50 yen, with more expensive ones from 70 to 90 yen at most. The size was usually small, from B6 (about postcard size) to B7 (half of B6 size) or B8 (half of B7), and many were from 24 to 48 pages in length. There were many without the name of artists and publisher or date of publication.

Japan's best known and very prolific comic artist, Tezuka Osamu[14] drafted 37 comic books between 1947 and 1953, mostly published by Osaka red comic book publishers, such as Tokōdō, Fuji Shobō, and Ikuei Shuppan. Therefore, the early works of Tezuka can be considered one kind of red comic book, clearly plagiarized by other red comic book artists. *Chōsoku Motakā* (High Speed Motorcar) (see Figure 7.5), for example, was produced by appropriating the matrices of *Ryūsenkei Jiken* (Stream Line Case) (see Figure 7.6), changing only the cover, and using 48 of the 62 pages of the original. With the popularity of Tezuka's comics at the time, it is conceivable that many other red comic books were blatant copies of his works, made illegally using the matrices of the original.

When a work became a hit in the comics world, a variant in red comic book form would show up. With the success of *Sazae-san*[15] by Hasegawa Machiko, for instance, a red comic book, *Shiruko-san* (by Sugimoto Machiko) with characters very similar to Sazae-san and her family, appeared, and the best-selling *Boken Tāzan* (Adventurous Tarzan) by Yokoi Fukujiro spurred *Tāzan Ma no Izumi* (Tarzan and the Devil's Fountain) (see Figure 7.7), *Yumo Tāzan* (Courageous Tarzan), *Tāzan no Ikari* (Wrath of Tarzan), and other Tarzan books.[16] After Tezuka Osamu's *Issennengo no Sekai* (The World One Thousand Years After) was released, red comic books such as Junpei Maki's *Sennengo no Sekai* (The World A Thousand Years After) and Hideo Kikuchi's *Chikyū Nisennen no Sekai*

Figure 7.5 Tezuka Osamu, *Chōsoku Motakā*, (Enomoto Horeikan, publication date unknown). Produced by illegally appropriating and using matrices of *Ryusenkei Jiken* by Tezuka Osamu. See Figure 7.6.

(Earth Year 2000) that copied it were published. The emergence of Tezuka's comics had certainly raised the quality of red comic books as well as boosted comic books for children as a whole.

Comic-strip artist Sakurai Shōichi of Osaka, born in 1933, wrote:

Around 1949, Tezuka Osamu produced pocket-size comic books besides (ordinary-size) comic books. They were A6 (about photograph) size comic books that opened to the side and were sold next to cards for children depicting baseball players, movie stars, and more recently cartoon and comic characters (*menko*) and *ramune* soda in candy stores. Such a tremendous hit in the comics world were these pocket-size comic books, the printing plates practically developed holes from countless reprinting.

(Sakurai, 1978)

Figure 7.6 Tezuka Osamu, *Ryusenkei Jiken* (Gorakusha, 1948).

Pocket comic books were probably copies of Tezuka comics. They were called rag books (*zokkibon*) or one-read books (*mikiribon*). Seeing his works occasionally plagiarized, Tezuka described in *Manga Shonen*[17], how these books were produced, sold in night stalls and such, and why they were extremely cheap (Tezuka 1953). By the flowing lines of his comics that could be easily imitated, Tezuka had greatly influenced young, aspiring comic strip artists.

Red comic books distinctly differed from comic books that had appeared up to then, by not generating characters with widespread popularity. *Norakuro*, *Tankutankuro*, and other comic books from before World War II became bestsellers; their main characters became the heroes of the day. No such heroes rose out of the diverse red comic books. As mentioned earlier, red comic books imitated the heroes and heroines of comics such as *Sazae-san* and *Tarzan* or turned stars of the movie or sports worlds into their main characters. *Gojira*

Figure 7.7 Artist unknown, *Tāzan Ma no Izumi*, (Enomoto Horeikan, publication date unknown). Influenced by Yokoi Fukujiro, *Boken Tāzan* (1948).

Nippon wo Yuku (Godzilla Travels Japan) (see Figure 7.8) took advantage of the popular movie *Godzilla* released in 1953; *Ganbare Rikidozan* (You Can Do It, Rikidozan) (see Figure 7.9) made a television star pro wrestler into its main character. Artists of these comic books all used the names or faces of stars and created their own stories about the stars.

Demise of Red Comic Books

Publication of red comic books reached its peak from 1948 to 1950 and the books vanished about ten years after their first appearance in 1947. One main reason was that the rise in prices due to inflation caused children to turn away from red comic books. In the 1950s, many red comic books were introduced that cost over 100 yen. Children consequently began leasing comic books for about

Figure 7.8 Artist unknown, *Gojira Nihon wo Yuku*, (Enomoto Horeikan, publication date unknown). A book which took advantage of the popular film, *Gojira* (Godzilla), first shown in 1953.

ten yen per copy from lending libraries. Red comic book publishers either went out of business or transformed into companies that published comic books intended for lending libraries. Many publishers appear to have chosen the latter course.

The Gordon W. Prange Collection of the University of Maryland in the United States is a collection of publications and magazines submitted to the allied forces for censorship during the occupation period. Collected here are nearly 1,000 comic books, making this, without a doubt, the world's largest collection of red comic books, and one that was made during the period that their publication reached its peak. Their contents have not been completely researched. No catalog of works is available, but the comic book collection was recorded onto 21 photographs in a study done by the newspaper *Sankei Shimbun* in 1994. The titles of 650 works can be discerned from the

Figure 7.9 Artist unknown, *Gambare Rikidozan*, (Enomoto Horeikan, publication date unknown). Used as its main character the popular professional wrestling television star, Rikidozan.

photographs, which have appeared in the eleventh (20 July 1994) issue of *Fushiga Kenkyū* (*Quarterly of Satirical Cartoon Studies*) which I edit.

Japanese comic books for children targeted pre-school or elementary school age children; red comic books were also mainly for an elementary school age readership. The lending libraries, frequented by large numbers of children in elementary and junior high school, sought from publishers cartoons that appealed to even a broader readership, as a means to increase profits.

This need for a larger market led to the launch of quintessential comic magazines meant for lending libraries, *Kage* (Shadow) (see Figure 7.10) in 1956, and *Machi* (Street) the following year. Carrying comics for junior high and high school adolescents, these successful endeavors inspired a flurry of similar comic magazines for lending libraries. The strips carried in these comic magazines were stimulated by pictorial story books and foreign films, and had stories with

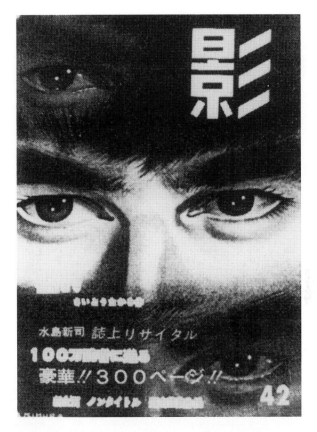

Figure 7.10 *Kage*, (Hinomaru Bunko, 1956), a monthly comic magazine leased from lending libraries.

realism, echoing the dreams and attitudes of junior high and high school students, as well as junior high school graduates in the workforce. These works were dubbed narrative comics (*gekiga*) in 1957 by cartoonist Tatsumi Yoshihiro of Osaka, and this became the commonly used term. In 1959, Sanpei Shirato started the gekiga called *Ninja Bugeichō* (Ninja Combat Scrolls) (see Figure 7.11), that caused a sensation. With a print run of 5,000 copies for each of the 17 volumes, the readership was probably in the 2.5 million range, with an average of 30 readers per copy through lending libraries. Read even by college students, such gekiga gradually became a medium of the masses.

The medium of the weekly magazine[18] played a major role in gekiga becoming accepted among the masses across generations. First, the weekly magazines for boys, *Shūkan Shōnen Magajin* and *Shūkan Shōnen Sande* appeared in 1959, followed in 1963 by the weeklies for girls *Shūkan Shōjō Furendo* and *Shūkan Māgaretto*. At the outset, these magazines carried comics,

Figure 7.11 Sanpei Shirato, *Ninja Bugeichō*, (Sanyosha, 1959). A popular gekiga in seventeen volumes. Fans extended to the high school student and college student populations.

illustrated tales, and stories not differing from the conventional monthly magazines for boys and girls, and therefore, they did not sell that well. In the latter half of the 1960s, however, they entered the limelight by carrying gekiga. *Shūkan Shōnen Magajin* made the breakthrough with the printing of the serial, *Kyojin no Hoshi*[19] (Hoshi of the Giants) starting from 1966, and *Ashita no Jo*[20](Tomorrow's Jo) starting from 1968, and with the popularity of these stories, the magazine's circulation grew to surpass one million in late 1966 and 1.5 million in 1969. Various magazines, as a result, began to place importance on gekiga and accordingly, increased their own circulation.

In 1967, the weekly magazines for youth, *Shūkan Manga Akushon* (Manga Action Weekly) and *Yangu Komikku* (Young Comic) were started and, in the

1970s, even weeklies for the general public began serializing gekiga, with the result that this genre became a part of the culture of the masses. Made available in train station kiosks, weeklies which carried serials of gekiga continued to grow in circulation with *Shūkan Shōnen Jump*, founded in 1968, reaching a circulation of more than six million in the 1990s. The readership was not limited to children, but comprised a wide range of people, from high school students to college students and businessmen. The magazine for youth founded in 1968, *Biggu Komikku* (Big Comic), was a monthly at first but in the following year was published twice a month. A related magazine, *Biggu Komikku Orijinaru* (Big Comic Original), was started in 1972. The popularity of the latter set the trend for gekiga to be referred to as comic (*komikku*) and, by the latter half of the 1970s, komikku became the commonly used term.

The huge success and popularity of Japanese comics today can be attributed to the transforming of red comic book artists into gekiga cartoonists, and the paramount role played by red book creator, Tezuka Osamu.

Notes

* The author's name and all names of Japanese persons in this text appear in the vernacular order of surname first and given name second. English names in parentheses ( ) are ones by which their referents are commonly known in English.
1 Japan's modern period, in this paper, is defined as the period from the collapse of the Tokugawa Shogunate in 1868 to the end of World War II in 1945.
2 A cartoon titled *Enoshima – Kamakura Chōtan Ryokō* in which a tall character Cho and a short character Tan appear.
3 Sino-Japanese War of 1894–1895, in which Japan fought against China for control over Korea's domestic affairs and won.
4 Russo-Japanese War, a war Japan fought in 1904–1905 against Russia for control over Korea and Manchuria.
5 Tagawa Suihō (1899–1989), cartoonist, whose *Norakuro* (Blackie the Stray) was a popular comic strip that appeared in *Shōnen Kurabu* (Boys' Club) from 1931.
6 *Fushiga Kenkyū*, No. 25 (publ. 20 January, 1998), p. 13.
7 Okamoto Ippei (1886–1948), a major cartoonist of the 1920s. His wife, Kanoko, was a poet and novelist; their son, Taro, was a painter who represented Japan's post-war western-style painting.
8 Story by Oda Shosei, illustrated by Kabashima Katsuichi. Appeared as a serial comic strip in *Asahi Graph (Gurafu)* in 1923 and published in form of six books between 1924 and 1925. It was influenced by British comic strips.
9 Story by Makino Taisei, illustrated by Imoto Suimei, serialized in 1929 in the *Yomiuri Shimbun* (Yomiuri Newspaper). It was published in book form in 1930 by Kodansha.
10 Work by Tagawa Suihō, appearing in a serial comic strip in *Shōnen Kurabu* (Boys' Club) in 1931. Ten editions before World War II and five editions after the war appeared. It is the first comic strip to have an animal as a main character.
11 Work by Sakamoto Gajo, serialized in *Yonen Kurabu* (Children's Club). A cyborg action story born in the days tanks and airplanes ruled supreme. It appeared in book form in 1935.
12 By Aso Yutaka (1898–1961). His serial comic *Nonki na Tōsan* was carried from 1923 in the upper left-hand corner of the front page of the evening edition of *Hochi*

Shimbun. This was the first four-frame serial comic strip to appear daily in a fixed space in a medium.

13 The first red comic book after the war was *Shin-Takarajima* (New Treasure Island) by Sakai Shichima and Tezuka Osamu, published from Ikuei Shuppan on 30 January 1947. Tezuka wrote at the end of the volume of *Shin-Takarajima* (3 October,1984) in *The Complete Collection of Tezuka Osamu's Works* published by Kodansha, 'This was the first comic book made right after World War II'.

14 Tezuka Osamu: comic-strip artist, animation artist, and medical doctor. His representative works include *Janguru Taitei* (Kimba, the White Lion), *Tetsuwan Atomu* (Mighty Atom), *Hinotori* (Phoenix 2772), *Burakku Jakku* (Blackjack), and *Adorufu ni Tsugu* (The Stories of Three Adolfs). In 1963, he began making Japan's first television animation series *Astro Boy* (animated version of Mighty Atom) and thereafter created other animation works which were also superb.

15 A four-frame cartoon appearing serially in *Yūkan Fukunichi, Shin-Yūkan, Asahi Shimbun,* and others. The complete 69 volumes were issued by Shimaisha and by Asahi Shimbunsha as the *Asahi Bunko* edition and by Kodansha International in twelve volumes, in English.

16 Tarzan comic books sold well also due to the popularity of the movie *Tarzan's Secret Treasure,* starring Johnny Weissmuller, a 1941 US movie shown in Japan in 1948.

17 Published by Gakudosha, 1948. Tezuka Osamu's early representative work, *Janguru Taitei* (Kimba, the White Lion) was serially carried in this magazine from 1950 to 1954.

18 In Japan, newspaper publishing companies published weekly magazines but from the latter 1950s, publishing houses also began to publish them. In the 1970s publishing houses carried *gekiga* (narrative comics) in the weekly magazines.

19 Story by Kajiwara Ikki, illustrated by Kawasaki Noboru.

20 Story by Takamori Asao, illustrated by Chiba Tetsuya. Kajiwara Ikki and Takamori Asao are the same person.

Part II

Representations and Portrayals

REDRAWING THE PAST: MODERN PRESENTATION OF ANCIENT CHINESE PHILOSOPHY IN THE CARTOONS OF TSAI CHIH-CHUNG

Shu-chu Wei

Tsai Chih-chung (b.1948, see Figure 8.1), one of the most prominent cartoonists in Taiwan, was born to a farmer's family in a small, isolated village in Hwatan, Changhwa, in the central region of the island. Encouraged by a teacher who did not believe that regular education was for everyone, he dropped out of the eighth grade and started his cartooning career in Taipei. The fifteen-year-old country lad assured his father that he had a job in the capital city and left his hometown with a small amount of money his father and brother-in-law had given him (Qiu 1992:118; Tsai 1997:106). He worked as a cartoonist in Taipei until he went into the army to fulfill his military duty in 1968. After completing military service, he decided to leave the field of cartoon magazines which he felt was too commercialized.

His next move was into animation, when a top film company chose him as the sole non-college graduate among 30 recruits in 1971. Five years later, he left to establish his own animation company. In 1981, he worked with a Hong Kong businessman to produce an animated film, *Lao Fuzi* (The Old Gentleman), which was awarded the best animation prize of the year by the Taiwanese government (Qiu 1992:118–120; Tsai 1986:5).

Tsai continued with his interest in cartoon drawing while managing his animation company. By 1983, his comic strips had become very popular, appearing regularly in major newspapers in Taiwan and elsewhere in Asia, including Hong Kong, Japan, Singapore, and Malaysia. Examples of his comic books in this period were *Da Zuixia* (The Drunken Swordsman), *Feilong Guojiang* (The Fat Dragon Crosses the River), *Daoshuai Duyanlong* (The One-Eyed Super-Thief), and *Guangtou Shentan* (The Bald Supersleuth). Through these works, he established a style of his own, illustrating humorous characters with simple, forceful lines. Eventually, Tsai chose to concentrate almost solely on cartoons and, in 1984, closed his animation company of 120 employees. His next step was to embark on a grand plan to illustrate Chinese history in cartoons. While on a flight to Japan to sell this plan, hoping to access a wider Asian market, he became engrossed in a book he had picked up to read and the grand plan shifted direction. The book was *Zhuangzi*, one of the classics of ancient

Figure 8.1 Tsai Chih-Chung's self-portrait.

Chinese Daoist thought. Tsai was so immensely absorbed with the ideas in *Zhuangzi* that he spent most of his stay in Japan drawing the book (Qiu 1992:120). The publication of *Ziran de Xiaosheng, Zhuangzi Shuo* (The Music of Nature, Zhuangzi Speaks) in 1986 marked the beginning of his cartoon series on ancient Chinese philosophy.

Mixing philosophy with cartoons did not seem a likely endeavor, as Tsai was well aware. Nevertheless, he wrote in the preface to the Chinese edition of *Zhuangzi Speaks*:

> An ancient book in classical Chinese does not interest the readers in general. But an ancient book presented in cartoons is different – it easily arouses the readers' curiosity, which leads them to first browse the pages, then study them in detail, and finally become interested in the original text ... By reading this comic book for merely thirty minutes, the reader will be able to understand the most important ideas in Zhuangzi's thoughts ...
>
> (Tsai 1986:11, my translation)

He was surely dealing with mission impossible. In addition to obvious obstacles of presenting complex thoughts through a seemingly 'simple' medium, many other difficulties existed. For example, Confucian thoughts have generally been considered didactic and dull, while cartoons are supposed to be interesting, funny, satiric, or provocative. How then does a cartoonist make serious Confucian thoughts interesting without creating distortions to the original? Laozi (also rendered as Lao-Tzu, meaning Master Lao, Lao being a family name) and Zhuangzi (Master Zhuang), the leading Daoist masters, are names known to many people, but only a few scholars and college students majoring in philosophy and Chinese literature would bother to read their books in difficult classical Chinese, as Tsai has pointed out. How can publishers market them to such indifferent readerships? Moreover, Laozi's ideas of the Dao (also known as Tao) are highly mystic and abstract, leading to the question, Can they be graphically illustrated at all?

Despite such concerns, Tsai Chih-chung found a publisher and, surprisingly, the sales of the comic book *Zhuangzi Speaks* were phenomenal; by 1994 the Chinese edition had gone through 114 printings. Its English translation is being used in college classrooms and never fails to amaze American students, who marvel at how such depth of thought is illustrated by cartoons. Tsai's subsequent comic book on Laozi in 1987 was another hit. Soon readers demanded a comic book on Confucius as well, and high school students even requested that it be published before the college entrance exam to help them prepare for the Chinese test, which includes Confucius' *The Analects*. Tsai responded by drawing two books on Confucius (1987 and 1988), the second one prefaced by a college professor from a traditionally conservative Chinese department. In 1989, he drew more comic strips on Zhuangzi and Laozi, published in the newspapers and later collected into book volumes. By 1993, it was reported that Tsai's comic books had sold 'a record 30 million copies' (Lent 1993:11) since 1986.

Such astronomical sales naturally pique one's curiosity. How did Tsai master his art to achieve all this? How faithful was he in presenting the most important Chinese philosophies in his cartoons? What does his success story tell us about today's Taiwan? This article attempts to answer these questions by studying Tsai's cartoon rendition of the most representative and influential Chinese philosophers – Confucius (551–479 B.C.E.), Laozi (probably in the earlier part of the 4th century BC), and Zhuangzi (c. 365–290 B.C.E.).

Supposedly, all three thinkers – possibly more than three, as some scholars doubt that there was a single author called Laozi in history – were active before and during the Warring States era (403–221 B.C.E.), a time when the central government, or the Emperor of the Zhou dynasty (?1027–256 B.C.E.), had lost control of China and feudal states fought for territorial occupation and political leadership. Interestingly, this chaotic period released enormous intellectual energy, as a hundred schools of thought contended, offering remedies for the socio-political problems not only to the state leaders but also to confused individuals. Some of their ideas are similar, while others clash. For instance, Laozi and Zhuangzi share views on human harmony with Nature and the two eventually were grouped together as masters of Daoism. Confucius advocates the merit of propriety in the performance of rituals, which the school of Laozi strongly opposes, even ridicules. Hundreds of books have been devoted to the study of these thoughts, so that to discuss even the major ideas would be beyond the scope of this chapter. Rather, I intend to concentrate on Tsai Chih-chung's art in presenting the three ancient philosophers, selecting illustrations which best depict important aspects of the philosophies and following the order in which these comic books were published.

Zhuangzi Speaks

The methods Zhuangzi employs to present his thoughts probably make it easier for a cartoonist to illustrate his book than do those of other philosophers. Zhuangzi uses parables and anecdotes in humorous ways and sometimes in satirical tones to highlight his unconventional ideas, which are often in direct conflict with the established stream of thought. His presentational modes provide space for the cartoonist to make the best use of his art to catch the funny nature of incidents depicted and to reveal Zhuangzi's provocative perspective.

Zhuangzi's main concerns are Nature and freedom, which seem to reflect contemporary Taiwanese anxiety about the environment and society. One introductory essay in Tsai's *Zhuangzi Speaks* hopes the book will serve to remind readers of the loss of the island's natural beauty and of the escalation of social ills as Taiwan industrializes (Tsai 1986:10). Indeed, having enjoyed more than two decades of the so-called 'economic boom', Taiwan has, at the same time, suffered from both environmental and spiritual pollution. Water and land are chemically contaminated; air is unhealthy for the lungs in numerous locations; and many people are interested in nothing more than material pursuit or quick monetary gains. Disgusted intellectuals have dubbed their own land the 'island of garbage' and 'island of greed'; some parents and educators created an 'Elementary School in the Forest' to escape what they called the 'forests of cement', that is, the choking cities. Thus, it cannot be accidental that Tsai placed the words *The Music of Nature* before *Zhuangzi Speaks* in the title of his first comic book on Chinese philosophy.

Zhuangzi advocates absolute freedom for human beings – freedom from all kinds of man-made restrictions, particularly preconceptions which limit human perspectives. To achieve freedom, one should observe Nature as it is in the raw and experience life in the limitless time and space of Nature. Tsai illustrates Zhuangzi's concept of Nature in an intriguing manner, though the pictures appear extremely simple.

In an episode which Tsai titles *Tiandi Riyue* (The Earth and the Sky) (Tsai 1986:71; English translation Tsai 1992:57), the first sentence – 'Does the sky move?' – comes from Chapter 14, *Tian Yun* (Movement of the Sky) in the original *Zhuangzi*. Tsai places his protagonist Zhuangzi, a representative of human beings, in the lower position in the frame of the column, and makes him stand on the surface of the earth, looking toward the sky and asking the question, which is written between Zhuangzi and the heavenly bodies. The question thus occupies the central position, signifying its importance. The earth is drawn in a circular line, which reflects modern astronomical knowledge that the earth is round instead of the ancient Chinese understanding of the earth as square. The sun, moon, and stars – represented by the well-known Dip – appear in the sky simultaneously to stand for all heavenly bodies. There are also two clouds close to the mountain at the end of the horizon. Since common sense tells us that clouds drift, transform, and disappear constantly, perhaps it is the clouds that move and not the sky.

The same technique is applied in the next column depicting the second question, 'Does the earth stand still?' Zhuangzi is seen standing on the surface of the earth watching a small plant as it grows. The activity of something growing from inside the earth is perhaps an indication that the earth grows and moves as well. Tsai's illustrations provide graphic explanations for the significance of these two questions which are not intended to be answered but to lead readers to careful observations of Nature.

Tsai (1986:58; 1992:44) illustrates Zhuangzi's Nature as a super hero (see Figure 8.2). In the philosopher's original text, *da kuai* (meaning large chunk, or the mass) is the term used to refer to Nature, which is presented as the force/creator that gives human beings body, vitality, age, and death. Tsai personifies da kuai by drawing the major elements in the universe into the human shape of a super hero who stands huge in front of the tiny comic figure Zhuangzi. Tsai's

自然像個大力士，
他有無窮的力量在運轉。

Figure 8.2 Nature as super hero from *Zhuangzi Speaks* (Tsai 1986:58).

super hero is made of water, land, wind, clouds, and the heavenly bodies of the sun, moon, and stars. This large mass in human shape is full of cosmic power, emanating from water splashing, the sun exerting its fiery force, and the wind blowing. This graphic personification of da kuai comes alive visually to explain more easily, and to more readers than words alone could do, the 'limitless strength' inherent in Zhuangzi's idea of natural force.

Illustrating Zhuangzi as the Master of Ceremony in this episode not only enhances the concept of Nature as all powerful but also adds a sense of humor. The MC, smiling proudly and raising one arm to show off muscle and strength, reminds the reader of an American animation, 'Popeye the Sailorman', a popular TV program in Taiwan for decades. The funny atmosphere derived from this MC/Popeye analogy serves to lighten the seriousness of topics concerning life and death, and in turn, suits Zhuangzi's belief that death, as well as life, is nothing but a natural phenomenon and therefore, 'the distinction between life and death will lose its significance', as Tsai's comic figure Zhuangzi the Commentator concludes.

The super hero's whistling wind full of musical notes is also seen in Tsai's illustration of *Dadi de Xiaosheng* (The Music of the Earth) (1986:30–33; 1992:16–18). In this episode, Mr. Nanguoziqi loses himself listening to the music of the earth. When he points out to his disciple, Ziyou, that the music of the earth is the sound of the wind, which itself is the breathing of the earth, Tsai illustrates the two characters sitting on earth listening to the wind (1986:31; 1992:17; see Figure 8.3, upper column), represented by sweeping and curving lines. As the lines flow across the space above the earth and around the two listeners, musical notes and scattered leaves follow. The musical notes are western, as very few Taiwanese recognize ancient Chinese notes. The leaves are crucial indicators that the wind is a natural force, especially in contrast with the music of people illustrated in a separate frame in a corner. Musical notes with scattered leaves create the music of Nature, whereas man-made instruments play one sound to the neglect of all other sounds. Only the music of Nature is capable of producing complete harmony.

The intriguing part of this parable occurs when Nanguoziqi explains that as the wind blows, the openings in the huge mountain trees respond. The openings, described as being like nostrils, mouths, ears, circles, mortars, deep pools, or shallow gullies, lend a graphic personification to the mountain trees (see Figure 8.3, lower column). The wind with its musical notes blows out of the trees' openings, which resemble human facial features. The man in the picture, Nanguoziqi, is completely immersed and 'lost' in the music of the earth. His hair, eyebrows, mustache, and beard are all blowing in the wind; his eyes are closed, as if not necessary. But one of his ears is illustrated as either moving with or moved by the music. Words alone can never bring us to the attention of this closeness between Nature and man.

For Zhuangzi, the highest state of harmony between Nature and man is for man to be one with Nature. This idea is best illustrated in 'The Dream of the

Figure 8.3 The Music of the Earth from *Zhuangzi Speaks* (Tsai 1986:31).

Butterfly' (1986:40; 1992:26), in which one cannot tell whether Zhuangzi is the butterfly or the butterfly is Zhuangzi. Tsai brings about this effect by drawing the butterfly having Zhuangzi's head and Zhuangzi having the butterfly's wings (see Figure 8.4).

The belief of the oneness between Nature and man leads Zhuangzi to advocate non-restriction for both man and animal. Animals, being creatures of Nature, should not be restricted by man or man-made devices. *Buyao Chuan Niubi* (Don't Ring the Bull's Nose) differentiates Nature from what is man-made by pointing out that 'four legs on horses and cows is natural' (1986:74; 1992:60). Tsai makes the cow and the horse look serenely happy and free from harnesses or nose rings as a demonstration of their being natural. To depict what is man-made, Tsai contrasts their contentment with two pictures of the horse and the cow in obvious surprise and annoyance at the harnesses.

To remain natural, Zhuangzi believes, man should strive to be free from the fear of death – the greatest restriction man has imposed on him/herself. The fear arises from our knowing nothing about death. Since we can never find out what happens after death, there exists a possibility that death may be 'so great that we'll end up regretting having ever lived', as is presented in an episode in the chapter on *Qiwu Lun* in *Zhuangzi*. This episode is rendered as *Liji de Kuqi* (Liji's Tears) in Tsai's comic book (1986:37; 1992:23). According to Zhuangzi's story about the famous beauty Liji, she cried sadly before being married to the Duke of Jin, but later regretted her tears when she realized what a comfortable life she had been provided in his court. To some people, Tsai's graphic depiction of Liji enjoying the material goods as a parable for the good life after death may seem

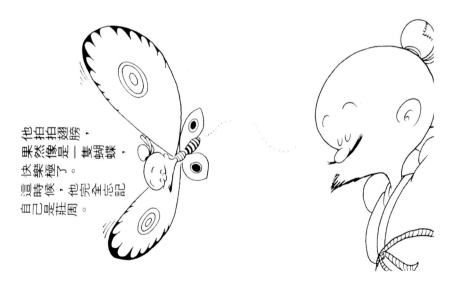

Figure 8.4 Zhuangzi the butterfly from *Zhuangzi Speaks* (Tsai 1986:40).

too far removed from the idea of natural living. However, they should have no problem understanding Zhuangzi's unique idea of happiness in death from reading *Zhuangzi Mengjian Kulou* (Zhuangzi Dreams of a Skeleton), taken from *Zhile* (The Utmost Happiness) in *Zhuangzi* (1986:86–87; 1992:72–73). In the pictures (see Figure 8.5), an all-smiling Zhuangzi attempts to lure the skeleton back to life from the death that it boasts allows it to have 'total comfort in being one with the world'. Zhuangzi's smiles connote human confidence in the belief that life is certainly better than death. Therefore, when the skeleton jumps away from the lure in disgust, the Zhuangzi in the dream is illustrated to stare in disbelief with eyes widely open. At the end, outside the frames of the cartoons, Zhuangzi the Commentator contemplates the philosophy of life and death by holding the skeleton in one hand in front of him, a posture reminiscent of Hamlet in the graveyard scene, which is not unfamiliar to many Taiwanese readers. Is Tsai telling us that Zhuangzi's thought on life and death is indeed a universal issue?

The remarks made by Tsai's Zhuangzi the Commentator are sometimes derived from the philosopher's original text, but other times are interpretations by Tsai himself (Tsaizi Speaks?). One does not have to agree with Tsai's comments. In theory, Zhuangzi's writing is open to interpretation by any means – translation, paraphrasing, or cartoons – as long as they help us understand his ideas. Zhuangzi employs this theory in *Deyu Wangquan* (Catch the Fish, Discard the Trap) (1986:112; 1992:98).

Laozi's Whispers of Wisdom

Like Zhuangzi, Laozi also advocates a life of simplicity and naturalness, and believes that, to live such a life, one should not interfere with the course of natural events. (The same principle applies to the way a sage ruler governs.) To have perfect harmony with Nature is to follow the Dao, but what Laozi means by the Dao is a complex, mysterious issue. Tsai illustrates Laozi as an old man carrying on his back a gourd, on which the Chinese character 'Dao' meaning 'way' is written or carved. The book *Dao De Jing* (or *Tao Te Ching*), whose authorship is attributed to Laozi, never connected the author with the gourd, but Tsai depicted Laozi as legend has it. According to popular belief developed in the formation of religious Daoism, the Daoists used gourds to carry the precious elixir pills, produced through alchemy and believed to possess magic powers capable of obtaining longevity and immortality. Tsai's Laozi may not have the magic pills in his gourd, but he is certainly carrying and delivering the Dao.

The Dao that is being preached in *Dao De Jing* is, as its first sentence states, something that cannot be explained by language or any other ordinary discourse. (That is why the word is seldom translated in a foreign language.) However, Dao is everywhere in the universe if we observe carefully. Water, essential to the myriad creatures and the most pliant, yet eroding, element residing everywhere in the lowly places of the universe, is presented by Laozi, or whomever the

161

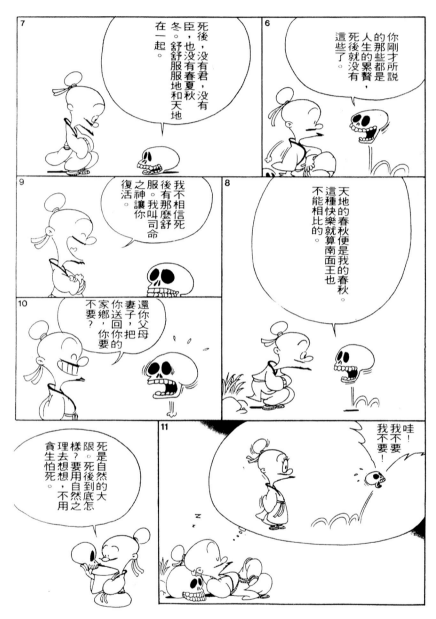

Figure 8.5 'Zhuangzi Dreams of a Skeleton' from *Zhuangzi Speaks* (Tsai 1986:87).

author of *Dao De Jing* may be, as the predominant metaphor of the Dao. This explains why Tsai's Laozi is often looking at a river or a pool, contemplating the essence of the Dao. In some instances, Laozi is depicted as sitting on the waves in a meditative posture (see Figure 8.6). Such unrealistic illustrations are designed to indicate the necessity for humans to follow the flow of water in the spirit of the Dao.

If Laozi's Dao cannot be explained by ordinary discourse, how then can it be illustrated, let alone by cartoons? While Laozi was forced to employ unusual devices such as figurative speeches and paradoxes to transmit the Dao, Tsai makes use of the Chinese character 'Dao' with help from the ancient Chinese *Taiji* (or *Taichi*) symbol and modern scientific knowledge of the universe. The Chinese character *Dao* a combination of a character for 'the head' and a running or walking radical, etymologically implying 'to go ahead', is usually rendered as 'the way' in English. By putting this Chinese character in his illustrations, Tsai presents graphically and ideologically a way to go to, to walk on, and to explore (see Figure 8.7).

The *Taiji* picture embodies the basic concept of the cosmic component in Daoism. The symbol has the yang/male/bright element and the yin/female/dark element interacting with and complementing each other in a circle that represents the universe (see Figure 8.8, note that both elements have an equal share of the circle). Laozi's cosmic system begins with 'nothingness' (*wu*) in which there were neither shapes nor forms. This state of nothingness, which is subtle and mysterious, is the underlying substance of the Dao. Dao then

水處於卑下的地
方，有道德的人
為人謙下。

Figure 8.6 Laozi sits on waves from *Laozi Speaks* (Tsai 1986:35).

163

Figure 8.7 The Chinese character Dao from *Laozi Speaks 2* (Tsai 1993:18).

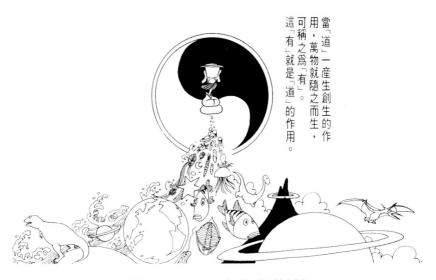

Figure 8.8 The *Taiji* symbol from *Laozi Speaks* (Tsai 1986:24).

produced the function of creation and a myriad things came forth – this is the state of 'being' (*you*), whose function is vast and limitless. Tsai uses the yang/male/bright element in the *Taiji* symbol to represent the state of 'nothingness', and the yin/female/dark element the state of 'being'. This depiction is wonderfully clever: the bright part of the *Taiji* picture is empty, the dark part is full. In terms of creation, the male element represents the substance of the Dao, while that of the female produces the myriad things, illustrated to include water, clouds, mountains, planets (one of which is apparently the Earth), the sun, the moon, stars, jelly fish, other species of fish, dinosaurs, a pterodactyl, seeds, leaves, and so on. The fact that some of the species have been long extinct connotes the beginning of creation. All of them pour forth from the *Taiji* symbol at the upper central position toward the lower section, covering the entire bottom edge and seemingly brimming over, indicating the limitlessness of the producing force. To complete this cosmic system, Tsai puts Laozi at the center of the circle: that is, the universe. The master sits on the substance of the Dao, touching both realms of the yin and the yang, and watching how the Dao functions in its creation process. In this example, Tsai's cartoon explicates without having to sacrifice the complexity of the subject.

In his *Laozi Speaks 2*, Tsai further illuminates Laozi's enigmatic Dao, using modern knowledge of physics and astronomy. Chapter 25 in *Dao De Jing* states that Dao is an ambiguous, integral mass of something that existed before the birth of heaven and earth; quiet (soundless) and void (shapeless), its independent and constant force moves around continually; and it is the source of all things in the universe. Laozi claimed that he did not know the name of this mass and chose to call it Dao. Some of these ideas are presented in the first chapter of Laozi's book, discussed in the paragraph above. New explanations of the Dao in this chapter are extremely subtle: for example, if the Dao is soundless and shapeless, it is probably untouchable and invisible, attributes which do not help a visual artist at all. Tsai's answer to this challenge is to have Laozi hold in his palm and contemplate the physics symbol for the atom. In some instances, Laozi is shown holding the Chinese character Dao in a posture strikingly similar. Juxtaposition of the two pictures (see Figure 8.9a/b) informs the reader that the atom symbol is intended to be the Dao. Whether the atom symbol is an appropriate substitute for the Dao can be debated, but in physics, the smallest component of an element, which is the source of energy, is possibly similar enough to something that is soundless, shapeless, and the creating force of the universe. It is graphically intriguing for us to see an ancient Chinese philosopher watching a modern scientific discovery in deep thought.

A similar example is found in the illustration in which Laozi sits at the center of the solar system thinking of the Dao (see Figure 8.10). Our knowledge of astronomy says it is the sun that sits at the center of the system, sending forth to the revolving planets its heat, energy, light, and other life-sustaining compounds. We are reminded by Tsai's illustration, then, that the way the sun functions in the solar system can apply, to some extent, to the way the Dao works in Laozi's

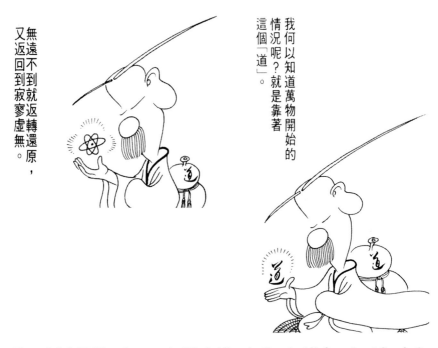

Figure 8.9a/b Holding the atom (p. 26); holding the Dao (p. 19) from *Laozi Speaks 2* (Tsai 1993).

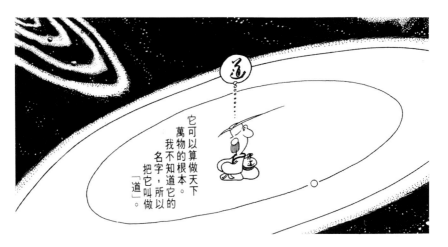

Figure 8.10 The Dao in the solar system from *Laozi Speaks 2* (Tsai 1993:25).

cosmic system. In this vein of interpretation, Tsai seems to imply that the sun functions in a way similar to that of his *Taiji* symbol. Luckily, Tsai found in his second comic book on Laozi a modern and scientific signifier to illustrate Laozi's Dao to readers who might think the *Taiji* symbol too archaic and too estranged from their common sense knowledge.

Confucian Teachings

Confucius, or *Kongzi* (Master Kong), spent his lifetime preaching and practicing the principles of ethics, education, and statesmanship. For a while, he worked as a high-ranking government official in his birth state and achieved widespread reputation as an accomplished administrator, but soon he became disappointed with the state lord who failed to bestow on him enough trust. So he took to travelling around the states with his students, selling his ideas on how to be a sage ruler to other state lords. Lords of the Warring States treated him with respect, but they were more interested in winning battles than becoming sage rulers. In his old age, he returned to his hometown and concentrated on teaching while compiling and editing books. After his death, his students collected their notes of his teaching in an anthology called *Lunyu* (The Analects). In the early period of the Han dynasty in the second century B.C.E., Confucian thought was adopted as state policy and has remained the most influential doctrine in China ever since.

To maintain social order, which is one of the major concerns in Confucian thought, rulers should direct the people to practice propriety (*li*, manners, rites) with genuine respect, and rulers as well as their officials should behave in exemplary manner. Tsai Chih-chung's cartoons reflect this basic teaching by showing people bowing all the time. They bow and kneel when they worship their ancestors (see Figure 8.11), during which rituals they follow the proper timing and procedures, offer the proper sacrifices, and wear the proper attire. One sees in Tsai's cartoons government administrators in their official robes offering sacrifices to the altar, in the process demonstrating good examples for people to follow. The text says that such practices will lead society to be harmonious and virtuous. What does this society look like? Tsai illustrates it in the lower column as he shows people smilingly and courteously offering food and money to the poor, and an intellectual greeting a farmer (the one wearing a straw hat) with deep bows, indicating equality and mutual respect between different social ranks. In the upper-right corner, behind the observer who is one of Confucius' students, people with happy expressions are doing business in the shops, in front of which a soldier strolls at ease, there being no need for his alert attention. Tsai brings to this small space of a column all sorts of people doing different things and interacting with one another. He breathes life into an abstract statement of a virtuous society.

Confucius was a devoted educator. Honored as the model teacher of all teachers, or Saint Teacher, his birthdate, believed to be 28 September, is

Figure 8.11 Propriety from *The Analects* (Tsai 1988:15).

designated as Teacher's Day in Taiwan, and *The Analects* is a required textbook in all Taiwanese high schools. *The Analects* teaches ethics, the most important subject in the Confucian curriculum. Confucius trained his students to be true gentlemen (*junzi*) who could proceed to become righteous state officials capable of assisting sage rulers. A close reading of *The Analects* reveals that he gave drastically varying advice to students who came to him with the same ethical question, as he believed that students had different personalities and needs and should be directed accordingly. He advised the students in gentle manner and tone, but never hesitated in offering moral guidance. An entry in Chapter 14 of *The Analects* records that one day Confucius heard one of his students, Zigong, ridicule other people's shortcomings. The Master said, 'Zigong, are you capable in every aspect? As for me, I don't have free time to do it'. One of many records demonstrating how Confucius taught his students, the teaching probably does not impress readers, especially those familiar with the book. But Tsai's cartoons made this incident lively and memorable (see Figure 8.12). In the first column, Zigong is shown laughing at a big guy who is angered by the ridicule, but restrains himself from taking action. The person in the middle seems dumb-founded by his

Figure 8.12 Confucius' teaching from *Confucius Speaks* (Tsai 1987a:107).

fellow student's rudeness. The second column has the Master Teacher standing tall between the two sides, pointing to Zigong and asking if he is a perfect person. The big guy smiles in contentment. The person in the middle wears an expression showing agreement with the teacher's comment. Both happily walk away from the scene. Zigong is not laughing any more: instead, he is sweating profusely; his eyes stare widely open, perhaps in disbelief at his misconduct or misfortune, while his mouth is shut, and the shadow on his cheek implies embarrassment. The exclamation mark above his head indicates that he realizes his mistake. The last column shows him bowing in shame in front of the teacher; there is even one teardrop falling from his face. Confucius sits there in his usual calmness, admonishing one of his beloved disciples. Tsai's cartoon characters enact an ordinary incident into an unforgettable scene. We also notice that the cartoonist's effort to enliven the scene of didacticism does not distort the content or method of the teaching.

Conclusion

Because no one knows for sure what these three ancient Chinese thinkers looked like, Tsai Chih-chung's renditions bear some scrutiny. Tsai's Zhuangzi is a young-looking comedian, constantly changing costumes and props as he alters his subjects, much like today's talk show hosts, and he does talk a lot, his mouth being a conspicuous feature of his large, bald head. In contrast, Confucius' and Laozi's mouths disappear underneath their long mustaches, making them look solemn. With their eyes closed most of the time, they seem to be always meditating or thinking about serious matters of the world, which reflects what they did in their lifetimes. While Zhuangzi's nose and ears appear small on his large head, these features are portrayed as huge and noticeable on Confucius and

Laozi. It is not difficult to interpret the size of their ears as an indication that they listened attentively, but why are they given those enormous noses? Is it an artistic necessity, or was Tsai simply having fun giving these two grave thinkers a comic appearance with noses more appropriate to clowns? Their eyebrows are also unusually long, especially Laozi's, which look almost like the brim of a hat around his forehead. Some Chinese believe that eyebrows grow white and long with age and call them 'longevity eyebrows' (*shoumei*). If wisdom comes with age, Tsai must be drawing portraits of two wise old men, which suits his subjects well. Whether this implies that Laozi is the wisest of the three is hard to determine without first consulting Tsai. What is clear is that Tsai's Confucius always looms large and tall in the midst of his earnest, loyal, and hard-working disciples, and Zhuangzi is, without doubt, the funniest and the most popular of the three.

In theory, becoming portrayals of the philosophers do not necessarily lead to appropriate illustration of their thoughts. Examples of Tsai's successful drawings discussed above, however, do present the philosophers' ideas more strikingly than words can do. In their crafty details, these cartoons reflect to a great extent the complexity of the original text. Although not all Tsai's cartoons render the thoughts with such a high level of intricacy, the selections above are excellent examples that will certainly attract readers to pursue further the philosophers' universes. Isn't this exactly what Tsai intended to do when he started illustrating Zhuangzi? He never claimed that his comic books on ancient Chinese philosophy could or should replace the original classics; instead, every Tsai book is provided with the original text and notes in the margins of the pages. We might be stunned by the staggering numbers of his readers who have wandered away from the cartoons to scout out the mystery of the margins.

GENDER INSUBORDINATION IN JAPANESE COMICS (*MANGA*) FOR GIRLS

Fusami Ōgi

Manga[1] are categorized according to readers' gender and age. In other words, manga are engendered texts with special ideological assumptions which divide the world into spheres for women and men. The focus of this chapter is on comics for girls (*shōjo manga*) with the purpose of determining whether the gender representations are subversive or whether they preserve the gender status quo. The period under study is the 1970s, thought to be a turning point in the representations of women in girls' comics.

Shōjo is a common word in Japanese meaning 'girls', yet at the same time, it also signifies an ideological institution of women based on Japanese modern femininity in the Meiji period: a feminine image based on westernization following Japan's centuries-long isolation and on the virtues of the so-called 'good wife and wise mother'. Both emphases were political policies of the Meiji administration.

According to Honda Masuko (Honda 1991:12–13; 1990:177–205), shōjo novels from the 1900s to the 1920s created the image of shōjo for the first time. The shōjo novels represented the dreams and illusions of girls who were neither children nor grown-ups – future mothers, but not yet at the age for marriage – who could not participate as members of society in the pre-war era after their graduation from elementary school. Shōjo appeared as innocent girls who were sedate, smiling, and unassuming. The representation of the shōjo was concerned more with describing her inner mind and feelings than with plot development.

How to present the images of the shōjo was an authorial problem more important than the development of the stories themselves. In fact, in these earlier works, illustrations were already significant. A shōjo novel or magazine story usually had two names on the title page, a writer's and an illustrator's.

Yoshiya Nobuko's *Hana Monogatari* (Flower Tales) (in *Shōjo Gahō* from 1916 to 1924) might have been the most popular novel for shōjo at that time. Yoshiya's novel was republished in 1939 with illustrations by Nakahara Junichi (see Figure 9.1)[2], one of the most popular illustrators of shōjo. We see the impressive black eyes there, which seem to have been from the start a crucial means of conveying a shōjo's emotions and mentality. The figure of the shōjo, by

Figure 9.1 From *Hana Monogatari* (Flower Tales) by Yoshiya Nobuko, illustrated by Nakahara Junichi, 1939 (Tōkyō: Kokusho Kankōkai, 1985)
Copyright © Sōji NAKAHARA / Kokusho Kankōkai 1997.

the hands of illustrators who studied European illustration styles and cultural motifs in the 1920s, also conveys her longing for a western lifestyle and shows the image of shōjo as an amalgam of Japan and the west (Aramata 1991:27). Such images of the shōjo were retained textually and visually through shōjo novels until the 1950s, at which time shōjo manga became popular as a genre for the shōjo[3].

Though the modern image of shōjo first appeared in the early twentieth century, the history of shōjo manga is not that old. Until the end of World War II, the world of manga had been exclusively dominated by male writers. Shōjo manga began in the late 1940s, authored for the most part by men who were already popular as writers of comics for boys, or *shōnen manga* (*Nippon*

1992:16). Thus, shōjo manga is not a genre invented by women but one developed for a female market. Early shōjo manga from the 1950s and 1960s offered fixed images of sentimental melodrama mostly concerned with motherhood (Kurihara 1995:90). Most heroines were mere children described from the viewpoint of male adults, while in shōjo novels like *Hana Monogatari,* on the other hand, shōjo were not confined to childish roles. Although their world only concerned girls before the age of marriage, women's relationships were more diverse and did not exclusively place an emphasis on their being 'daughters'. Their feelings of love and respect came from their sense of equality as individuals.

Before the 1970s, shōjo manga promoted icons which preserved Japanese modern femininity under the name of shōjo, and women were only passive recipients of the images, not creators. However, as the number of women writers increased, the nature of shōjo manga began to change, so the 1970s should be considered a turning point in writing 'women' into shōjo manga.

The 1970s as a Turning Point

The 1970s in Japan was a significant decade in which women developed a clear self-identity through changes in labor practices, introduction of new ideas from the western feminist movement, and the development of the mass media. The 1970s in Japan, as Ueno Chizuko (1995:686) remarks, constituted a turning point for women in the work force. The economic growth of the 1950s and 1960s had enforced heterosexual gender roles: men at work and women at home. Whereas in the 1960s only 30 per cent of young women in their early twenties had jobs and even those usually retired after two or three years to be married, in the 1970s, 70 per cent were employed. However, as Ueno herself and others assert (Tanaka 1995; Siota 1994; Satō 1979), in this decade, the changes in women's roles did not completely alter their views on gender.

While the second wave of the western feminist movement warned women of the dangers of merely pursuing equal opportunity with men, Japanese women strengthened their shared identity as 'women'. In spite of the increasing number of working women, most of them were housewives and part-time workers, whose labor was obviously secondary (Ueno 1995:700). That maintained the defined roles of women and only led to the status of 'working' housewives being improved.

As long as they pursued equal opportunity with men, women would never reconsider the heterosexual system itself which caused their alienation. Rather, the movement emphasized women's consciousness as 'women'. Women also absorbed representations of conventional gender roles through the various media, of course, and they developed a strong sense of identity within the patriarchal framework (Tanaka 1995:345; Satō 1979:37). In the 1970s, Japanese women tried to find their own ways of life; however, they tried to do so within the category of 'women' and this reinforced the established gender ideology and got in the way of attaining their own subjectivity beyond the fixed label of 'women'.

By the early 1970s, most writers and readers of shōjo manga were women, as the genre became one for women by women. Consciousness-raising in the 1970s also seems to have emphasized the conventional category of women, but I submit that about that time, shōjo manga also planted a subversive seed in the fixed category 'woman', in that representations not centering on women's issues emerged.

In the 1960s and 1970s special techniques were developed to separate shōjo manga from shōnen manga, or the male tradition. For example, Ōtsuka Eiji (1994:60–61) claims that shōnen manga present a story, while shōjo manga are concerned with how to express the character's personality and feelings. According to him, a traditional shōnen manga represents only the surface, while in a scene from shōjo manga, everything, including the background, represents the heroine's feelings (see Figures 9.2, 9.3 and 9.4). Shōjo manga make good use of the effect of silence to represent characters' inner worlds, thoughts, feelings, past, and memories.

Such attention to inner feelings appears most obviously in the presentation of characters' eyes. Huge orbs with stars have been notorious in shōjo manga, especially those of westernized figures with curly hair and long arms and legs. However, those outlandish eyes represent well a concern with the characters' inner being. The more gorgeous his or her eyes, the more important the character, and subcharacters rarely have bigger eyes than those of main characters.

Moreover, the manga's concern with feminine images created a special space in which flowers sometimes bloom only to emphasize the characters' feelings and characteristics, somewhat like the extradiegetic effect of music in films. In Figure 9.2, which shows a tennis game between two girls, the flowers at the top emphasize the girls' passionate feelings as rivals. Figure 9.3 encapsulates a key moment when a boy finds a picture of a girl; the flowers floating about emphasize the girl's femininity or let the reader vaguely imagine appropriate romantic relationships. More effective use of space in shōjo manga led to the deformation of frames (Yomota 1994:40). Early Japanese comics used a western format, with each frame arranged consistently, both vertically and horizontally. But as seen in Figures 9.2 and 9.3, these works ignored frame size, even their very existence, and in the process, created a new dimension within the limited space. The technique was widespread in shōjo manga but rare in shōnen manga at that time.

Such a flexible framework allowed space to control time too, as seen in Figure 9.4. Shōjo manga often employ a technique which combines the fade, dissolve, and flashback approaches of films[4]. One example presents a young couple, known to each other since childhood, meeting once again through the power of fate. Using no frames, but rather the entire page itself, suggests to readers that they can imagine these two characters' romantic bond as one destined beyond time and space. No long-winded verbal explanations are necessary. Even though

Figure 9.2 Yamamoto Suzuka, 1975, *Ace wo Nerae!* (Be an Ace!), vol.5, p. 55, Tōkyō: Shūeisha.
Copyright © Suzuka YAMAMOTO / Shūeisha 1997.

in this case the implicit ideal promoted is the comparatively progressive western notion of individual heterosexual romances, such silent paperwork provides women with an opportunity to represent themselves in their own way, expanding socially limited space and time. Their method might be counted as 'écriture féminine': Hélène Cixous (1976) claimed 'woman must write woman' and

175

Figure 9.3 Ōshima Yumiko, 1988 (1974), *Umi ni irunowa* (The one who is in the sea), p. 334, Tōkyō: Shōgakukan.

suggested that the writing of the female body is a revolutionary act which would 'give her back her pleasures' and explode the structures of conventional male language and thought. Shōjo manga was at least becoming a genre in which women could present their thoughts and express themselves.

Representations of shōjo manga around the 1970s were of two types in terms of gender: one placed female characters in the center and presented their lives, perhaps at the same time reinforcing the traditional images of shōjo; the other avoided centering on 'women' as subjects, and thus subverted the gender

Figure 9.4 Tachikake Hideko, 1979 (1977), *Ame no furu hi ha Soba ni ite* (Be with Me When It Is Raining), p. 111, Tōkyō: Shūeisha.
Copyright © Hideko TACHIKAKE / Shūeisha 1997.

convention of previous shōjo manga. Works by one important group of women writers in this period, the 'hana no 24 nengumi' or 'Magnificent 24s'[5], adopted this latter strategy. The group got its name because they were all born about 1949, the 24th year of the Shōwa period. Presenting 'women' in an independent way, such women writers gradually established shōjo manga as a genre apart from the male tradition. Modifying non-women as protagonists, the 'Magnificent 24s' offered many antidotes to conventional gender roles and raised questions concerning gender itself.

177

Some women writers retained an emphasis on women but altered the typical representations. In this category, ordinary girls, rather than idealized figures, gradually became the main characters, as women writers placed their heroines at the readers' own level. Love was the theme that made their characters 'women', offering a common inner concern among female readers and writers. In the 1960s, Mizuno Hideko began representing 'women', not shōjo in a traditional sense, in the world of shōjo manga (Bessatsu Taiyō 1 1991:72). What made her characters 'women' rather than 'children' was the theme of heterosexual love. Her work was much influenced by romantic Hollywood movies like those starring Audrey Hepburn. The heroines always had unslanted eyes and usually westernized names, and lived in huge edifices like western castles, which reflected the shōjo's dream of the day. They longed for a modern American life and European elegance, in contrast to the reality of their daily lives in post-war Japan. Maki Miyako, one of the pioneer women writers, made her first heroine a ballerina, perhaps because of her strong longing for a wealthy western lifestyle; in actuality she had lived amid a long stretch of burned ruins after the war (Maki 1991:70–71). Westernized romantic images consolidated the shōjo's desire to part from depressing daily matters through the theme of love, and the motif became dominant in the world of shōjo manga in the 1970s.

Juxtaposing exotic European images and ordinary Japanese girls, women writers presented various cute character types in the 1970s. Most women writers of that time were about the same age as their target readers. For example, the '*Ribon* Comics Group', one important body of the first category of writers, wrote stories as if they spoke for readers who could not express their feelings to the opposite sex because of their pubescent shyness. Most characters could not say anything that was as eloquent as their eye contact, even though they were thinking all the time of how they could convey emotional feelings to their future boyfriends. Showing those inner emotional struggles, shōjo manga depicted a concern about ordinary daily lives involving family and friends. Despite those shy girls' cute westernized rooms, frilly dresses and curly hair, they were characters with which readers could identify. Concerning other cultural phenomena of that time, Ōtsuka (1995:18) remarks that those cute shōjo images were not limited to the world of manga; they stimulated much shōjo paraphernalia designed for female consumption.

Thus, the first category of shōjo manga was mainly concerned with how to be loved in a heterosexual relationship, that is, how to identify with the objectification as a future 'woman'. To write for girls at their own levels, women writers adopted a strategy of self-representation, at the same time they reinforced prior images of shōjo. Although they wrote about female individuals and tried to offer their various feelings of love as a common theme of women, unless they destabilized the naturalized heterosexual gender roles, they would, after all, only impose traditional restraints of femininity upon themselves. Women could enjoy such gender images only if they agreed with their supposed position as an object of male desire. Feminist film critic E. Ann Kaplan

(1983:26) remarks that, assigned the place of object, 'she' is the 'recipient of male desire' and her sexual pleasure in this position can be constructed only around 'her own objectification'.

In order to present 'women', the women writers perpetuated the image, but in their own manner. To effectively visualize inner feelings, they invented techniques which have come to be regarded as characteristics of shōjo manga. However, as long as they explore 'women' only within the category of shōjo manga, they remain mere image-promoters rather than image-makers. Their voice is that of 'women' reinforcing the heterosexual gender roles and preserving the patriarchal ideology.

The 'Magnificent 24s'

However, as I indicated earlier, a second category of shōjo writers appeared in the 1970s, creating manga which often lacked foreground women subjects and issues of specific interest to women. Such representations were effectively offered by the 'Magnificent 24s' in the 1970s. In general, manga writers can be classified according to their publishers and magazines; ordinarily each contracts with one specific publisher once s/he begins a career. Each magazine or publisher has a target audience in mind and grooms popular writers to produce accordingly. In the same way, writers of the 1970s were closely associated with their publishers and then their magazines' titles. For example, the '*Ribon* Comics Group' takes its name from the title of a particular magazine. However, the 'Magnificent 24s' did not conform to this rule of identification with publisher and magazine. Significantly, the membership of this group, despite its familiarity to Japanese readers, has not been definitively settled yet[6]. The name signifies the revolutionary effects of the texts of the 1970s and remains separate from the publishers' names but *not* from the category of shōjo manga. This fact provides a crucial perspective from which to examine the fixed gender ideology of the genre, from which the 'Magnificent 24s' were born and which they would challenge.

The 'Magnificent 24s' offered the first manga by women writers, inspiring enough to be read and criticized by males (Yonezawa 1991:4). As they opened the world of shōjo manga to male readers, the women writers made them recognize that these works were not narrowly focused only on women, but also operated on a broader literary level. However, the theme of gender seemed to be ignored by male critics and readers, who did not challenge the traditionally male dominant codes of manga. For example, manga critic Murakami Tomohiko, when he analyzes texts by Ōshima Yumiko, one of the 'Magnificent 24s', examines her use of gender as part of traditional melodrama rather than as a challenge to the engendered category of shōjo. Murakami says Ōshima's originality lies in her attempt to present shōjo differently, using a traditional framework of melodrama, even while the rest of the 'Magnificent 24s' abandon it. Although Murakami talks about various gender roles appearing in her texts, he seems to miss the crucial points, even dealing with the theme of a sexual

179

transformation from male to female as a dreamlike idea which only adds a touch of comedy to the text (Murakami 1979:74).

Presenting gender in various ways, the texts of the 'Magnificent 24s' do challenge the concept of shōjo and destabilize the traditional codes of heterosexuality. However, these texts are not free from those defined codes in so far as they are productions of the gendered category shōjo manga. Here, I would like to consider carefully the meaning of the shōjo whose existence such critics and readers witness in the representations by the 'Magnificent 24s', even though their shōjo characters began to diminish in number and emphasis.

What determines shōjo manga is, first of all, the genre category which is, in turn, based on the gender category. The code of shōjo leads readers and writers to imagine they are experiencing something meant for shōjo. Aramata Hiroshi (1977:28) remarks that all manga written by women can be called shōjo manga. His remark not only suggests that to write manga was becoming a way of self-representation for women, but also that the category of shōjo manga was being heavily engendered as well. Even now, the category still marks the texts written under the name of shōjo manga. Readings of those texts have been limited under the code of shōjo.

Since the 1970s, homosexuality has been one of the more popular themes of shōjo manga. Pioneers of the theme were the early 'Magnificent 24' artists Takemiya Keiko and Hagio Moto. Usually with the use of male narrators, they presented manga from male characters' points of view. Their texts using boys as main protagonists contrasted sharply with the proto-world of shōjo manga before the 1970s, when what were identified as shōjo manga existed only because shōjo appeared as main characters or narrators, primarily as objects of identification for women of the same age. Shōjo manga lacking women characters and subjects of interest to women challenged the traditional code of the shōjo precisely because they were published under the name of that engendered category.

After seven years of publishers' rejections, in 1976, Takemiya was finally able to publish her masterpiece *Kaze to Ki no Uta* (Song of Breeze and Tree), which seriously took up the juvenile love theme by centering on two boys. The publication became a sensation, not only because it introduced for the first time homosexual scenes to the world of manga, but also because it came out as part of a shōjo manga. The opening of the text (see Figure 9.5) is radical because in the process of imagining shōjo, readers are not allowed to be mere receivers of the image. The scene of the naked male bodies embracing emphatically visualizes the absence of the shōjo, introducing two taboo subjects into the view of the presumed shōjo reader: boys' bodies and their libidinal agency. Despite the absence of women's bodies, by showing what does not exist for the familiar category of shōjo, the image stimulates readers to reconsider the existing notions of gender, at the same time forcing them to see what the prevailing category has preserved and excluded. Here, the readers are not just receivers of the image, but take part in image-making[7].

180

FUSAMI ŌGI

Figure 9.5 Takemiya Keiko, 1995 (1976), *Kaze to Ki no Uta* (Song of Breeze and Tree), p. 8–9, Tōkyō: Hakusensha Bunko.
Copyright © Keiko TAKEMIYA / Hakusensha Bunko 1997.

Before Takemiya's *Kaze to Ki no Uta,* Hagio had already published *Tōma no Shinzō* (The Heart of Thomas) in 1974 (see Figure 9.6), the original version of which, *Jūichigatsu no Gimunajiumu* (Gymnasium in November), appeared in 1971. Lacking the sexual scenes of Takemiya's work, *Tōma no Shinzō* presents the world of teenage boys in a German gymnasium and how they suffer through a boy's suicide. In the story, women appear variously as mother, sister, or strict grandmother, but never as primary characters. They are just seen and understood from the boys' points of view. As her reason for choosing the homosexual world of boys over girls, Hagio (1981:90) explained that she could not imagine any beautiful images of homosexual relationships involving shōjo's bodies. However, in spite of Hagio's disingenuous answer, readers still see shōjo in her representations of a world where women do not clearly exist.

Some readers/critics attempt to present women's inner worlds which have been repressed under male dominant codes; they claim that such representations show a narcissistic world of shōjo, using the bodies of the other sex (Takatori 1978:52). Others contend that male characters involved in homosexuality in shōjo manga emanate from the shōjo's desire, which has been repressed under male discourse (Fujimoto 1990:184; Honda 1988:29; Yonezawa 1991:77). But one must ask, where is the shōjo and what allows her to examine the shōjo in a

Figure 9.6 Hagio Moto, 1995 (1974), *Jūichigatsu no Gimunajiumu* (Gymnasium in November), p. 3, Tōkyō: Shōgakukan.
Copyright © Moto HAGIO / Shōgakukan 1997.

text without female bodies? The self-evident but likely to be denied answer is that these representations have been published under the name of shōjo manga, a genre presupposing readers will be shōjo. Here one should note that readers, even males, are all engendered – hailed in the Althusserian sense – by the category of shōjo. In these representations, which do not show women as central, the shōjo type unveils itself as a code and an institution.

In the structure of such a world, shōjo manga need not visually show female bodies in order to present shōjo. Instead, readers are forced to collaborate in making the position of the shōjo. Adopting non-female bodies, the representations in shōjo manga create the shōjo at the ideological level, while showing what shōjo cannot readily comprehend: that is, something beyond the category of shōjo. Adapting the theme of sexuality using boys, the writers create a secure sexual gaze for shōjo, who by convention lack libidinal agency, while they are also unveiling a code of sexuality which the category shōjo itself cannot contain. They show an impossible and therefore non-threatening situation in the process of their image-making of shōjo.

By using men, those texts allow girls to emancipate themselves as women without enduring the sexual suffering of the patriarchal discourse. Additionally, they represent the impossibility of active sexual participation by the figures of women which have been accepted within the category of shōjo. The secure gaze which does not cause anxiety for women readers may even entertain them. However, at the same time, the misogyny voiced by the characters and the text's marginalization of women permit the erased women to reconsider gender itself (Fujimoto 1990:184). Moreover, even the western setting in those texts might become a parody of shōjo conventions, by providing a taste of exoticism. Using non-Japanese backgrounds may allow women to enjoy this exoticism, but the lack of women characters and subjects of interest to women also allows them to reconsider the established feminine beauty of shōjo – an ideological institution involving standards of modern beauty for Japanese women.

Those texts which lack women may seem to abandon the qualities which make up the shōjo, but, in fact, they do not. As long as they operate under the name of shōjo manga, their challenge to the engendered category of shōjo actually parodies it. Under the name of shōjo manga, the detailed description of each character's inner feelings by the 'Magnificent 24s' seems to emphasize the characteristics of the engendered category. At the same time, the texts centering on men often expand the themes into primarily male domains of politics and history, in addition to 'love'.

The representations by the 'Magnificent 24s' have created in shōjo manga a genre more like the 'novel,' whereby a human drama of considerable length is presented. For example, Takemiya's *Kaze to Ki no Uta* centers on love between boys, but also takes up their various complicated family backgrounds, as well as the misunderstandings and conflicts caused by social problems in nineteenth century France, that is, racial discrimination, prostitution, social class conflict, and so on. The work has been republished in ten volumes, each of about 330 pages. In another story, Hagio's *Tōma no Shinzō*, a boy suffers from an inferiority complex caused by racial problems. Even in her work on vampires, *Pō no Ichizoku* (The Poes) (1972), Hagio develops the plot of a boy's life over a 200-year period, even filling out a genealogy of the boy's family. The central concern is the human struggle with life and death, rather than the romantic fantasy of vampires with eternal life, which would clearly be beyond the category shōjo.

Tezuka Osamu and the Origins of Shōjo Manga

In fact, Hagio talks about an important influence on her writings by Tezuka Osamu, a pioneer in the world of manga (Hagio 1981:86–7)[8], who claims that he himself introduced tragic effects for the first time to manga (Ishinomori

1989:123). Tezuka's text made Hagio realize that manga were not necessarily comedies or humorous texts, though that is the original nuance of the word manga.

However, in terms of gender, Tezuka maintained an extremely conservative view. Despite having written *Ribon no Kishi* (The Knight of the Ribbon)[9] 1953, sometimes referred to as the first shōjo manga narrative, Tezuka seems never to have admitted he was a writer in that genre. To him, shōjo manga were for women, not for him. Writing such stories must have been an embarrassment, since he had not read any shōjo magazines before he wrote *Ribon no Kishi* (Tezuka 1988:70). *Ribon no Kishi* is a fantasy of a princess who mistakenly receives both boy's and girl's souls before her birth. If we regard this work as indeed the beginning of shōjo manga, we find that gender was a concern from the outset. However, in *Ribon no Kishi,* the text preserves the characters' gender, based on a heterosexual division of the two conventional gender roles. The heroine is new in that she plays two gender roles simultaneously, even though the story tries to 'correct' her ambivalent tendencies and make her a true female. Once the heroine has a single soul – the female one, of course – she immediately begins to use feminine speech and to cook and clean for her future husband. Thus, *Ribon no Kishi* is based on a predictably masculine view of manga.

Tezuka's views can be further clarified by comparing his shōjo manga and those of the 'Magnificent 24s' in terms of gender and transvestitism. From 1972 to 1974, Ikeda Riyoko, one of the 'Magnificent 24s', gained huge success by writing about a cross-dressing woman in her famous manga, *Versailles no Bara* (Roses of Versailles), which presents the adventures of a woman guard, Oscar, in the French Court during the French Revolution. This text gradually shifts from presenting a woman's life to depicting a person free from fixed gender ideology. At first Oscar seems to reinscribe the feminine, longing to be a woman in spite of wearing male clothes. However, by wearing male clothes Oscar gradually reveals what 'she' cannot do, and at the same time 'she' does what she can do by not being a woman. In other words, the text unveils the ideological construction of femininity through her cross-dressing. On the one hand, this story portrays various other women's tragic lives, including that of Marie Antoinette, another heroine of this story who plays all the possible female roles: daughter, wife, princess, queen, lover, and mother. On the other hand, working as a guard to protect the people, Oscar gradually awakens herself as a human being. All she has is her love, her body, and her occupation, each marked by her clothes. When Oscar dies on the day of the fall of the Bastille, she recognizes the love she has experienced as the deepest of human pleasures.

Thus the gender treatments by Tezuka and Ikeda are in sharp contrast with each other. Tezuka's shōjo manga texts locate themselves in fantasy, but in terms of gender roles they stick to conventionality, rearranging everything within heterosexual boundaries that preserve the category 'woman' in shōjo manga. On the other hand, Ikeda's use of cross-dressing shows how feminine clothes oppress women and hinder self-assertion.

From Tezuka to the 'Magnificent 24s,' representations of manga changed significantly. Tezuka's texts, modelled on realistic novels, opened the world of manga to adults, characterizing them not only as entertainment but also as serious human drama. Characteristics engendered as masculine, when they appear in shōjo manga, however, parody conventional masculinity by showing the male world under the name of shōjo. In the 1970s, representations of women by women writers successfully motivated a challenge to male-dominant discourses. Moreover, the representations of shōjo manga, containing what is beyond the category of shōjo, have offered women writers an effective way of working within and yet challenging the male discourses, and thereby foregrounding other categories in terms of gender.

Conclusion

Today, shōjo manga remains a primary category of comics, but it is not the same category first generated. Besides, what shōjo manga once introduced now splits into new textual categories such as 'ladies comics'[10] and the so-called yaoi manga[11], which are subversive even in relation to the traditional gender concepts of shōjo manga itself. Moreover, techniques of traditional shōjo manga have now been adopted in manga for boys or adult males.

As an engendered category, shōjo manga should be seen as a genre that uses multiple dimensions of gender and provokes other categories of writings into maintaining conventionality in terms of gender. It acts like an item of clothing which anyone can wear, but the way it is worn creates an individuality and sometimes even works as subversion, a process which never lets the wearer look the same as before. Parodying the conventions of the category of shōjo, these manga raise questions about gender itself, while representing the drama of the dreams and illusions of generically defined girls.

Notes

1 In general manga can be considered a synonym for comics or cartoons. However, the term manga also suggests something closer to novels which have drawings as well as text. Manga is a particularly interesting part of the popular culture of both Japan and the west which has been little examined in the academic world. In fact, manga is still often regarded as trash culture. Even so, it seems gradually to be gaining consideration as a new literary genre in Japan. Since about 1994, manga have been republished in the book-size paperback format used for traditional fiction, so, finding old manga for research purposes was rather easy, but to collect the original publication information was difficult because publishers often do not supply information about the original format in the republished books. Such treatment may reflect a conservative view which does not value manga as materials for scholarly study. Furthermore, most libraries in Japan do not have manga, even though 40 per cent of the annual print publication in Japan is manga (Yonezawa 1997:860) and almost half the space of a typical bookstore is occupied by manga. The following two libraries are for manga: Hiroshima City Manga Library (*Hiroshima shi manga*

toshokan) and Contemporary Manga Library (*Gendai manga toshokan*). Hiroshima City Manga Library started in 1997 as the first public library for manga in Japan (http://www.tourism.city.hiroshima.jp/level7/f0401manga.html). Contemporary Manga Library is private, and we need to pay 100 yen per book borrowed (http://www.st.rim.or.jp/~hikaru-i/naiki/).

2 Each figure shows one manga page, which should be read from right to left and from top to bottom. Only Figure 9.5 shows two pages.

3 For example, *Shōjo Club*, a major magazine for shōjo started in 1923, had 336 pages in 1935, only nine pages of which were manga. The rest consisted of literary genres such as novels or essays. In 1955, 95 pages were novels and tales, and manga totaled only 54 pages. In 1962 *Shōjo Club* ceased publication, and instead, *Shūkan Shōjo Friend*, a weekly magazine of shōjo manga was launched (Nagatani 1995:128).

4 Interestingly, this technique is quite similar to what is sometimes called the 'memory play', one of the innovations of American playwright Tennessee Williams.

5 Fujimoto Yukari (1991) has translated 'hana no 24 nengumi' as 'Magnificent 24s' and I will use her translation throughout my chapter.

6 Hagio Moto, Takemiya Keiko, Ōshima Yumiko, and Yamagishi Ryōko are always counted as 'Magnificent 24s'. Ōtsuka adds Ichijō Yukari, one of the '*Ribon* Comics Group' (Ōtsuka 1997:53). Kure Tomofusa adds Ikeda Riyoko, Kimura Minori, Kurata Emi, and Satonaka Machiko (Kure 1997). Nakajima Azusa adds Kihara Toshie, Ikeda Riyoko, and Aoike Yasuko (Nakajima 1991:88–89). Takemiya Keiko created *Kaze to Ki no Uta* for *Shōjo Comic* brought out by Shōgakukan which also published Hagio Moto's *Tōma no Shinzō*. Ōshima Yumiko wrote her early works for *Bessatsu Shōjo Comic*, published by Shōgakukan; Yamagishi Ryōko for *Ribon*, and Kihara Toshie, for *Bessatsu Margaret*, both published by Shūeisha. Ichijō Yukari has written for *Ribon,* while Ikeda Riyoko did *Roses of Versailles* for *Shūkan Margaret*, also published by Shūeisha, and Satonaka Machiko and Aoike Yasuko have written for Kōdansha.

7 An American colleague made the interesting comment that to the western eye the boys in Figure 9.5 or Figure 9.6 might appear to be girls because of their soft bodies and big eyes with long lashes. Consequently, the scene in Figure 9.5 would look like two lesbians in bed.

8 Hagio read Tezuka's 'Shinsengumi' (which literally signifies a special samurai group during the transition from the Edo to the Meiji period), published in *Shōnen Book* (Book for Boys) from January (No. 1) to October (No. 10) in 1963.

9 *Ribon no kishi*, which literally means a knight of the ribbon, was translated as *Princess Knight* (Tezuka 1979:4).

10 'Ladies' comics' are for women in their twenties or older. They became popular in the late 1980s (Takeuchi 1995:154). Now about 80 kinds of ladies' comics are published per month (Yonezawa 1996:1066). Most of them deal with women's lives, particularly marriage and love affairs. Some take up social problems related to women's problems, pregnancy, birth, child-raising, and work.

11 *Yaoi*, an underground manga for girls, appeared about 1986. *Yaoi* parodies existing *anime* or manga by playfully presenting two male characters as a homosexual couple. The name *yaoi* comes from three Japanese phrases, *yama nashi* (without climax), *ochi nashi* (without ending), *imi nashi* (without meaning). Since 1994, several issues of *yaoi* have been published (Yonezawa 1996:1069). Perhaps *yaoi* is a new genre which represents what cannot be tolerated within the literal confines of shōjo manga. This new category seems to be part of shōjo manga because of its surface appearance, but it often contains sexually explicit depictions of boys' bodies, which most girls would find pornographic.

MALAYSIA'S MAD MAGAZINES: IMAGES OF FEMALES AND MALES IN MALAY CULTURE

Ronald Provencher

Social Commentary and Malay Humor Magazines

During the past 20 years, two Malay-language magazines, *Wanita* (Woman) and *Gila-Gila* (Mad), have contended for the honor of having the largest number of readers in Malaysia. Until 1994, *Wanita*, a magazine especially for modern Malaysian women, had the largest circulation. Since then, *Gila-Gila*, a cartoon and humor magazine renowned among Malays for its social commentary has become more popular than *Wanita*. Much of this latest success of *Gila-Gila* may be attributed to an increase in the number and quality of cartoons and humorous articles especially for female readers. Also, the magazine has retained its usual (mostly Malay) audience by continuing to address a wide variety of cultural, social, economic, and political issues in ways that delight the young and old, poor and rich, weak and powerful, female and male.

These humor magazines are published in Malay language, the national language of Malaysia and the native language of Malays, who comprise a bare Islamic majority in the nation. Both deal with traditionalist and modernist Islamic issues. But *Gila-Gila* is more concerned than *Wanita* with strongly controversial issues, those issues that provide the most delicious humor, issues such as the relationship of Islam and western modernization to female roles in contemporary Malaysian society. Malays, whatever their gender, and whether they are Malay traditionalists, Islamic revivalists, or western modernists, have a strong interest in the ways that traditional gender roles have been affected by the impact of cultural and social change on their society. And, whatever their gender, Malays savor humor as they savor food ... the flavor should not be too simple and it must be spicy. This was part of the rationale for the development of a new humor magazine by one of the cartoonists who regularly deals with matters of gender in *Gila-Gila*, the popular female cartoonist Cabai (a professional name referring to an especially spicy type of chili pepper).

The new magazine, *Cabai*, first published 1 April 1997, is subtitled 'Exclusively for Women' (*eksklusif untuk wanita*), the name of the women's interest section in *Gila-Gila*. Although technically published by an independent corporation, Cabai Productions, it is in fact part of the Creative Enterprise community of publications that publishes *Gila-Gila*. This is one of many examples of how Creative Enterprise, throughout its history, has allowed its artists to pioneer new types of publications until they succeed, and then it absorbs them, thereby avoiding losses to the whole corporation through investment in unpopular ideas, but capitalizing on the few ideas that actually enjoy commercial success. One might think that, after the success of *Cabai*, *Gila-Gila* would reduce its coverage of women's issues to avoid competition, but that has not been the case.

Much of the humor in *Gila-Gila* (and contemporary Malay society) involves the figurative use of traditional and other currently fashionable texts to represent different points of view regarding important social issues, such as gender roles. This chapter interprets several typical instances of this 'play of tropes' in cartoons and essay features of *Gila-Gila* and *Cabai* during a period of intense Malay attention to the roles of women in contemporary Malaysian society.

Bases of Interpretation: cultural and social contexts of gender humor

A frequently cited review of the anthropology of gender in Southeast Asia focuses on the differential distribution of female and male prestige as it is affected by tensions between historically different social and cultural institutions such as seniority, matrifocality, and Islam, and by the recent impact of nationalism, economic development, and world-wide popular culture (Ong 1989). These parameters of consistency, flexibility, and change in gender roles are common contexts within which metaphors, similes, and other tropes of Malaysian (especially Malay) cultures are played by cartoonists and humor writers for the amusement of their fans. The various sorts of Chinese and Indian cultures of Malaysia are occasionally visited by cartoonists and humorists, but regional Malay cultures and dialects provide the basis for most of their texts relating to gender humor. Although some of these regional Malay cultures, such as that of the state of Negri Sembilan in Peninsular Malaysia, differ significantly in the details of gender roles, some generalizations can be stated about Malay conceptions of gender (see Peletz 1996).

Seniority, the expectation that an older person involved in an instance of social interaction will be shown greater respect than a younger person, is one of the basic parameters of traditional Malay social organization. Seniority refers to the culturally encoded requirement for younger persons to honor even slightly older persons through formalities of speech, gesture, and posture. It is present in kinship terms that distinguish large age differences between generations (great-grandparents, grandparents, parents, children, grandchildren and great-grand-children), and also terms that distinguish between the smaller increments of age in the birth order of siblings born from the same womb. The latter are probably most central to the genius of Malay social organization (see McKinley 1975). Moreover, both 'generational' and 'sibling' seniority terms are regularly used, unselfconsciously, among co-members of extended kinship groups and non-kin social and occupational groups. Gender is a basic variable in these terms of address and reference in that terms for older persons (who deserve most respect) specify gender, but terms for younger persons do not. Noting gender, not simply femaleness or maleness, is the basic indication of respect. Gender unnoted indicates junior rank, gender noted indicates senior rank compared to that of the person speaking.

Third person singular pronouns ('he' and 'she', 'his' and 'hers'), on the other hand, do not take note of gender, only rank. In American English we have struggled to deal with the problem of whether to use 'he' or 'she' or both alternately when the gender of the person referred to is unknown or inconsequential. A solution to this 'problem' that I have occasionally suggested to my gender-conscious colleagues, 'it' or 'its,' has not been appreciated except as a demeaning jest, because 'it' is commonly thought to be even lower ranking than 'she' or 'her' in American English. But Malay speakers do say the pronoun 'it' (*dia* or *ia*) even when they know the gender of the person referred to. If the person referred to is of high rank the term used differs (for example, 'its honor' [*beliau*]), but this more respectful pronoun is applied regardless of gender. These details are important here only because they show that gender (as compared to biological sex) is a set of cultural constructions that can differ greatly from society to society and from language to language, and because they indicate that in some important respects the Malay system of knowledge, although strongly focussed on differences in social rank, is not particularly focused on ranking gender differences.

All Malays, by definition in the federal constitution of Malaysia, are Muslims. Many people of western culture falsely assume that all Muslim cultures are strongly patriarchial and patrilineal, that only men may rule, and that property is inherited only by males through males. This is especially not true of traditional Malay cultures. For example, there are a number of instances in the classical history of Malay kingdoms in which queens ruled. Some, it is true, were placed on the throne by a husband who had resigned in order to follow a more thoroughly religious life (see Wessing and Provencher 1988). But in other instances, such as the Malay kingdoms of Patani and Kelantan from the sixteenth into the eighteenth centuries C.E., queens were heirs to the throne and ruled in their own right (see Mohd 1993:48–86). Also, at the present time among non-royal Malays, it is frequently the case that a daughter, especially she who took care of the parents in their old age, has a stronger claim than the eldest son to inherit their parents' house and its adjoining land.

The overall gender of the house itself is female. Its heart or core, the main sleeping and living space of its inhabitants, is called the 'mother of the house' (*ibu rumah*) in the same way that the capital of a country is called 'mother of the country' (*ibu negeri* or *ibu negara*) and the thumb is called 'mother of the fingers' (*ibu jari*). Modern academic literature on gender informs us, of course, that throughout the world houses are commonly said to be female, because they

189

are viewed as private (female) regions rather than as public (male) regions such as markets. However, in some parts of the traditional Malay world (for example, the state of Kelantan), markets are viewed as female rather than male regions or as regions without a particular gender identification (for example, the state of Selangor). Also, it is important to note that Malays recognize that particular parts of a house are more appropriate than others for functions dominated by males or by females, but from a Malay perspective, even this recognition is more centered in different 'registers' or 'levels' of courtesy than in different genders.

In these and other matters, senior females continue to enjoy respect and control within the context of traditional law (*adat*) in Malay culture. And, although Islamic revivalist movements that tend to restrain the presence and participation of women in public sectors have gained political power and some popular support in Malaysia during the last three decades, a strong majority of Malay females continues to select traditional law rather than Islamic reformism as their standard. Many others, especially young women, have been attracted to standards associated with western consumerism. Nonetheless, the Islamic revivalist perspective on gender is a powerful part of the social and cultural context that Malays, female or male, must negotiate in everyday life. Gaining more influence than it now enjoys, it could place Malay females firmly within private domains, restraining their participation in public affairs such as business, education, entertainment, and politics; but not necessarily. As Wazir (1992:230) notes, no form of social organization guarantees or obviates male domination of females. 'Male domination only becomes absolute when women have, through history, come to accept the limitations of their own power in relation to men'. That Malay women, on average, continue to refuse to accept such limitations, and even assert their own dominance, is a more salient part of the context of gender humor than Islamic revivalism or even western modernism.

Malay women – who, as girls, helped their mothers and grandmothers keep house, wash and iron clothes, cook, tend younger siblings (and in rural areas, chickens, ducks, goats, gardens, orchards, and plantations), in training for the time when their own daughters would help them manage a household – commonly have an 'attitude' about the basic nature of men, as being irresponsible regarding the ordinary business of life. From the perspective of many, perhaps most, Malay women, men are responsible for ritual, not for everyday life; and they are often not to be trusted even with the practical aspects of ritual. When men are deeply involved in the preparation of various sorts of 'ritual feasts' (*kenduri*), for example, a few expert women serve behind the scenes as advisors on the purchase, preparation, and serving of the food; because men are not to be trusted with such important practical matters. In most instances, and especially if the ritual feast celebrates a deeply religious event and there are male participants who are from other households, women do not eat together with the men in the formal space set aside for the ritual meal; rather, they eat informally in the space for food preparation, because formal ritual is supposed to be men's work. Nonetheless, male guests, knowing that no event as complex as a really superb

190

ritual feast in the Malay world could possibly come to fruition without the hands of a woman, often inquire about who the female feast advisor is. This gendered division of labor, with men performing and witnessing rituals and women directing and attending to practical matters, including the preparation of food for rituals, is part of the basis for the commonly heard exclamations of frustrated Malay women, especially wives ... 'Men are like children!'

Modern western consumerism is a very important part of the context of gender humor in Malay society. Just as Islamic revivalism may reduce the public status of females by confining them to private places and by making them very private persons in public places, so modern consumerism may reduce the status of females by defining them as mere commodities or assemblages of commodities rather than as particular persons. Many young Malays have embraced modern consumerism; but some of them and some of their elders have not. The tensions between Malay traditionalism, Islamic revivalism, and modern consumerism, and the impact of these tensions on gender relations are important themes in modern Malay humor. Finally, traditions are not just parts of different cultural pasts; traditions exist in the present, and they differ according to different kinds of social statuses such as gender, age, and class, and according to different kinds of economic spaces such as residential, work, and recreational communities.

Example Interpretations of Cartoons about Malay Gender Roles and Traditions

'Who is big?' (Sapa Besar)

This single page feature in the first issue of *Cabai* begins with a man greeting his male friend, Din, who has just arrived at his door (see Figure 10.1). He notes that even though Din has recently married he seems to go everywhere by himself, and he asks Din where the wife is. Din tells him that the wife is just outside the door. Then the man of the house asks Din why he did not ask her to come in with him. Din motions his friend to step outside the house where Din's gigantic wife is standing. As Din's friend collapses upon seeing the wife, who is almost as tall as the two-story house, Din asks 'How can I invite her in ... she won't fit!' (*Nak ajak camana...tak muat!*). The everyday meaning of the title of the cartoon feature, 'who is biggest?' commonly also means 'who is most senior?', 'who is highest ranking?' or 'who is the boss?' Din's wife is physically the biggest and she is probably also the boss of Din's household. This is in spite of the probability that, like most Malay wives, she is called 'younger sibling' (*adik* or *dik*) by Din and she probably calls her husband 'older male sibling' (*abang* or *bang*).

Malay traditionalism is the most relevant interpretive context for this cartoon. This is evidenced by the architecture of the house, the clothing of the man in the house (sarong and sleeveless shirt) and of the wife standing outside the door (knee length gown [*kebaya*] worn over a sarong), and by the traditional custom of a recently married man visiting relatives and close friends to show off a new wife.

191

Figure 10.1 'Who Is Big?' (*SAPA BESAR?*) by Ajoule. *Cabai*, 1 April 1997, p. 89. Courtesy of Cabai Media Corporation Sdn, Bhd.

Feast of the first day of the month of Shawwal (Hari Lebaran)

This front cover cartoon of an issue of *Gila-Gila* shows a happy housewife arriving at her door with two large bags of goods, her gleeful children, and a truckload of new furnishing for her household (see Figure 10.2). Her neighbors have gathered around to watch the unloading of the great pile of new things from truck to house, while her husband, attracted from the house out onto the porch by the noise and commotion, seems shocked and is stuttering: 'That ... that ... Is all of that ours, Mah?' (*Tu ... tu kita punya semua tu, Mah?*). To which his ebullient wife replies: 'The discount was enormous ... 70 per cent, 80 per cent,

Figure 10.2 Cover cartoon, by Jaafar Taib. *Gila-Gila*, 15 March 1992, front cover. Courtesy of Creative Enterprise Sdn. Bhd.

wow … wow … wow … wow' (*Diskaun hebat Bang … 70 peratus, 80 peratus … la… la … la … la …*).

Malay traditionalism, modern consumerism, and Islamic revivalism are all important parts of the contemporary cultural context that gives meaning to the scene captured in this cartoon. The happy wife addresses her husband as *Bang*, short for *abang*, which in this case means 'husband', but its basic meaning is 'older male sibling'. It is a term of respect indicating that the speaker is of somewhat lower social rank than the person addressed. However, senior rank and respect are not always directly associated with power over the purse.

193

Traditionally, Malay wives controlled household budgets, but Malay husbands usually managed the budget for larger purchases. I believe modern consumerism has been associated with greater empowerment of Malay women over all kinds of purchases, including expensive furniture, houses, automobiles, businesses, and land which so seldom, nowadays, are paid for in lump sums. Modern consumerism has involved the expansion of credit and ownership in ways that have empowered women. At the same time, consumerism has made additions to religious celebrations that expand the financial role of the managers of the household budget, the wives. In times long past, the day following the end of the Fasting Month (*Ramadan*), the first day of the month of *Shawwal*, was essentially a religious-social occasion during which persons of junior rank made gestures of respect to their elders and social superiors, who in turn provided fancy food and refreshments. Young adults who had traveled beyond their native community came home to visit their parents. Children were usually provided with a new set of clothes. Over time, as consumerism expanded, more and more households feasted their neighbors and relatives at a more and more expensive level. The annual replacement of items of clothing also expanded, and the replacement of household furnishing on an annual basis became popular. This change did not occur in a cross-cultural vacuum; Malays drew moral support for these developments from similar changes in the celebrations of other Malaysian communities (for example, Christian Chinese Christmas and Chinese New Year). Finally, even Islamic revivalism contributed to the modern development of this expensive religious holiday in the sense that Muslim pride demanded that the celebration of 1 Shawwal be as grand as the 'holidays of consumption' for other Malaysians.

'Dutch wives', new wives and modesty

Another front cover cartoon of *Gila-Gila* shows a middle-aged couple in bed. Talking in his sleep, cuddling his 'Dutch wife' pillow (*bini belanda*), the husband is promising a woman of his dream, whom he calls 'Hamidah' as he moans with pleasure, that he will marry her this year (see Figure 10.3). The wife to whom he is already married is wide-awake, sitting up, with a look of unhappy discovery on her face. Although obviously younger than her husband, she may have babies, children, teenagers, and even young adult offspring who require or expect some support from her household budget. The cover of her bedstead, the mirrored vanity with modern cosmetics, and the fact that her husband probably dreams of taking another, younger wife suggests that she is at least upper middle class, because getting a second, third, or fourth wife is a mark of a man's economic and social success. Probably, she is the everyday head and fiscal manager of her own household, an exemplar of what Malay men are talking about when they tease each other about being subject to 'queen control'.

Her husband is now in deep trouble! Although, according to Islamic law, he can have up to four wives, he must treat his wives and their children equally, and

194

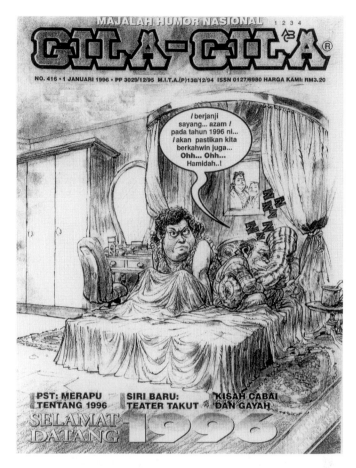

Figure 10.3. Cover cartoon, by Jaafar Taib. *Gila-Gila*, 1 January 1996, front cover. Courtesy of Creative Enterprise Sdn. Bhd.

this ordinarily requires him to maintain a separate household for each wife. Also, according to law, he must obtain permission from his wife or wives before he can marry a new wife. A wife does not give such permission easily, not only because of lost affection, but even more because of lost financial resources for herself, her children, and even her aged parents, because modern Malay men commonly, although not always, surrender the day-to-day management of family finances to their wives. A few Malay women whose husbands are truly wealthy are proud to be the first wife of a man wealthy enough to support one or more additional households, legitimized by an unusual religion, Islam. Most Malay women believe that marriage should involve one woman and one man, and that males who take advantage of an 'antiquated' religious law are simply 'horny' or 'itchy'

195

(*gatal*). Many Malay males believe that women are the 'itchy' ones and that women by wearing provocative clothing cause men to be 'itchy'. Many middle-aged and elderly Malay women, too, comment openly on clothing that is immodest, but many young women are attracted to immodest modern fashions of 'California' style.

The cover cartoon of an issue of *Cabai* shows a grandmother and granddaughter in traditional Malay formal dress staring at a young Malay woman who is dressed in skimpy casual modern 'California' style (*berkalifornya*) and talking casually on her cellular telephone (see Figure 10.4). The grandmother says: 'Look at that warped person ... when you are grown and successful ... let's not forget our sense of decency and propriety ... remember

Figure 10.4 Cover cartoon by Cabai. *Cabai*, 1 May 1997, front cover. Courtesy of Cabai Media Corporation Sdn, Bhd.

196

that' (*Tengok tu Doyah, Bila dah besar ... dah berjaya, Jangan pulak kita lupa adat resam dan budaya kita, ingat tu ...*). And the granddaughter is staring with a look of delight on her face and saying 'Wow!' (*Wahhh ...*).

A one page feature in the June 1997 issue of *Cabai*, titled 'Coffee Hot One' (see Figure 10.5), begins with a series of three panels showing beautiful young women modeling different bare-shouldered, skimpy-skirted evening gowns before a large audience. It is a modern fashion show. The next panel shows a grim-faced middle-aged Malay woman in traditional clothing and a beautiful young woman in skimpy fashionable dress saying: 'And the illusion continues' (*Rekaan seterusnya*). In the following panel, the middle-aged woman, with angry and pointing finger yells: 'Aha ... that's him' (*Ha ... itu pun dia!*). In the

Figure 10.5 'Coffee Hot One' by Kelisa. *Cabai*, 1 June 1997, p. 8.
Courtesy of Cabai Media Corporation Sdn, Bhd.

197

last panel the middle-aged woman is on the stage pointing down into the audience at an older man seated at the very edge of the stage. She is saying: 'You horny old man. I'm busy cooking and you are busy here. Go home! Go home!' (*Orang tua gatal. Orang sibuk nak masak dia sibuk kat sini. Balik! Balik!*). He is saying: 'Shhhh ... speak a little more slowly and softly, you evil spirit)!' (*Isyk ... cakap pelan-pelan sikit, yang!*).

More about queen control and men as children

That the wife's role as household manager is more comprehensive than merely controlling the budget is illustrated in two other examples, both of which were published in issues of *Cabai*. The first of these examples, a more or less regular one-page cartoon feature titled 'Mithali's Wife' (*Isteri Mithali*), was published in the first May Day issue of the magazine (see Figure 10.6). The wife is shown dancing and singing in a celebratory fashion in her kitchen. Her husband, sitting in his easy chair on the verandah, hears her commotion and asks: 'What is it that makes you so very happy?' (*apa yang kamu gembirikan sangat tu*?). She replies: 'Gosh ... tomorrow is the first day of the month of May ... Worker's Day' [*Ala ... esokkan satu hari bulan Mei ... Hari Pekerja*]. She chuckles aloud, and he thinks to himself: 'God help me ... it looks like I am going to have to cook, wash clothes, straighten up the house, wash the dishes and so-on-and-so-forth' (*Tau dah nampaknya esok aku kena masak, basuh baju, mengemas rumah, basuh pinggan ... bla ... bla ... bla ...*). Most Malay boys and men do help with housework, and many are pretty good at it, but they claim not to like it, especially when scolded for not doing it properly.

A full-page silent cartoon feature in another issue of *Cabai* further illustrates this last point (see Figure 10.7). The title of the feature is 'It looks just the same.' A middle-aged wife is scolding her husband. He has a bored look on his face, because he is used to her scolding him. As she scolds he notices a magic lamp at his feet. He picks it up and rubs it and a genie appears who asks what he wants. He tells the genie that he wants his wife to be changed into a beautiful young girl. In a magical puff, his wife changes into a beautiful young girl. But she continues to scold him as if he were a child.

The cover for the special women's section inside the 15 June 1997 issue of *Gila-Gila* titled 'Crazy Minny – Not for Males' (*Minahleter – Bukan Untuk Lelaki*) deals directly with the child-like quality of men from both female and male pespectives (see Figure 10.8). It shows Grandpa and two of his grandsons waving a banner and beating a drum as they parade through the community celebrating a championship won by the Selangor soccer team. A modern young woman dressed in tight western jeans and T-shirt (probably Crazy Minny herself) is talking to her mother or perhaps her aunt, who is dressed in modest traditional Malay clothes, saying: 'Males, just for the sake of soccer, are ready to be stupid and indecorous'. A note at the bottom of the cartoon reads: 'One

Figure 10.6 'Mithali's Wife' (*ISTERI MITHALI*) by Vikey. *Cabai*, 1 May 1997, p. 4. Courtesy of Cabai Media Corporation Sdn, Bhd.

reason why males are special is that they are gifted at pretending' (that the Selangor soccer team might actually win a championship).

Malay women also like to win

A feature 'From Taiping With Love' in an issue of *Gila-Gila* shows the heroine of the feature, Mon, a large good-hearted young lady (who really loves her little mother), playing the part of Jebat in a full costume portrayal, for village children, of the classic tale of the duel between the greatest Malay knights of Melaka, Hang Tuah and Hang Jebat (see Figure 10.9). A young man, who like

Figure 10.7 'It Looks Just the Same' (*SERUPA JUGAK*) by Baba Chua. *Cabai*, 1 June 1997, p. 85.
Courtesy of Cabai Media Corporation Sdn, Bhd.

most villagers is smaller than Mon, plays the part of Hang Tuah. The cartoon begins with the young man who is playing the part of Hang Tuah saying, according to script: 'For shame ... dishonorable Jebat, you must come down here ... Here is Tuah come to demand retribution ... Let us join in a competition of strength!' (*Cis ... Jebat derhaka, turunlah kau ... ni Tuah datang ingin menuntut bela ... Marilah kita beradu tenaga!*). One of the little kids says: 'Wow ... this is really heavy stuff when elder brother Mat and elder sister Mon do drama' (*Wah ... hebat betul Abang Mat dengan Kak Mon berdrama*). The next picture shows Mon, in her costume as the dishonored hero Jebat, leaping with short sword (*kris*) high in the air and yelling a war cry. The last scene shows

Figure 10.8 Cover cartoon for inside magazine 'Crazy Minny – Not for Males' (*Minahleter – Bukan Untuk Lelaki*) by Azam. *Gila-Gila*, 15 June 1997, p. 73. Courtesy of Creative Enterprise Sdn. Bhd.

that Jebat, as played by Mon, and contrary to the classical version of the story, has won the battle easily. Abang Mat is complaining: 'Enough Mon! ... Have you forgotten the history of Hang Tuah? ... At the end of the story it was Hang Tuah who won! ... Ouch ... ouch ... ouch!' (*Sudah Mon! ...You lupa ke sejarah Hang Tuah?. . . Ending cerita Hang Tuah yang menang! . . . Adoi . . . adoi . . . doi!*). Mon, holding her friend's arms behind his back and sticking the point of her sword in the back of his neck, says: 'I don't care, I just want to win!' (*I tak kira, I nak menang jugak!*).

This choice of traditional story as the context for a Malay woman to best a Malay man is itself significant. The hero Jebat was Hang Tuah's best friend, and

Figure 10.9 'From Taiping With Love' by Rashid Asmawi. *Gila-Gila*, 15 June 1997, p. 51. Courtesy of Creative Enterprise Sdn. Bhd.

the reason for which Hang Tuah was sent to capture or kill him was unjust – for the selfish pride of the Sultan for whom they both worked. Jebat is seen by many, perhaps most, Malays as the real hero of the story for his resistance to unjust authority. Many Malay women feel that they too suffer honorably, if certainly not silently, in a society that in certain ways constrains their new economic possibilities, their freedom to enjoy life fully, and the chance of realizing all their talents. They feel that they deserve to win more often.

Concluding Remarks

These example texts from Malay humor magazines are very different from the texts about gender relations in the magazine *Wanita*, which is patterned on the 'slick' magazines for upper-class and upwardly mobile women of the modern western world, such as *Vogue* or *Good Housekeeping*. *Wanita*, the women's magazine that competes head-to-head with *Gila-Gila* for the greatest circulation, is a more likely target of government censorship because its readership includes numerous Chinese and Indian Malaysians as well as Malays, and because one of the legal bases for government censorship is that a publication insults the dignity of an ethnic community. Also, *Wanita* publishes in a very formal register of Malay language, that of the official national language (*Bahasa Kebangsaan*);

whilst *Gila-Gila* publishes in the low registers of informal localized dialects of Malay. Perhaps because of these factors, *Wanita* does not dig as deeply into gender issues as the Malay humor magazines.

Wanita, like the verandah of the traditional Malay house, is a formal place where outsiders and other persons of rank are courteously entertained. *Gila-Gila* or *Cabai*, like the kitchen of the traditional Malay house, is an informal place where immediate members of the family loll about, enjoying relaxed and quarrelsome good humor. Texts from the Malay humor magazines are much less likely targets of government censorship because they can be seen as 'not serious' and are written in the 'informal' lower registers and local dialects of Malay language thought not to be easily understood by non-Malay Malaysians. As in the traditional kitchen (a place of informal registers of language and courtesy), so in the Malay humor magazine, informality rules and censorship is inappropriate.

That Malay humor magazines so frequently deal with matters of gender involves recent economic and social changes that are related to gender roles in the Malay house. Traditionally, a senior person's gender must be noted as the minimal act of respect, but a senior male is not necessarily more respected than a senior female. In fact, in the kitchen and other informal parts of the house not frequently visited by outsiders, Mom is often the boss; and if she isn't, she is probably working on it. Moreover, used to control of her home and, in most recent decades, realistically hopeful of an expanding household budget that will take her further into the modern world of expensive consumer goods, she may have begun to extend her dominance over her husband into behavioral regions beyond the house. In the context of traditional Malay culture this could be a breach of respect. But in the context of modern Kuala Lumpur, with its many novel behavioral regions (such as furniture stores, shopping malls, night clubs, and fashion shows) that are not easily sorted into traditional informal and formal categories, who is to say that she is embarrassingly wrong or actually right? Usually, her husband would like to be boss, too; he has a traditional claim to lead in family and personal matters located in behavioral regions beyond the house. But now his wife and other Malay women have come to claim important roles in many of those same economic and social spaces ... behavioral regions not yet well defined by tradition. These are matters of rank and courtesy, the very heart of Malay culture and society, and worthy of the interest of Malays, whatever their gender.

11

IMAGES OF THE ENEMY IN THE WARTIME *MANGA* MAGAZINE, 1941–1945

Rei Okamoto

Introduction

Manga was one of the few Japanese cartoon magazines that survived wartime restructuring and came out regularly during the first half of the 1940s[1]. In the pre-war era, however, this type of magazine had prevailed as an influential mass medium. Cartoon magazines gradually became rooted in Japanese journalism with the creation of Charles Wirgman's *Japan Punch* in Yokohama in the late nineteenth century. Some cartoons blatantly criticized the government, as seen in *Marumaru Chimbun* (1877–1907) during the Popular Rights movement in the Meiji Period (1868–1912) and in the left-leaning fourth *Tokyo Puck* (1928–1941) in the early Shōwa Period (1926–1989). As the state's attempt to control the media intensified in the 1930s, however, the cartoonists involved in the proletarian movement were severely suppressed and the number of humor magazines decreased through the restructuring of the media under the mobilization law of the New Order.

Manga started in November 1940 as an organ of the New Cartoonists Association of Japan (Shin Nippon Mangaka Kyōkai), a body founded to conform to the New Order, being published monthly until late 1944. Like other media, it supported and voluntarily promoted the official ideology, and consequently 'helped to create a public consensus in favor of government policy' (Shillony 1981:93). The political and social cartoons in *Manga* consisted of various codes and signs which reflected how the enemies – most notably the United States, Great Britain, and China – were perceived under direct and indirect influence of wartime state censorship. During the war, cartoonists directed their criticisms not at their own government but at enemies of Japan, for which they were later criticized as shamefully submitting to and collaborating with state propaganda[2].

John Dower (1986) has shown in *War without Mercy* that visual images such as cartoons were among the most powerful representations of popular wartime perceptions of 'the pure Self and the demonic Other'. Drawing on Dower's analysis of Japanese wartime graphic images, this chapter attempts to study *Manga* magazine as a mass-medium text in which wartime ideological representations were inscribed and embedded. Another objective is to identify the history of cartoon magazines and situate it within the development of Japanese journalism. Thus, this study begins with a history of Japanese cartoon magazines, as a mass medium, up to the Pacific War[3], and discusses the history and format of *Manga*. It then analyzes both visual and verbal elements of the cartoons in *Manga* in order to determine the types of representations of the enemy.

Pre-war and Wartime History of Cartoon Magazines

Birth of cartoon magazines

Once the country opened its borders to foreign trade in the 1850s after more than 200 years of seclusion, the Japanese became profoundly influenced by a number of western visitors and the technologies that came with them. Among them was Charles Wirgman, an Englishman who arrived in Japan in 1861 as a correspondent for the *Illustrated London News*. He created Japan's first cartoon magazine, *The Japan Punch* (1862–1887), to inform the foreign community in Yokohama of Japan's politics and society (Shimizu 1991). Named after the British humor magazine, *The Japan Punch* included cartoons on all pages. Until about 1877, Wirgman's cartoons often addressed Japanese politics, society, and people, after which topics were limited to news items from within the foreign community in Yokohama (Shimizu 1985). As such, Wirgman's cartoons are valuable historical records of the changes in a Japanese society that hastily transformed from feudal to modern (Shimizu 1987). *The Japan Punch,* with about ten pages, made use of Japanese techniques: printed by woodblock (though, beginning in 1883, lithography was used) on Japanese paper (*washi*), and stitched in Japanese style (Schodt 1983; Shimizu 1991).

With a circulation of a few hundred, the magazine quickly became popular among foreigners; in 1865, Wirgman began publishing it on a monthly basis. *The Japan Punch* made a considerable impact on Japanese comic art[4], to the extent that *ponchi*, a word derived from the title of this magazine, quickly replaced the words that previously meant 'caricature' (Shimizu 1985, 1991)[5].

In 1874, a Japanese artist, Kawanabe Kyōsai, teamed up with novelist Kanagaki Robun and created *Eshimbun Nipponchi* (The Illustrated Newspaper Japan), the first cartoon magazine published by the Japanese. The influence of *The Japan Punch* on its style and content was apparent, not to mention the use of the word *ponchi* in its title, as a pun on 'the land of Japan' and 'Japanese ponchi'. Although its second issue was also its last, it is noteworthy as the first attempt to publish a Japanese magazine filled with cartoons (Shimizu 1991).

Political cartoons in humor magazines of the Meiji Period (1868–1912)

During the years before and after the imperial restoration of 1868, Japan experienced a radical shift in its social structure, from a traditional feudal to a modern industrial society. When the Popular Rights movement extended throughout the nation in 1874, a weekly cartoon magazine, *Marumaru Chimbun* (1877–1907), aided its growth by severely satirizing the government. The magazine was founded by Nomura Fumio, who, believing in the necessity to learn from the Europeans, had gone to England to study. Four years later, Nomura brought back several issues of *Punch* and volumes of caricature books. He showed them to an artist, Honda Kinkichirō, who then created a new type of cartoon that was a mixture of the western (*Punch*) and traditional Japanese styles. Honda was in charge of the cartoons of *Marumaru Chimbun* from 1877 to 1882 and from 1893 to 1894. The magazine was thus directly influenced by *Punch*, rather than by Wirgman's *The Japan Punch*. *Marumaru Chimbun*'s political and social cartoons were earnestly welcomed by young intellectuals interested in both politics and literature. Introduction of zinc etching accelerated the speed of printing, allowing for mass production of the magazine. Coupled with the development of the national transportation system and mail service, this technology enabled the magazine to greatly expand its circulation and sphere of influence. *Marumaru Chimbun* was published every Saturday with a peak circulation of 15,000 (Shimizu 1985, 1991). To reach a wider audience, cartoon captions were written in both Japanese and English (Schodt 1983).

Besides Honda, well-known artists who drew cartoons for *Marumaru Chimbun* were Kobayashi Kiyochika and Taguchi Beisaku. Honda and Taguchi together had much to do with the creation of narrative strips. Possibly learning from *Punch*, Honda drew a six-panel cartoon in an affiliated magazine of *Marumaru Chimbun*, *Kibidango* (No. 143, 27 July 1881), the first Japanese narrative cartoon. Taguchi, in charge of cartoons in *Marumaru Chimbun* from 1894 to 1903, created the first serialized short narrative cartoon in 1896, a six-panel cartoon continued for three issues (Shimizu 1991)[6].

As well as *The Japan Punch*, the bi-weekly *Tobae* (1887–1890), a foreign-language magazine published during the Meiji Period, had a tremendous impact on Japanese comic art. It was started by a French artist, George Bigot, who came to Japan in 1882 originally to study Japanese art. Bigot drew cartoons for *Marumaru Chimbun* for a while, before starting his own humor magazine in Yokohama in 1887[7]. Of its 70 issues, the first 41 contained cartoons with captions in French and Japanese, targeted at both the foreign community and Japanese intellectuals. Considering that the price of *Marumaru Chimbun* was 5 sen[8], *Tobae*'s 80 sen cover cost was rather expensive for the reading public (Sakai and Shimizu 1985; Shimizu 1991). Bigot drew cartoons that satirized both Japanese government and society, much in the tradition of France's Honoré Daumier (Schodt 1983)[9].

Kitazawa Rakuten and the first Tokyo Puck

Kitazawa Rakuten was nineteen years old when he began working for an English weekly newspaper, *Box of Curios*, in Yokohama in 1896. There, he was an assistant to Frank Nankivell, an Australian cartoonist, and became strongly influenced by western, primarily American, cartoons. He soon joined Fukuzawa Yukichi's daily *Jiji Shimpō*, where he was put in charge of a Sunday *Jiji Manga* page, newly created in 1902 and totally devoted to cartoons. Having studied American Sunday funnies, Kitazawa created for the paper serialized comic strips with humorous protagonists, such as a farmer and an artisan visiting Tokyo from a rural area (Shimizu 1991).

After his newspaper stint, Kitazawa started a large-sized color cartoon magazine, *Tokyo Puck* (1905–1912), the first of its kind in Japan. Its success was sensational, reaching a 100,000 circulation within a year (Ishiko 1988). *Tokyo Puck* became bi-weekly in its second year, and appeared every ten days the following year. All pages featured cartoons accompanied by captions in Japanese, Chinese, and English, targeting international markets such as Korea, Taiwan, and China. The range of topics had been naturally extended to include international affairs. The success of the magazine enabled Kitazawa to devote his life to creating cartoons, thus making him the first professional cartoonist. All artists before him had drawn cartoons only as side jobs. Kitazawa constantly studied western cartoons within the context of journalism, and eventually proposed a new style of ponchi (the quality of which had begun to decline) that could compete with western counterparts. To make them distinctive, he renamed the new type of cartoons *manga*, a term still widely used for single-panel cartoons, comic strips, comic books and magazines, and often, even for animated cartoons[10].

Tokyo Puck stimulated a rash of new cartoon magazines, many containing the word 'Puck' in their titles and imitating Kitazawa's magazine in style and content. *Osaka Puck* was among them, one of the few magazines that was created in this period and survived the Pacific War (Sakai and Shimizu 1985; Shimizu 1985).

Introduction of American funnies and new movements of cartoonists

During the Taishō Period (1912–1926), a number of western, especially American, comic strips were introduced to Japanese newspapers and cartoon magazines. George McManus's 'Bringing up Father' was the most famous imported comic strip, which began serialization in the *Asahi Gurafu* in 1923. The American funnies greatly influenced young Japanese cartoonists (Shimizu 1985). For example, cartoonist Sugiura Yukio recalled that he looked forward to reading 'Bringing up Father' when he was at elementary school. Still active in cartooning, Sugiura admitted that the influence of the comic strip on his drawing style continues to exist[11].

After Kitazawa quit the editorship of the original *Tokyo Puck* in 1912, three editions followed – the second *Tokyo Puck*, 1912–1915, the third, 1919–1923, and the fourth, 1928–1941 – each published by a different editor and featuring different cartoonists. For instance, the rising cartoonists of the Taishō Period, such as Okamoto Ippei, Shimokawa Hekoten, and Ogawa Jihei, created cartoons for the third *Tokyo Puck*, which was smaller in format but contained more pages. Shimokawa Ken'ichirō, a journalist, reissued the fourth *Tokyo Puck* and supported many young cartoonists. Among them were the proletarian cartoonists – Yanase Masamu, Suyama Keiichi, Iwamatsu Jun, and Matsuyama Fumio – who created radical leftist cartoons attacking the capitalists and the rich. The proletarian cartoon movement began in the early 1920s and virtually died out by the mid-1930s due to repression by the state. Many of the movement's cartoonists were arrested and tortured by the Special Higher Police in charge of suppressing such movements (Usami 1981; Ishiko 1988; Ide 1996).

In 1932, the New Cartoonists Faction Group (Shin Manga-ha Shūdan) was organized by a body of young cartoonists who adopted the style of foreign, especially American, comics. The principal aims of this organization were to promote its members as a group, not as individual artists, and to seek publishing outlets for themselves. Journalism had been developed and big publishing houses prospered, the best known of these being, Asahi, Mainichi, and Yomiuri in the newspaper field, and Bungei Shunjū, Shōgakkan, and Kōdansha in magazines. However, these publishers usually worked only with established cartoonists such as Okamoto and would not even meet with obscure cartoonists, let alone hire them.

Having experienced the heyday of the proletarian movement, young (and then-anonymous) cartoonists, Kondō Hidezō, Sugiura Yukio, and Yokoyama Ryūichi, thought that acting as an organized group like the proletarian cartoonists would pave the way to success[12]. With the strength of a corporate organization and uniqueness of their western-flavored drawing style, the group successfully achieved a share in an industry previously monopolized by a few established cartoonists. It also promoted 'nonsense cartoons', which contained less dialogue and more humor than the traditional Japanese style. The creation of 'nonsense cartoons' can be attributed to the introduction of American funnies in the 1920s and the strong influence they had on many young Japanese cartoonists. As the group met its goals, its leaders, Kondō, Yokoyama, and Sugiura, established themselves as popular cartoonists (Katayori 1980; Shimizu 1985; Teramitsu 1990).

Cartoon magazines during the Pacific War (1941–1945)

Japan's aggressive intentions in east Asia were made clear by the 1931 bombing of the tracks of the South Manchuria Railways (Manchurian Incident) and the subsequent establishment of Manchukuo in 1932. Relations between Japan and China became increasingly strained, until the 1937 China Incident prompted a full-scale war between the two countries.

As the state control intensified, magazines and newspapers were merged under the mobilization law of the New Order. One result was a smaller number of publications (Kasza 1988); consequently, only limited outlets were left for cartoonists, primarily in the following three categories: newspaper comic strips which promoted national solidarity[13]; single-panel cartoons in cartoon magazines which mainly defamed the enemy; and propaganda leaflets targeted at enemy troops and the Asian populace. The New Order also affected the structure of the profession, as several cartoonist organizations were integrated into one – the New Cartoonists Association of Japan (Shin Nippon Mangaka Kyōkai) (Shimizu 1971; Schodt 1983). The following analysis focuses on the second category, cartoon magazines, by analyzing single-panel cartoons appearing in *Manga*[14].

History of *Manga*

One of the few cartoon magazines permitted publication during wartime was *Manga*, started in November 1940 as an organ of the New Cartoonists Association of Japan[15]. This magazine contained single-panel political and social cartoons, several comic strips, and illustrated articles. Political cartoons militantly attacked and ridiculed enemy countries and their leaders, whereas social cartoons bore characteristics similar to newspaper comic strips.

According to Minejima (1984), *Manga* magazine was started in the following manner: Kondō Hidezō, one of the leaders of the New Cartoonists Faction Group, was introduced to Yamashita Zenzō, who was eager to create a new cartoon magazine. Kondō's idea was to start a magazine as an organ of the New Cartoonists Association of Japan to gain easier access to government-rationed paper. Yamashita established the publishing unit, Mangasha, and took charge of sales, with Kondō as the chief editor.

The first issue (November) of *Manga* was published on 29 October 1940, as a 'new citizens' magazine' (Saitama Kenritsu Bijutsukan 1993:140). It consisted of 24 pages, plus four two-color pages bound by a full-color cover. About 15,000 copies were printed and made available for sale at 30 sen per copy, but 50 per cent went uncirculated.

After about a year, the *Manga* management changed because of financial difficulties. The magazine eventually became a commercial enterprise with no direct relationship to the New Cartoonists Association of Japan, which was virtually an organization in name only. One month after the phrase, 'recommended by the Propaganda Division of the Imperial Rule Assistance Association (Taisei Yokusankai)', first appeared on the cover of the July 1941 issue, the motto 'official magazine of the New Cartoonists Association of Japan' was dropped (Minejima 1984)[16].

When Sugao Sadayoshi became the new manager of *Manga* in June 1941, Kondō, as editor, asked him to ensure that cartoonists be well compensated, which they were. Kondō worked hard to nurture young cartoonists, providing abundant space for good cartoons regardless of the fame of the cartoonist and encouraging amateur cartoonists with prize money. Some of the latter, such as Katō Yoshirō and Taniuchi Rokurō, became well known after the war (Minejima 1984; Kimoto 1985).

Manga started to sell well in early 1942 when the military achieved a sweeping victory over the Allies. By that time, it had gained greater public awareness, as the total number of magazines decreased because of publication control, and as the suppressed wartime public welcomed the humor of its cartoons. At its peak, *Manga* reached a circulation of 200,000. As the war progressed, its contents became increasingly propagandistic, characteristic of other media under wartime thought control.

Manga was discontinued near the end of the Pacific War when the publisher and the printer were completely burned out during the air raid of Tokyo on 29 November 1944. Although Sugao immediately began efforts to revive *Manga*, gathering paper and searching for another printer, the next issue of only eight pages on rough paper did not appear until April 1945. Sugao published the eight-page May 1945 issue in August, and after the war ended on 15 August, the June/ July, October, and November issues, each made up of sixteen pages, were distributed in late 1945 (Minejima 1984).

Format of *Manga*

Manga used a variety of journalistic styles and typically had several two-page, two-color (red and black) single-panel cartoons, several serialized comic strips, and illustrated essays, mainly written and drawn by cartoonists. For example, the December 1940 issue of 36 pages contained: two one-page (two-color), one two-page (two-color), and fifteen small single-panel cartoons; five comic strips; six illustrated essays; and three articles without illustrations. The number of pages decreased as the war progressed, but the basic content, namely the emphasis on single-panel cartoons, did not change much. The November 1944 issue of eighteen pages, for instance, included two one-page (two-color), one two-page (two-color), and fifteen small single-panel cartoons, one comic strip, and three illustrated essays.

Through the end of 1944, the cover of the magazine stayed full-color. Editor Kondō drew caricatures of the leaders of both the Axis and Allied countries on the full-color covers and two-color inside pages of *Manga*, but, without question, his most popular characters were Winston Churchill and Franklin Roosevelt[17]. He also chose Japanese political and military figures as his subjects. Although various cartoonists drew the front covers of earlier issues, Kondō almost exclusively assumed that responsibility after June 1941. With the exception of those of Roosevelt and Churchill, Kondō's cover caricatures were not overly exaggerated. Particularly the faces of the Japanese (ministers and a general), shown smiling broadly, were depicted like portraits. On the other hand, Kondō's Roosevelt and Churchill were usually portrayed as evil monsters or battered and weary losers.

Analysis of *Manga*

Major themes carried in the magazine were antagonistic and derogatory satires of the enemy, often personified by caricatures of the enemy leadership, as well as depictions of wartime life in Japan. The former degraded the enemy and tried to evoke hateful and contemptuous feelings from readers, while depictions of the domestic scene tended to promote national unity and raise morale by praising wartime virtues such as saving, diligence, and cooperation.

In his analysis of wartime popular culture of Japan, Dower (1986) has categorized the portrayal of the enemy in Japanese graphic images as animals, demons with human traits, and humans with depraved, degenerate, or demonic impulses. He also indicated that representing the demonic nature of the enemy through the leaders produced two different effects. First, it gave the enemy a sense of personality, individuality, and humanity. At the same time, it may have helped the Japanese form the association of the demonic nature with the enemy leaders.

Viewed in this light, a close look at the images of the enemy leadership reveals how the characteristics of each enemy country and power relations between these countries were reflected in *Manga* magazine. Thus, the following analysis focuses on the images of the enemy leaders – specifically, Roosevelt, Churchill, and Chiang Kai-shek – depicted in *Manga*, by looking at their personality and unique traits and the relationship of the leaders to one another when being portrayed together. It also pays attention to the change of emphasis in these representations over time.

Franklin Roosevelt: an old, weary gentleman

Roosevelt was the most popularly used figure in the magazine. Especially in the early years of the war, he was portrayed as a well-dressed old man with a silk hat, tuxedo, and bow tie. As the war progressed, he began appearing in rags. He was variously disguised as boxer, cowboy, soccer player, sailor, and pilot[18].

He was also randomly depicted as an animal, and as Dower (1986) suggested, there was no particular pattern to such portrayals. For instance, on one occasion, he was a dog standing on his hind legs, kept on a dollar-shaped chain while being kicked by a man's leg that read 'Jewish conglomerate'. At other times, he was a dove with knife-shaped claws and muzzle-shaped wings and tail, octopus with a helmet, grasshopper attacking ears of rice (representing Japan), and gorilla sitting on a big tank[19].

But the most prominent manifestation of Roosevelt related to Dower's categories of demon with human face, or human with demonic impulses. Even when depicted as a human, the marks of the animal, such as 'claws, fangs, animal hindquarters, a tail, small horns' (Dower 1986:244), were often used to suggest Roosevelt changing into, or existing as, a demon. Examples included the American president as an old man with sharp nails and a skull-and-crossbones mark on his chest, crucified by an aggravated Jesus; as a man with a small horn, as in the 'A Send-off by the Satan' cartoon (see Figure 11.1); and as a green-colored monster with fangs. Another cartoon showed horned Roosevelt throwing birdseed to numerous chickens following him, and read, 'How long can this birdseed lure Americans?'[20].

Figure 11.1 'A Send-off by the Satan' by Kondō Hidezō (March 1941:20–21).

As the war progressed, topics in the magazine centered on the European theater and the enemy country's domestic affairs – for example, Roosevelt's campaign for a fourth term in 1944[21]. A reason for this switch of emphasis related to the increased difficulty of dealing with the war in the Pacific theater once the setbacks began in mid-1942. When the war situation was mentioned, the treatment of the enemy tended to be more brutal and grotesque in the later years of the war. For example, a caricature of Roosevelt by Tauchi Masao in the October 1944 issue, titled 'Increase the Production for the Revenge', called for determination to defend 'our sacred land' against the abominable enemy. The manifestation of Roosevelt was at once hateful and miserable, with an extremely skinny body and sharp nails, and with a foot fixed on an island (possibly the Marianas) with a dagger, an eye pierced by a *kanzashi* hairpin. His naked belly was barely covered with a torn US flag, his hands chained with a Japanese fighter that was followed by countless reinforcements taking off from the island that bore Mt. Fuji. This issue of *Manga* was soon followed by the first air raid on Tokyo by the US B-29s in November 1944.

Winston Churchill: a fat, cruel man with a cigar

Churchill, the leader of Great Britain, was also a cartoonists' favorite. Alone, he appeared to be less popular than Roosevelt, and he was often coupled with the president, usually disguised as a woman in those cartoons, as will be discussed below. When portrayed alone, Churchill was fat, evil-looking, and ferocious, always with a cigar in his mouth. His facial and bodily features were often exaggerated: for example, receding hair, extended belly, and sagging cheeks.

Images of Churchill changed variously: from a Napoleon using a Yugoslavian woman as a bullet shield; to a man in Scottish kilt, hanging from his shoulder a big purse instead of bagpipes; by way of a kilt-dressed executioner of the Tower of London[22]. He was often depicted as a cold-blooded male chauvinist, a sharp contrast to the images of him as a woman when coupled with Roosevelt. He took advantage of helpless countries personified as women, such as Yugoslavia, India, China, the Netherlands, and Australia[23].

The most malicious of all was an example of Churchill as a demon, Kondō's portrayal of him as a fake Dharma on the cover of the December 1943 issue. Churchill, completely bald and wrapped in a surplice, held a bone (instead of a cigar) in his mouth and a bloodied whip in his hand. His eyes looked wicked, almost insane. Both slobber dripping from his mouth (showing a little fang) and a pound-shaped earring hanging from his lobe indicated his greediness. The title of this cartoon read: 'A Fake Dharma Rampant in India' – the Chinese characters used for 'Dharma' here mean 'a slobbery demon'.

Chiang Kai-shek: a pathetic, wily loser

Chiang Kai-shek, Generalissimo of the Nationalist government, was perceived in the cartoons as representative of Japan's long-term enemy, China. He was the center of attention in *Manga* much less frequently than Roosevelt and Churchill – implying Japan's contemptuous attitude toward China deeply rooted in the popular consciousness, as Ienaga (1978) has suggested. When Chiang appeared, he was always pictured as being in trouble. The magazine stressed that, after all, he was just a skinny, miserable ringleader who had recklessly challenged Japan. The cartoons depicted Chiang as emaciated – a seedy man with sunken cheeks and usually with a Band-Aid stuck to his face. In one cartoon, he was shown living in an air-raid shelter, from which he made a phone call to England to make sure the country still existed. In another cartoon, his doctor recommended that he continue sunbathing, while Chiang's skinny belly was exposed to a beam of light through a narrow hole of the shelter[24]. His troubled situation was emphasized in several cartoons. For example, in a 1942 cartoon titled 'Present Arms!: A Military Review in Chungking', Chiang inspected his soldiers, most of whom had no armaments. In another cartoon titled 'My Dear Master, America' in the June 1944 issue, the lined-up soldiers, all looking exactly like Chiang, appeared perplexed but loyally saluted two American officers flirting with Chiang's wife.

213

Relationship of Roosevelt and Churchill

As pointed out earlier, Roosevelt and Churchill were often paired in *Manga*. Since wartime popular practice was to label the United States and Great Britain collectively (for instance, 'devilish Americans and English' [*kichiku bei-ei*]), this pairing seems natural. The usual pattern of presenting the relationship was to show Churchill dependent on Roosevelt or Roosevelt taking advantage of Churchill, manifested in depictions of Roosevelt as physically bigger than Churchill, unequal positioning of the two, and portrayal of Churchill as a woman.

An example of the first manifestation was a cartoon by Ishikawa Shinsuke titled 'The Reversed Role of the Robbers A and B' in the November 1941 issue (p. 6): Roosevelt and Churchill had captured a dark-skinned skinny man wearing a rectangular-shaped hat that read 'peoples in Southeast Asia'. Instead of robbing him, Churchill made him hold a long knife that read 'resistance to Japan' and Roosevelt gave him a money bag with a dollar sign. The caption read: 'Here! We'll give you this and also this'. Churchill, in a beret and sporting a Band-Aid on his forehead, was the same height as the robbed man but twice as round, while his height was only up to the chest of the well-dressed Roosevelt.

Concerning unequal positioning, several cartoons showed Churchill being carried either on the back or shoulders of Roosevelt: one in a cartoon by Kondō in the January 1943 issue, titled 'Carry Me on Your Shoulders' (p. 17), portrayed Churchill sitting on Roosevelt's shoulders and saluting him. Roosevelt was flexing his arm, showing his insignificant biceps that read 'resistance'; his left eye was swollen as though it had been punched. The caption reads: 'I'm a loyal aide-de-camp of the US president'. Another example of unequal positioning was a December 1943 cartoon by Kondō titled 'Splendid Achievements in Multiple Areas' (p. 14–15), ridiculing Roosevelt's disconcerting battle in the sea. Dressed in a black suit, with his arms stretched out and his buttocks on fire, the president balanced himself on one foot which was placed on Churchill's head sticking out of the surface of the ocean. Each held a small glass of red liquor that read 'the three nations' conference'[25]. In the meantime, a number of US fighters were going down in flames, and US battleships were being hit and sunk. This visual image indicated that Roosevelt, faced with insurmountable difficulties, was in a shaky position toward Europe, and that he was trying to save himself at the expense of his sinking ally, Churchill.

The portrayal of Churchill as a woman seems odd because the physical traits given to Churchill in *Manga* cartoons were not in the least feminine. To the contrary, he was shown as a male chauvinist when not in Roosevelt's company. Showing him as a woman when with Roosevelt reinforced the image that England had to rely on and be protected by the United States. However, Roosevelt in these images was usually weary, injured, and at a loss what to do.

For instance, in early 1942, when Japanese forces were sweeping the battles in the Pacific theater, a cartoon titled 'The US and British Warmongers Complaining about Their Complete Defeat' (see Figure 11.2) presented Churchill, in a long dress bound by rocket bombs and wearing a crown (most likely mimicking the Queen of England), crying hard while holding a handkerchief in his hand and a bunch of weapons under his hairy arm. Roosevelt was pictured as run ragged; his left arm was in a sling, as he leaned on a cane, holding a bent bayonet with a US national flag in tatters. The caption read: 'It really is a tragic but brave resolution to challenge (Japan) with a long-drawn-out guerrilla war'.

Other examples of Churchill disguised as a woman were evident in 1944 cartoons, all of which caricatured the trouble that the United States and England experienced because of diplomatic relations with the Soviet Union. A cartoon titled 'Sharing the Pathetic Umbrella' introduced Churchill and Roosevelt as a couple sharing one umbrella that is torn by the Soviet Union during a thunderstorm. Another titled 'An Exhausting Dance' showed them as a dancing couple manipulated by a Soviet conductor. And still another titled 'Propaganda Is of High Priority: a Chorus with Tears' depicted them as a couple singing together into a microphone that symbolized the Soviet Union. In all of them, Churchill was female and Roosevelt male[26].

Figure 11.2 'The US and British Warmongers Complaining about Their Complete Defeat' by Ikeda Eiji (February 1942:4–5).

Relationship of the three leaders

When Roosevelt, Churchill, and Chiang were depicted together in *Manga*, the focus shifts to emphasize Chiang's insignificance compared to the other two leaders. The inequity of power between Roosevelt and Churchill became less obvious when Chiang joined the party, although several cartoons still depicted Churchill as a woman. For example, in a cartoon by Kondō in the June 1942 issue, 'Spies May Be Right Next to You' (p. 17), the three enemy leaders, pretending to be ordinary Japanese people, were walking down the street, Chiang disguised as a carpenter, Roosevelt as an old man in a national uniform, and Churchill as a woman in a *kimono*. All three were portrayed with shifty eyes, an indication that they were not to be trusted.

Chiang's powerless position was emphasized by presenting him physically small or positioning him at the end of the lined-up leaders. For example, he was placed in a small basket as the crying baby of a chained couple (Roosevelt as husband, Churchill as wife) in 'Vespers', a July 1942 caricature by Kondō drawing on Millet's 'The Angelus' (p. 18–19). Others situated him behind Roosevelt and Churchill, either standing on the deck of a wrecked submarine that displayed the acronym 'ABCD', floating in the sea in a barrel, being chased by a Japanese motorboat, or sitting on an exhausted elephant that was supposed to aim toward Burma[27].

In addition, Chiang was sometimes turned into a non-human, manipulated or exploited by other allies. In the May 1944 issue, for instance, a two-page cartoon titled 'Joint Operations of Counter Attack by America, Britain, and China' (see Figure 11.3) transformed Chiang into a giant turtle, bleeding from his mouth, on whose shell was written, 'the military base for China, America, and England'. Roosevelt was portrayed sitting on the shell with a blank strategy plan and a compass in front of him, and Churchill, with a pirate outfit and a skull and crossbones on his hat, clinging to his waist. The caption read: 'Ladies and gentlemen, the circus is starting'. On the May 1941 cover, Akiyoshi Kaoru depicted Chiang, along with Churchill, as a cactus planted in a pot, being watered from a sprinkling can (with the US flag) held by a hand with sharp nails.

Conclusion

The images in *Manga* magazine, one of the influential mass media publications during the war (Ishiko 1994), vividly illustrated the Japanese perception of the enemy. Wartime cartoonists who made contributions to *Manga* relentlessly attacked the enemy, frequently using images of the enemy leadership to make their point. The graphic representations of the enemy leaders – Roosevelt, Churchill, and Chiang Kai-shek – indicated distinctive patterns peculiar to each and to their relationship with one another.

Roosevelt, by far the most popular subject in *Manga*, was depicted as an old, weary, and clueless leader of the United States obsessed with money. In the early

Figure 11.3 'Joint Operations of Counter Attack by America, Britain, and China' by Kanda Eijirō (May 1944:10–11).

years, he was well-dressed, but as the war progressed, he appeared in rags. He was also portrayed as the chief of the Allies, though untrustworthy, who sometimes manipulated and took advantage of the other two leaders. Churchill, when alone, appeared as a fat, grim-looking man with a cigar. He was depicted as a male chauvinist who exploited helpless countries personified as women; but with Roosevelt, he was disguised as a dependent woman. Chiang, less popular than Roosevelt and Churchill, was described as a pathetic loser with a feeble body. When together with the other two, his inferior status was marked by positioning him last or by featuring him as a non-human creature.

Power relations of the three leaders were established visually through gender, relative size, and unequal positioning. The most striking configuration is, as mentioned above, the images of the female Churchill when coupled with Roosevelt. Interestingly, this kind of portrayal of the British prime minister was only manifest in single-panel cartoons in *Manga*, not in the other two genres of wartime comic art – newspaper comic strips and propaganda leaflets – in which the US and British leaders were frequently referred to together as well (Okamoto 1999).

It is ironic that many of the contributors to the magazine (such as Kondō, Yokoyama, and Sugiura) were tremendously influenced by western cartoons, whose style was welcomed by the Japanese audience as sophisticated and refreshing. In order to degrade western leaders, the cartoonists used the style and technique that developed from their constant yearning for and imitation of their western counterparts. As discussed in this study, cartoonists were inspired by both Japanese and western themes in various genres such as politics, art, and religion. Thus, western thoughts and popular perceptions affected their view, such as the reference of the Jew as manipulator of the war that was observed in *Manga* cartoons as well as in other media (Shillony 1981; Dower 1986).

We must understand that the three major comic art genres in wartime Japan each assumed a different audience. *Manga* was written for domestic adult readers who had interest in foreign affairs, whereas the newspaper strip was targeted at Japanese families, including children, and the cartoon leaflets were directed at foreign audiences such as Indians, the US–Australian troops, Chinese, and so on. Since *Manga* magazine's audience was narrowly focused, the encoded message conveyed values assumed to be widely held by the Japanese who were informed about foreign relations. The unequal power relations between Roosevelt and Churchill, then, seem to engender a consensus about a hierarchy in world politics. Furthermore, the encoding of this inequality in terms of gender must have exploited the popular perception of the time – women as the weak and dependent.

Is it possible to know how these images were actually read by their intended audience? Were they easily accepted? Or were they received somewhat critically? Minejima (1984) indicates that, in fact, caricatures of the enemy leadership (especially those done by Kondō) were widely quoted in wartime media and helped visually shape Japanese perception of enemy leaders.

The emphasis of enemy portrayal on different characteristics and topics changed during the course of the war. Earlier, the enemy leadership was portrayed as being miserably defeated or at least driven into a corner by Japan. Then, after the Japanese experienced setbacks in the Pacific theater, the focus shifted to the European theater and to domestic affairs in enemy countries. When US air raids on Japanese cities became a real threat, *Manga* cartoons presented increasingly cruel and grotesque images of the enemy, while calling for a resolute manner in defending their homeland against the detestable enemy. In short, the representational mode of enemy portrayal transformed from caricature to monstrosity. This also marks a significant shift in the juxtaposition of the Self and the Other over time. Earlier in the war, cartoons depicted a brave, youthful Japanese hero cornering weary human enemies personified by their leaders. Later, the magazine often carried images of Japanese citizens collectively defending their country against the gigantic, demonic enemy.

The dehumanization effect became more apparent later in the war, thus images of the enemy leaders drifted away from realism. These visual images no longer conveyed the recognizable, believable Other. Instead, response to the enemy became a bare emotional outcry of the cartoonists as they attempted to evoke the audience's hatred toward the enemy. This tendency toward the monstrous may be seen as a form of visual lyricism, at once more visceral and less concerned with the reality of nations at war.

218

Notes

1 Another surviving the war was *Osaka Puck* (1906–1950), which was originally created to emulate the style of the first version of *Tokyo Puck*, but ended up surviving longer than its model. Although regional, its popularity among local readers in the Kansai area made it the longest-lived cartoon magazine in Japan (Shimizu 1985). With its title changed to *Manga Nippon* in 1943, the magazine continued publication until January 1945 (Saitama Kenritsu Bijutsukan 1993). This study focuses on single-panel cartoons published in *Manga*, which was circulated nationwide, compared to the regional *Osaka Puck*.
2 For example, see Ishiko Junzō (1970, 1994) and Ishiko Jun (1988). These are among the few studies that have paid attention to Japanese wartime cartoons.
3 Although the history of Japanese comic art can be traced to the twelfth century, the following section focuses on the history of modern comic art, when it came to be widely accepted as a mass medium and read by a mass audience.
4 See Shimizu (1987) for details on Wirgman and *The Japan Punch*.
5 Previously, various terms referred to 'caricature', such as *tobae*, *zaree*, *giga*, and *kyōga* (Shimizu 1991).
6 The title of this cartoon was 'Enoshima, Kamakura, Chō-tan Ryokō' (Mr. Tall and Mr. Short Travel Enoshima and Kamakura).
7 Bigot actually published the first *Tobae* in Tokyo in 1884, but it was discontinued after the first issue.
8 *Sen* is a unit of Japanese currency used in the pre-war era. It is one hundredth of one yen.
9 See Shimizu (1986, 1992) for Bigot's works and detailed analysis. Also, see three volumes of a collection of Bigot's sketches (Haga *et al.* 1989).
10 The term manga did exist in the early nineteenth century. For example, it was used in the title of a series of books, *Hokusai Manga*, a compilation of drawings of a famous *ukiyo-e* woodblock artist, Katsushika Hokusai. However, the term then just meant 'essays by picture' (Shimizu 1985, 1991).
11 Sugiura Yukio, interview with the author, January 12, 1994.
12 Sugiura Yukio, interview with the author, January 12, 1994.
13 See Okamoto (1993, 1997) for analyses of the images in a Japanese wartime comic strip.
14 The wartime issues of *Manga* used for the analysis of this chapter are: February through June, August, September, November, and December 1941; February through August, October through December, and special issue 1942; January through July, September, November, and December 1943; January through November 1944; and May 1945. I would like to thank Shimizu Isao, who owns the Archive of Modern Japanese Cartoons (Nihon Manga Shiryōkan), for letting me use his collection of *Manga* magazine and for giving me invaluable information.
15 Minejima (1984) introduced an episode concerning the foundation of this organization. Cartoonists of other groups such as the Sankō Manga Studio (a group of Kitazawa's disciples), desperate to survive restructuring of the industry, convinced members of the New Cartoonists Faction Group to voluntarily form an integrated cartoonist organization. This incident indicates how powerful the New Cartoonists Faction Group was at that time.
16 The phrase also disappeared from the cover after the April 1943 issue. It is not clear whether the magazine received any material support from the Association for being recommended by a division. According to Minejima (1984), the management of *Manga* expected the recommendation to ensure the acquisition of paper, but the magazine remained a commercial enterprise. Therefore, it is probably not accurate to call *Manga* a 'government humor magazine' (Dower 1986:257–258).

17 On the available front covers (43 issues in total), Churchill appeared six times and Roosevelt seven times. It is noteworthy that Roosevelt appeared on the cover more frequently in the later period.

18 These are, respectively, by Yokoi Fukujirō, April 1941:19; by Kondō Hidezō, October 1944, on the cover, March 1944:14–15, September 1944:7, and May 1944, on the cover; and by Ikeda Eiji, February 1944:11.

19 By Kondō, March 1942:17 and February 1941, on the back cover; by Ikeda, September 1943:14–15; by Tauchi Masao, August 1944:10–11; and by Yasumoto Ryōichi, August 1944:14, respectively.

20 The first three examples all by Kondō, April 1944:11, March 1941:20–21, and February 1943, on the cover; and the fourth by Yokoyama Ryūichi, April 1943:3.

21 For example, cartoons by Matsushita Ichio (March 1944:2), Kondō (August 1944:7), Yasumoto (August 1944:14), and Kanda (October 1944:7), all satirized Roosevelt's desperate struggle to win the election.

22 By Ono Saseo, May 1941, on the back cover; by Kondō, August 1942, cover; and by Yasumoto, June 1943:13, respectively.

23 India as a woman appeared in a cartoon by Sugiura Yukio, April 1942:20; the rest in a cartoon by Ishikawa Shinsuke, November 1942:3.

24 By Yokoyama, February 1941:27; by Ishikawa, August 1942:20; by Fujii Tomu, June 1942:20; and by Kondō, p. 7–8, respectively.

25 This probably points to the Cairo Conference in November 1943, that led to the Cairo Declaration, signed by Roosevelt, Churchill, and Chiang.

26 These are, respectively, by Tauchi, p.14, and by Kanda, on the back cover, both in the May 1944 issue; and by Shiota Eijirō, June 1944:7.

27 These are, respectively, by Kondō, July 1942:18–19; and by Ikeda, May 1942:18–19, August 1942:18–19, and March 1943:18–19.

REFERENCES

Introduction

Croizier, Ralph C. 1998 'A great leap forward for modern Chinese art history? recent publications in China and the United States – a review article,' *The Journal of Asian Studies* 57(3), pp. 786–93.

Lent, John A. 1992 'Chinese comic art: historical and contemporary perspectives,' *Asian Culture* 20 (4), pp. 27–46.

—— 1995 'Easy-going Daddy, Kaptayn Barbell, and Unmad: American influences upon Asian comics,' *Inks*, November, pp. 59–72.

—— 1999 *Pulp Demons: international dimensions of the postwar anti-comics campaign*, Cranbury, NJ: Associated University Presses.

Mair, Victor H. 1988 *Painting and Performance: Chinese picture recitation and its Indian genesis*, Honolulu: University of Hawaii Press.

Peng, Shan 1980 'Picture story books of China,' *Asian Culture*, January, pp. 2–3.

Rao, Aruna 1995 'Immortal picture-stories: comic art in early Indian art' in John A. Lent (ed.) *Asian Popular Culture*, Boulder: Westview, pp. 159–174.

Schodt, Frederik L. 1983 *Manga! Manga!: the world of Japanese comics*, Tōkyō: Kodansha International.

Shi Jicai 1989 'Introduction' in Hua Junwu (ed.) *Cartoons from Contemporary China*, Beijing: New World Press, pp. 12–15.

Zhu Guorong 1990 *China Art: the ultimate*, Shanghai: Knowledge Publishing House.

Chapter 1

Anderson, Benedict 1990 'Cartoons and monuments: The evolution of political communication under the New Order,' in *Language and Power: exploring political cultures in Indonesia,* Ithaca: Cornell University Press, pp. 152–193.

Athonk 1994 *Bad Times Story*, Yogyakarta: Pure Black.

Berman, Laine 1999 'Strategies of positioning in the discourses of the Indonesian state,' in M. van Langenhove and R. Harré (eds) *Positioning Theory: moral contexts of intentional action,* Oxford: Blackwell, pp. 138–159.

—— 1998a *Speaking Through the Silence: narratives, social conventions, and power in Java,* New York: Oxford University Press.

—— 1998b 'Ayam Majapahit meets Kung Fu Boy: the death of the Indonesian comic,' *Comic Edge.* 21: June, p. 19.

Brotoseno and Marto Art 1993 *Ontran-Ontran ing Muria* (Chaos in Muria), Jepara: TPI.

REFERENCES

Dogfight 1996 Yogyakarta: Core Comics.

Freire, Paulo [1970]1993 *Pedagogy of the Oppressed,* New York: Continuum.

Gara-Gara Sepatu (All because of shoes), 1986 Jakarta: Goltum Agency.

Hai 1995a 'Si Sarmun ke New York' (Sarmun goes to New York), 8/XIX, 21 February, pp. 58–60.

Hai 1995b 'Antihero dalam komik' (Antiheroes in comics), 21/XIX, 30 May, pp. 66–68.

Heryanto, Ariel 1990 'The making of language: developmentalism in Indonesia,' *Prisma: The Indonesian indicator,* 50, pp. 40–53.

Jakarta Post 1996 'Comic craze boosts the Indonesian comics industry,' 1 August.

Jakarta Post 1994 'Press bans spur new debate on openness,' 23 June.

JeJAL 1994 'Mas Malio,' January.

JeJAL 1994 'Mbah Boro,' June.

Kompas 1992 'Panji Koming,' January.

Kosasih, R.A. 1978 *Bharatayudha, Seri 1–3,* Bandung: Benalines.

Lent, John A. 1993 'Southeast Asian cartooning: Comics in Philippines, Singapore and Indonesia,' *Asian Culture,* Winter 1993, pp. 11–23.

Lindsay, Timothy 1987 'Captain Marvel meets Prince Rama: 'Pop' and the Ramayana in Javanese culture,' *Prisma: The Indonesian Indicator,* 43, pp. 38–52.

Miklauho-Maklai, B. 1991 *Exposing Society's Wounds: some aspects of contemporary Indonesian art since 1966,* Adelaide: Flinders University Asian Studies Monograph No. 5.

Musuh dalam Selimut (Enemy in a Blanket) 1982 Bandung: Sutawijaya Group.

Peacock, James 1968 *Rites of Modernization: symbols and social aspects of Indonesian proletarian drama,* Chicago: University of Chicago Press.

Phillipe, Robert 1982 *Political Graphics: art as a weapon* (translated by James Ramsay), Oxford: Phaidon Press.

Pos Kota 1994 'Doyok,' 7 September.

Selingkuh 1996 Yogyakarta: Komik Selingkuh.

Siegel, James 1986 *Solo in the New Order: language and hierarchy in an Indonesian city,* Princeton: Princeton University Press.

Stairway to the Dog 1996 Yogyakarta: Core Comics.

Suara Merdeka 1996a 'Comeback-nya Panji Tengkorak' (The comeback of Panji Skull), 9 November.

Suara Merdeka 1996b 'Jagoan, figur abadi dalam komik' (Heroes, eternal figures in comics), 9 November.

Suara Merdeka 1993 'Pak Bei,' 27 June.

Tabrani, Primadi 1998 'Pencarian identitas: aspek komunikatif bahasa rupa komik Indonesia' (Searching for identity: communicative aspects of language in Indonesian comics), paper presented at National Comic Seminar, 7 February 1998, National Library, Jakarta.

Tanggaku Kirik 1996 Yogyakarta: Core Comics.

Tempo 1993 'OPINI' (Opinion), 28 August.

Tempo 1988 'Si Jin Kui dalam imajinasi Oto' (Si Jin Kui in Oto's imagination), 30 April, p. 90.

Warren, Carol 1998 'Mediating modernity in Bali,' *International Journal of Cultural Studies,* vol.1(1), pp. 83–108.

Weda Kusuma, I Nyoman 1998 'Komik sebagai warisan budaya' (Comics as a cultural inheritance), paper presented at National Comic Seminar, 7 February 1998, National Library, Jakarta.

Wirosardjono, Soetjipto 1998 'Renungan tentang fungsi komik dalam masyarakat Indonesia' (Thoughts about the function of the comic in Indonesian society), paper presented at National Comic Seminar, 7 February 1998, National Library, Jakarta.

222

Zaimar, Okke 1998 'Aspek komunikatif dalam komik Indonesia' (Communicative aspects of Indonesian comics), paper presented at National Comic Seminar, 7 February 1998, National Library, Jakarta.

Chapter 2

Baria, F. 1992 'A twist in the tale,' *Mid-Day*, 19 February, pp. 4–5.

Bhramania, G. 1995 Interview with Aruna Rao, Bombay, India, 24 October.

Business Standard 1984 'The comic culture,' 29 November, p. 6.

Ceulemans, M. and G. Fauconnier 1979 *Mass Media: the image, role, and social conditions of woman – a collection and analysis of research materials,* Paris: Unesco.

Chakravarty, S. S. 1993 *National Identity in Indian Popular Cinema, 1947–1987*, Austin: University of Texas Press.

Chatterjee, P. 1986 *Nationalist Thought and the Colonial World: a derivative discourse?* London: Zed.

—— 1990 'The nationalist resolution of the women's question' in K. Sangari and S. Vaid (eds.) *Recasting Women: essays in Indian colonial history,* New Brunswick: Rutgers University Press, pp. 233–53.

Craig, S. 1992 *Men, Masculinity and the Media*, Thousand Oaks: Sage.

Dorfman, A. and A. Mattelart 1971 *How To Read Donald Duck: imperialist ideology in the Disney comic,* New York: International General.

Eisner, W. 1992 *Comics and Sequential Art,* Princeton, WI: Kitchen Sink Press, Inc.

Fernandes, L. 1993 Interview with Aruna Rao, Bombay, India, 18 June.

Fuller, C. J. 1992 *The Camphor Flame: popular Hinduism and society in India,* Princeton: Princeton University Press.

Gallagher, M. 1983 *The Portrayal and Participation of Women in the Media,* Paris: Unesco.

Gangadhar, V. 1988 'Anant Pai and his Amar Chitra Kathas,' *Reader's Digest*, August, pp. 137–141.

Gupta, M. 1995 Interview with Aruna Rao, New Delhi, India, 20 December.

Halbe, E.B. 1993 Interview with Aruna Rao, Bombay, India, 15 June.

Hornblower, M. 1993 'Beyond Mickey Mouse: comics grow up and go global,' *Time*, 142:18, pp. 42–48.

Joshi, O.P. 1986 'Contents, consumers and creators of comics in India,' in Alphons Silbermann and H.- D. Dyroff (eds), *Comics and Visual Culture: research studies from ten countries,* New York: K.G. Saur, pp. 213–224.

Kapada, S. 1986 'The story of Amar Chitra Katha,' *Free Press Journal*, 26 July, pp. 6–7.

Kothandaraman, B. 1989 'Colorful yarns – and how! Indian comics in English,' in R.S. Sharma et al. (eds), *Literature and Popular Culture*, Hyderabad: Cauvery Publications, pp. 16–20.

Krishnan, P. and A. Dighe 1990 *Affirmation and Denial: construction of femininity on Indian television*, New Delhi: Sage.

Kumar, K. 1983 'Confused ideals in fantasy land,' *The Telegraph*, 8 May, p. 7.

Kumar, M. 1995 Interview with Aruna Rao, New Delhi, India, 16 December.

Mani, L. 1992 'Cultural theory, colonial texts: reading eyewitness accounts of widow burning,' in L. Grossberg et al. (eds) *Cultural Studies*, New York: Routledge, pp. 88–126.

McCloud, S. 1993 *Understanding Comics*, Northampton, MA: Kitchen Sink Press.

Nehru, J. 1937 'Address to Indian Science Congress,' *Mainstream* 1986 (Nehru-Indira Birth anniversary Special) 9, November.

Parekh, M. 1991 'ACK: the closing chapters,' *Business World*, 20 November–3 December, pp. 17–18.

Pai, A. 1993 Interview with Aruna Rao, Bombay, India, 16 June.
Pai, A. 1995 Interview with Aruna Rao, Bombay, India, 24 October.
Pran 1995 Interview with Aruna Rao, New Delhi, India, 17 December.
Puri, R. 1993 Interview with Aruna Rao, Bombay, India, 15 June.
Puri, R. 1995 Interview with Aruna Rao, Bombay, India, 23 October.
Rai, G. 1995 Interview with Aruna Rao, New Delhi, India, 23 December.
Rao, A. 1995 'Immortal picture-stories: comic art in early Indian art,' in J.A. Lent (ed.), *Asian Popular Culture*, Boulder: Westview Press, pp. 159–174.
Reddi, U.V. 1985 'An Indian perspective on youth culture,' *Communications Research*, 12(3), pp. 373–380.
Signorielli, N. 1986 *Role Portrayal and Stereotyping on Television*, London: Greenwood Press.
Singh, C.U. 1982 'Fortune from fantasy,' *India Today*, September 30, pp. 146–147.
Spear, P. 1990 *A History of India: Volume 2*, London: Penguin.
Subbarao 1993 Interview with Aruna Rao, Bombay, India, 18 June.
Subbarao 1995 Interview with Aruna Rao, Bombay, India, 20 October.
Suraiya, B. 1984 'Comics emerge from the satchel as the voice of India's heritage,' *Far Eastern Economic Review*, 2 February, pp. 38–39.
Surti, Abid 1995 Interview with Aruna Rao, Bombay, India, 22 October.
The Telegraph 1983 'ACK's: distorted history or education?,' 13 November, p. 8.
Uppal, J. 1995 Interview with Aruna Rao, Bombay, India, 20 October.
Waeerkar, R. 1993 Interview with Aruna Rao, Bombay, India, 16 June.
Waeerkar, R. 1995 Interview with Aruna Rao, Bombay, India, 25 October.
Wertham, F. 1954 *Seduction of the Innocent*, London: Museum Press.

Chapter 3

Primary Sources

Chen Yuewen, and Lin Yulou (illus.)1968 *Xiaolanqiu Dada* (Little Basketball Dada), Taipei: Ministry of Education.
He Linken, and Gao Shanlan (illus.) 1968 *Xiao Gushou* (The Little Drummer), Taipei: Ministry of Education.
Lin Liang, and Zhao Guozong (illus.) 1980 *Papa*, Taipei: Xinyi.
—— 1978 *Mama*, Taipei: Xinyi.
—— and Wang Shi (illus.) 1971 *Caihong Jie* (Rainbow Street), Taipei: Ministry of Education.
Liu Xingqin 1992 (1958) *Asan Ge Da Shenpo You Taibei* (Brother Asan and Great Auntie Visit Taipei), Taipei: Lianjing.
Pan Qijun, and Zhou Chunjiang (illus.) 1969 *Laoxiejiang yu Gou* (The Old Cobbler and the Dog), Taipei: Ministry of Education.
Tang Yitao, and Cao Junyan (illus.) 1968 *Maoqi de Yuanbao* (The Steaming Silver Nuggets), Taipei: Ministry of Education.
Xi Song 1979a *San ge Huaidongxi* (Three Bad Creatures), Taipei: Xinyi.
—— 1979b *Taohua Yuan* (Peach Blossom Spring), Taipei: Xinyi.
Xia Shude (ed.) 1969 *Keren Dao* (Here Comes the Guest), Taipei: Ministry of Education.
Xie Wuzhang, and Zhang Zhengcheng (illus.) 1981 *Dongwu de Ge* (Songs of Animals), Taipei: Xinyi.
Ye Hongjia 1990 (1958) *Zhuge Silang Dadou Shuangjiamian* (Zhuge Silang Fights against the Two Masks), Taipei: Guxiang Chuban Gongsi.

Zheng Rui, and Zhao Guozong (illus.) 1969 *Dongtian li de Bailingniao* (A Singing Bird in Winter), Taipei: Ministry of Education.
Zhongguo Tonghua (Chinese Folktales) 12 vols. 1982, Taipei: Hansheng.
Zhu Jiefan (ed.), and Huang Changhui (illus.) 1967 *Jier Wowoti* (The Rooster Crows), Taipei: Ministry of Education.

Secondary Sources

Bader, Barbara 1976 *American Picturebooks from Noah's Ark to The Beast Within*, New York: Macmillan.
Bang, Molly 1991 *Picture This: perception and composition*, Boston: Bulfinch/Little, Brown.
Bhabha, Homi K. 1994 *The Location of Culture*, London: Routledge.
Griffiths, Gareth 1996 'The post-colonial project: critical approaches and problems,' in Bruce King (ed.) *New National and Post-colonial Literatures*, Oxford: Clarendon, pp. 164–177.
Hong Wenqiong 1994 *Taiwan Ertong Wenxueshi* (History of Children's Literature in Taiwan), Taipei: Chuanwen.
King, Bruce 1996 'New centres of consciousness: new, post-colonial, and international English literature,' in Bruce King (ed.) *New National and Post-colonial Literatures*, Oxford: Clarendon, pp. 3–26.
Lin Wenyi 1979 'Shei chuan Zhongguo manhua de xiayiba xinhuo?: jieshao shiyi wei xinku er zhoyue de Zhongguo manhuajia' (Who is to carry on the torch for the Chinese cartoon?: an introduction of eleven hard-working and outstanding Chinese cartoonists), *Shuping Shumu* (Book Reviews and Bibliography) 75, pp. 2–33.
Moebius, William 1986 'Introduction to picturebook codes,' *Word and Image* 2 (2), pp. 141–158.
Said, Edward 1978 *Orientalism*, London: Routledge; New York: Pantheon.

Chapter 4

Asiaweek 1980 'Axa stirs a storm,' 19 October, p. 84.
Collette, Aubrey 1948 *Ceylon Since Soulbury. Part I. A History in Cartoons by Collette*, Colombo: Times of Ceylon.
—— 1970 *The World of Sun Tan*, Hong Kong: Asia Magazine.
Comics Journal 1993 'World censorship watch: South Asia,' August, p. 37.
Dharmasiri, Albert 1993 Interview with John A. Lent, Colombo, Sri Lanka, 19 July.
Dayananda, Paliyagoda 1993 Interview with John A. Lent, Colombo, Sri Lanka, 15 July.
Dorakumbure, W. B. 1990 'Exhibition of cartoons by Wijesoma,' *The Island*, 21 August, pp. 6–7.
Hettigoda, Winnie 1993 Interview with John A. Lent, Colombo, Sri Lanka, 18 July.
—— 1996 Correspondence with John A. Lent, 11 September.
—— 1997 Correspondence with John A. Lent, 24 April.
Karunanayake, Nandana 1990 *Broadcasting in Sri Lanka: potential and performance*, Colombo.
Mahindapala, D. H. L. 1993 Interview with John A. Lent, Colombo, Sri Lanka, 20 July.
Medagama, K. M. K. 1993 Interview with John A. Lent, Colombo, Sri Lanka, 14 July.
Media 1981 'Comic war looms in Sri Lanka,' March, p. 11.
Opatha, S.C. 1993 Interviews with John A. Lent, Colombo, Sri Lanka, 17 and 20 July.
Perera, Camillus 1993 Interview with John A. Lent, Colombo, Sri Lanka, 19 July.

Piyadassi, Venerable Nayaka Thera 1993 Interview with John A. Lent, Colombo, Sri Lanka, 16 July.

Ratnayake, Janaka 1993 Interview with John A. Lent, Colombo, Sri Lanka, 15 July.

Rifas, Leonard 1995 'Cartooning in Sri Lanka: a precarious tightrope act,' in John A. Lent (ed.) 1992 *Asian Popular Culture*, Boulder: Westview, pp. 109–125.

Rupasinghe, Bennete 1993 Interview with John A. Lent, Colombo, Sri Lanka, 19 July.

Siriwardena, Wasantha 1993a Interview with John A. Lent, Colombo, Sri Lanka, 16 July.

—— 1993b Correspondence with John A. Lent, 26 August.

Wickramanayake, W. P. 1993 Interview with John A. Lent, Colombo, Sri Lanka, 17 July.

Wijesoma, W. R. 1993 Interviews with John A. Lent, Colombo, Sri Lanka, 15 and 17 July.

Yoonoos, Jiffry 1993 Interview with John A. Lent, Colombo, Sri Lanka, 19 July.

Chapter 5

A Ying 1957 *Zhongguo lianhuan tuhua shi* (The History of Chinese Illustrated Story Books), Beijing: People's Art Press (Renmin meishu chubanshe).

Bai Chunxiong *et al.* 1989 'Zhongguo lianhuanhua fazhan tushi' (Illustrated History of the Development of Chinese *Lianhuanhua*) *Lianhuanhua yishu* (Picture Stories Art) 10 (2) p. 114–129; 12 (4) p. 77–127.

Bi Keguan, and Huang Yuanlin 1986 *Zhongguo mahhua shi* (History of Chinese Comics), Beijing: Culture and Art Publishing House (Wenhua yishu chubanshe).

Chen Guangyi 1979 'Lianhuanhua mingchen de youlai' (The Origin of the Term *Lianhuanhua*), *Lianhuanhua yanjiu* 15, pp. 66–69, 71.

Ding Su 1928 'Wo de zhiyou Bochen' (My Best Friend Bochen), *Shanghai manhua* 18.

He Youzhi 1996 Interview with Kuiyi Shen, 14 August.

Huang Ruogu, and WangYiqiu 1989 'Yige dute de lianhuanhua faxingwang' (The Unique Distribution System of Lianhuanhua), *Lianhuanhua yishu* 11:3, pp. 115–119.

——, and —— 1993 'Shanghai lianhuanhua jianshi' (A Concise History of *Lianhuanhua* in Shanghai), *Shanghai meishu tongxun* (Shanghai Art Information) 25 December, pp. 12–23.

Ling Tao 1981 'Yi Shen Manyun laoshi' (A Memory about My Teacher Shen Manyun), *Lianhuanhua yanjiu* 25, pp. 82–88.

Lu Shicheng 1981 'Dute de faxingwang' (A Special Distribution System), *Lianhuanhua yanjiu* 21, pp. 51–53, 27.

Shanghai Manhua 1928 'Several words of the founders,' p. 2, 1.

Shen Bochen 1918 'Benkan de zeren' (The Responsibilities of the Magazine), *Shanghai Puck* 1.

Wang Yamin *et al.* 1994 *Zhongguo manhua shuxi–Feng Zikai* (The Series of Chinese Cartoons, Feng Zikai), Shijiazhuang: Hebei Educational Publishing House (Hebei jiaoyu chubanshe).

Wang Yiqiu 1995 Interview with Kuiyi Shen, 17 December.

Wang Zimei 1935 'Zhongguo manhua de fazhan yu zhanwang' (The Evolution and Prospect of Chinese Cartoons), *Manhua shenghuo* 2, p. 2.

Xie Bo 1991 *Ye Qianyu zhuan* (Biography of Ye Qianyu), Changchun: Jilin Art Publishing House (Jilin meishu chubanshe).

Xu Zhihao1992 *1911–1949 Zhongguo meishu qikan guoyanlu* (1911–1949, Survey of Chinese Art Periodicals), Shanghai: Shanghai Calligraphy and Painting Publishing House (Shanghai shuhua chubanshe).

Xuan Wenjie 1980 'Diyijie quanguo manhua zhanlanhui' (The First National Cartoon Exhibition), *Beijing Daily*, 14 December.

Zhao Hongben 1978 'Congshi lianhuanhua chuangzuo sishiqinian (1931–39)' (Producing Lianhuanhua for Forty-seven Years, the Years 1931–39), *Lianhuanhua yanjiu* 13, pp. 55–62.
Zhao Jiabi 1981 'Lu Xun he lianhuanhua' (Lu Xun and lianhuanhua), *Lianhuanhua luncong*.
Zheng Yimei 1979 'Dui jiwei manhuajia de huiyi' (A Memory to Some Cartoonists), *Fengci yu youmo* 3.
Zhu Guangqian 1980 'Huiyi laoyou Feng Zikai' (A Memory of My Old Friend Feng Zikai), *Art World* 1, p. 25.
Zhu Guangzheng 1982 'Huiyi wo de fuqin Zhu Runzai' (A Memory of My Father Zhu Runzai), in *Zhu Runzai lianhuanhua xuan* (Selected Lianhuanhua of Zhu Runzai), Beijing: People's Art Press (Renmin meishu chubanshe), pp. 51–58.

Chapter 6

Andrews, Julia F. 1994 *Painters and Politics in the People's Republic of China, 1949–1979*, Berkeley: University of California Press.
Apter, Emily 1991 *Feminizing the Fetish: psychoanalysis and narrative obsession in turn-of-the-century France*, Ithaca: Cornell University Press.
Banyue (The Half-Moon Journal), September 1921–November 1925, Zhou Shoujuan (ed.), Shanghai, Dadong Shuju.
Bao Tianxiao 1971 *Chuanyinglou Huiyi Lu* (Reminiscences of the Bracelet Shadow Chamber), Hong Kong: Dahua Chubanshe.
Bi Keguan 1982 *Zhongguo Manhua Shi* (A History of Chinese Cartoons), Ji'nan: Shandong Renmin Chubanshe.
BYHB (*Beiyang Huabao*) (The Pei-yang Pictorial News), July 1926–July 1937, Wu Qiuchen (ed.), 1,587 issues, Tianjin; rpt. Beijing: Shumu Wenxian Chubanshe, 1985.
Cohn, Don J. (ed.) 1987 *Vignettes from the Chinese: lithographs from Shanghai in the late nineteenth century*, Hong Kong: Chinese University of Hong Kong, Renditions Paperback.
Dianshizhai Huabao (The Dianshizhai Pictorial), May 1884–December 1898, Wu Youru (ed.), 473 issues, Shanghai: Dianshizhai.
DLMH = Duli Manhua (Oriental Puck), September 1935–February 1936, Zhang Guangyu (ed.), 9 issues, Shanghai: Duli Chubanshe.
Elvin, Mark 1989 'Tales of *shen* and *xin*: body-person and heart-mind in China during the last 150 years,' in M. Feher (ed.) *Fragments for a History of the Human Body*, New York: Zone Books, v.2, pp. 266–349.
Feiyingge Huabao (The Feiyingge Pictorial), August 1890–March 1894, Wu Youru (ed.), 132 issues, Shanghai: Feiyingge.
Hay, John 1994 'The body invisible in Chinese art?' in A. Zito and T. Barlow (eds) *Body, Subject and Power in China*, Chicago: University of Chicago Press, pp. 42–77.
Henriot, Christian 1994 'Chinese courtesans in late Qing and early Republican Shanghai (1849–1925),' *East Asian History* 8 (December), pp. 33–52.
Hershatter, Gail 1994 'Modernizing sex, sexing modernity: prostitution in early twentieth-century Shanghai,' in C. Gilmartin, G. Hershatter, L. Rofel, and T. White (eds) *Engendering China: woman, culture, and the state*, Cambridge, Mass.: Harvard University Press, pp. 147–174.
Hucker, Charles O. 1975 *China's Imperial Past: an introduction of Chinese history and culture*, Stanford: Stanford University Press.
Hung, Chang-tai 1994 *War and Popular Culture: resistance in modern China, 1937–1945*, Berkeley: University of California Press.

Liu, Ts'un-yan (ed.) 1984 *Chinese Middlebrow Fiction: from the Ch'ing and early Republican eras*, Hong Kong: Chinese University Press.

Lu Xun [Lu Hsun] 1960 *Lu Hsun, Selected Works*, v. 3, Peking: Foreign Languages Press.

LY (*Liangyou*) (The Young Companion), February 1926–October 1945, Shanghai: Liangyou Chuban Gongsi.

MacKinnon, Stephen R. 1997 'Toward a history of the Chinese press in the Republican period,' *Modern China* 23:1 (January), pp. 3–32.

Manhua Jie (Modern Puck), April–December 1936, Wang Dunqing (ed.), 8 issues, Shanghai: Manhua Jianshe she.

QQDY (*Qingqing Dianying*) (The Chin-Chin Screen), April 1934–April 1949, Yan Ciping (ed.), Shanghai: Qingqing Dianying She.

Raffle Zahi (The Raffle), 1895, with Cartoonist H. W. G. Hayter, Shanghai: Kelly and Walsh.

Shidai Manhua (Modern Sketch), January 1934–June 1937, 39 issues, Lu Shaofei (ed.), Shanghai: Shidai Tushu Gongsi.

Tang Zhenchang (ed.) 1993 *Jindai Shanghai Fanhua Lu* (Splendors and Glamors of Modern Shanghai), Hong Kong: Shangwu.

Wakeman, Frederic, Jr. 1995 'Licensing leisure: the Chinese Nationalists' attempt to regulate Shanghai, 1927–49,' *Journal of Asian Studies* 54:1 (February), pp. 19–42.

Wang, David Der-wei 1997 *Fin-de-Siècle Splendor: repressed modernities of late Qing fiction, 1849–1911*, Stanford: Stanford University Press.

Wu Xiangzhu (ed.) 1958 *Dianshizhai Huabao de Shishi Fengsu Hua* (Illustrations of Folk Custom and Current Events in the Dianshizhai Pictorial), Beijing: Renmin Meishu Chubanshe.

Wu Hung 1996 *The Double Screen: medium and representation in Chinese painting*, Chicago: University of Chicago Press.

Wu Youru 1908 *Wu Youru Huabao* (A Treasury of Wu Youru's Illustrations), rpt. Shanghai: Shanghai Guji Chubanshe, 1983.

Wu Zuxiang, Duanmu Hongliang, and Shi Ying (eds.) 1991 *Zhongguo Jindai Wenxue Daxi: xiaoshuo ji* (A Treasury of Early Modern Chinese Literature: fiction volumes), v. 1, Shanghai: Shanghai Shudian.

Xiao Jianqing 1936a *Manhua Shanghai* (Shanghai in Cartoons), Shanghai: Jingwei Shuju.

—— 1936b *Shehui Manhua* (Society in Cartoons), Shanghai: Jingwei Shuju.

Xiaoshuo Daguan (The Grand Magazine), August 1915–June 1921, Bao Tianxiao (ed.), Shanghai: Wenming Shuju.

Xiaoshuo Shibao (Fiction Times), October 1909–November 1917, Bao Tianxiao (ed.), Shanghai: Youzheng Shuju.

Xu Min 1994 'Shi, chang, you–wan Qing Shanghai shehui shenghuo yipie' (Literatus, prostitute, actor: a glimpse of social life in late Qing Shanghai), *Ershiyi Shiji* 23 (June), pp. 34–41.

Ye Xiaoqing 1990 '*Dianshizhai Huabao* zhongde Shanghai pingmin wenhua' (Shanghai plebeian culture in *The Dianshizhai Pictorial*), *Ershiyi Shiji* 1 (October), pp. 36–47.

Zhang, Yingjin 1996 *The City in Modern Chinese Literature and Film: configurations of space, time, and gender*, Stanford: Stanford University Press.

Zhang Zhongli (ed.) 1990 *Jindai Shanghai Chengshi Yanjiu* (Urban Studies on Modern Shanghai), Shanghai: Shanghai Renmin Chubanshe.

Zheng Jiazhen 1992 *Xianggang Manhua Chunqiu* (A History of Hong Kong Cartoons), Hong Kong: Sanlian Shudian.

Chapter 7

Matumoto Reiji and Hidaka Satoshi 1980 *Manga Rekishi Dai Hakubutsukan* (Great Historical Museum of Manga) Tōkyō: Buronzusha.

Nakano Haruyuki 1993 *Tezuka Osamu to Rojiura no Mangakatachi* (Osamu Tezuka and Comic Artists of Red Comic Book) Tōkyō: Chikumashobo.

Oshiro Noboru, Tezuka Osamu, Matumoto Reiji 1982 *Oh! Manga*. Tōkyō: Shobunsha.

Sakurai Shoichi 1978 *Watashi wa Gekiga no Shikakenin datta* (Call Me 'The *Gekiga* (narrative comics) Mastermind') Tōkyō: Eipuriru Shuppan.

Shimizu Isao 1989 *'Manga Shōnen' to Akahon Manga* (The Magazine for Boys Manga Shonen and Red Comic Books) Tōkyō: Zoonsha.

—— 1991 *Manga no Rekishi* (History of Japanese Cartoon) Tōkyō: Iwanamishoten.

Tezuka Osamu June 1953, 'Zokkibon, Mikirinbon wa naze tsukurarerunoka' (Why Zokkibon and Mikiribon, reprint edition of red books, are made) in Shimizu, *Manga Shonen.*

YonezawaYoshihiro 1996 *Shōnen Manga no Sekai* (The World of Boy's Comic) *I (1945–1960) The extra number of Graphic Magazine,* Taiyo, Tōkyō: Heibonsha.

Comics referenced

Hideo, Kikuchi (publication date unknown) *Chikyu Nisennen no Sekai* (Earth Year 2000), Enomoto Horeikan.

Junpei, Maki (publication date unknown) *Sennengo no Sekai* (The World A Thousand Years After), Enomoto Horeikan.

Sugimoto, Machiko (publication date unknown) *Shiruko-san* (publisher unknown)

Tezuka Osamu (1948) *Issennengo no Sekai* (The World One Thousand Years After), Tokodo.

—— (1948) *Ryusenkei Jiken* (Stream Line Case), Gorakusha 1948.

Ganbare Rikidozan (You Can Do It, Rikidozan) (publication date unknown) Enomoto Horeikan.

Gojira Nippon wo yuku (Godzilla Travels Japan) (publication date unknown) Enomoto Horeikan

Kage (Shadow) 1956, Hinomaru Bunko.

Machi (Street) Sentoraru Shuppan.

Chosoku Motaka (High Speed Motorcar), publication date unknown, Enomoto Horeikan

Chapter 8

Lent, John A. 1993 'The renaissance of Taiwan's cartoon arts,' *Asian Culture* 21 (1), reprinted, Taipei: Asian Pacific Cultural Center, pp. 1–17.

Qiu, Jiayi 1992 'Tsai Chih-chung: manhua shijie duxingxia' (Tsai Chih-chung: the independent warrior in the world of cartoons), *Zhanlue Shengchanli* 439, pp. 118–120.

Tsai, Chih-chung 1997 'Manhuajia yanzhong de Taiwan jingji 50 nian – Tsai Chih-chung de manhua riji' (50 years of Taiwan's economy in the eyes of a cartoonist – Tsai Chih-chung's diary in cartoons), in Wen Shiren *Taiwan Jingji de Kunan yu Chengzhang* (Hardship and Growth in Taiwan's Economy), Taipei: Dakuai Wenhua, pp. 93–115.

—— 1995 *The Tao Speaks: Lao-tzu's whispers of wisdom* (translated by Brian Bruya), New York: Doubleday.

—— 1993 *Zhizhe de Diyu, Laozi Shuo 2* (Whispers of Wisdom, Laozi Speaks 2), Taipei: Shibao Wenhua, Manhua Congshu 167.

—— 1992 *Zhuangzi Speaks: the music of nature* (translated by Brian Bruya), Princeton: Princeton University Press.

—— 1988 *Ruzhe de Zhengyan, Lunyu* (Confucian Advice, the Analects), Taipei: Shibao Wenhua, Manhua Congshu 57.

—— 1987a *Renzhe de Dingning, Kongzi Shuo* (A Humanitarian's Admonition, Confucius Speaks), Taipei: Shibao Wenhua, Manhua Congshu 27.

—— 1987b *Zhizhe de Diyu, Laozi Shuo* (Whispers of Wisdom, Laozi Speaks), Taipei: Shibao Wenhua, Manhua Congshu 18.

—— 1986 *Ziran de Xiaosheng, Zhuangzi Shuo* (The Music of Nature, Zhuangzi Speaks), Taipei: Shibao Wenhua, Manhua Congshu 14.

Chapter 9

Abel, Elizabeth and Emily K. Abel (eds) 1983 *The Signs Reader: women, gender & scholarship*, Chicago: The University of Chicago Press.

Aramata Hiroshi 1977 'Chō shōjo no gūwa' (A fable of super *shōjo*), in Takeuchi, *Manga Hihyō Taikei* 2, pp. 9–31.

—— 1991 'Yumemiru sōshoku' (Dreaming decoration), in Bessatsu Taiyō 2, (op.cit.), vol.2, pp. 26–27.

Bessatsu Taiyō 1991 *Shōjo Manga no Sekai* (The World of *Shōjo Manga*) 2 vols., Tōkyō: Heibonsha.

Childers, Joseph and Gary Hentzi (eds) 1995 *The Columbia Dictionary of Modern Literary and Cultural Criticism*, New York: Columbia University Press.

Cixous, Hélène 1976 'Laugh of medusa,' in Abel and Abel (op.cit.), pp. 279–297.

Fujiyama-Fanselow, Kumiko and Atsuko Kameda (eds) 1995 *Japanese Women: new feminist perspectives on the past, present, and future*, New York: The Feminist Press.

Fujimoto Yukari 1990 'Onna no ryōsei guyū, otoko no han inyō' (Trans-gender phenomenon in comics), *Gendai no Esupuri* 277, pp. 177–209.

—— 1991 'A life-size mirror: women's self-representation in girls' comics,' *Review of Japanese Culture and Society* Vol. IV, Saitama, Japan: Center for Inter-Cultural Studies and Education, Jōsai University, pp. 53–57.

Hagio Moto and Yoshimoto Ryūmei 1981 'Jikohyōgen toshite no shōjo manga' (*Shōjo manga* as self representation), in *Eureka* 13:9, pp. 82–119.

Honda Masuko 1991 'Senjika no shōjo zasshi' (Magazines for girls during the war), in Ōtsuka, *Shōjo Zasshi Ron*, (op.cit.), pp. 7–43.

—— 1990 *Jogakusei no Keifu* (Archeology of Female Students), Tōkyō: Seitosha.

—— 1988 'Shōjo katari,' in *Shōjo Ron,* Tōkyō: Seikyūsha, pp. 9–37.

Ishinomori Shōtarō 1989 *Manga Chō Shinka Ron* (Comic Evolution), Tōkyō: Kawaide Shobō Shinsha.

Kaplan, E. Ann 1983 *Women and Film: both sides of the camera*, New York: Routledge.

Kure Tomofusa 1997 *Gendai Manga no Zentaizō* (General Features of Contemporary *Manga*), Tōkyō: Futabasha.

Kurihara Yōko 1995 'Uta no naka no hahaoyazō' (Maternal images in songs), *Feminism in Japan* 7, Tōkyō: Iwanami Shoten, pp. 85–96.

Maki Miyako 1991 'Anokoro' (Those days), in Bessatsu Taiyō, (op.cit.), vol.1, pp. 70–71.

Murakami Tomohiko 1979 'Yume no naka no nichijyō: Ōshima Yumiko' (Daily Matters in Dreams: Ōshima Yumiko), in Takeuchi and Murakami, *Manga Hihyō Taikei* (op.cit.), vol.2, pp. 72–85.

Nagatani Kunio 1995 *Nippon Manga Zasshi Meikan* (Directory of Japanese Manga Magazines), Tōkyō: Data House.

Nakajima Azusa 1991 'Mizō no jidai' (Unprecedented age), in Bessatsu Taiyō (op.cit.), vol.2, pp. 88–89.

Nippon Mangaka Meikan 500 (Japanese Cartoonists 500 List) 1992, Tōkyō: Akua Planning.

Ōtsuka Eiji 1997 *Shōjo Minzokugaku* (*Shōjo* Ethnology), Tōkyō: Kōbunsha.

—— 1995 *Ribon no Furoku to Otomechikku no Jidai* (Free Gifts Appended to *Ribon* and Cute Period), Tōkyō: Chikuma Shobō.

—— 1994 *Sengo Manga no Hyōgen Kūkan* (Representing Space in *Manga* after 1945), Kyōto: Hōzōkan.

—— (ed) 1991 *Shōjo Zasshi Ron* (Examining Magazines for Girls), Tōkyō: Tōkyō Shoseki.

Satō Yōko 1979 '70 nendai ni okeru joseitachi no tatakai' (Women's struggles in the 1970s), *Shisō no Kagaku* 100, Tōkyō: Shisō no Kagakusha, pp. 20–29.

Shiota Sakiko 1992 'Gendai feminism to nihon no shakai seisaku' (Feminism and Japanese social policy), *Feminism in Japan* 4, Tōkyō: Iwanami Shoten, pp. 113–133.

Shuppan Shihyō Nenpyō 1996 (Annual Report of Publication) 1996, Tōkyō: Shuppankagaku Kenkyūjo.

Tanaka Kazuko 1995 'The New Feminist Movement in Japan, 1970–90,' in Fujiyama-Fanselow, *Japanese Women*, (op.cit.), pp. 343–352.

Takatori Ei 1978 'Tozasareta kūkan kara no romanticism' (Romanticism in the closed space), in Takeuchi and Murakami, *Manga Hihyō Taikei* (op.cit.), vol.2, pp. 48–58.

Takeuchi Osamu 1995 *Sengo Manga 50nenshi* (History of *Manga* for 50 Years After the War), Tōkyō: Chikuma Shobō.

Takeuchi Osamu and Murakami Tomohiko (eds.) 1989 *Manga Hihyō Taikei* (Criticism on *Manga*) 3 vols., Tōkyō: Heibonsha.

Tezuka Osamu 1996–7 *Tezuka Osamu Manga Zenshū* (*Tezuka Osamu Manga* Collection) Supplements 9 vols, Tōkyō: Kōdansha.

—— 1988 'Manga to no deai' (Encounter with *manga*), in *Tezuka Osamu Manga Zenshū*, vol.9, pp. 15–98.

—— 1979 *Tezuka Osamu Manga Zenshū* 85, 86 (*Tezuka Osamu Manga* Collection), Tōkyō: Kōdansha.

Ueno Chizuko 1995 'Rōdō gainen no gender ka' (Gendering the work force), in Wakita, *Gender no Nihonshi* (op.cit.), vol.2, pp. 679–710.

Wakita Haruko (ed.) 1995 *Gender no Nihonshi* (History of Gender) 2 vols., Tōkyō: Tōkyō University Press.

Yomota Inuhiko 1994 *Manga Genron* (The Principles of *Manga*), Tōkyō: Chikuma Shobō.

Yonezawa Yasuhiro 1997 '*Manga* bunka' (*Manga* culture), in *Gendai Yōgo no Kisochishiki* (Basic Knowledge on Contemporary Terms), Tōkyō: Jiyū Kokuminsha, pp. 860–864.

—— 1996 '*Manga* bunka' (*Manga* culture), in *Gendai Yōgo no Kisochishiki* (Basic Knowledge Concerning Contemporary Terms), Tōkyō: Jiyū Kokuminsha, pp. 1064–1068.

—— 1991 'Shōjo manga no genzai, kako, mirai' (The present, past, and future of *shōjo manga*), in Bessatsu Taiyō (op.cit.), vol.1, pp. 4–9.

Chapter 10

Djamour, Judith 1959 *Malay Kinship and Marriage in Singapore*, London: Athlone Press.

McKinley, Robert 1975 *A Knife Cutting Water: child transfers and siblingship urban Malays*, Ph.D. dissertation, University of Michigan.

Mohd. Zamberi A. Malek 1993 *Umat Islam Patani: sejarah dan politik*, Shah Alam: Penerbit HIZBI.

Ong, Aihwa 1989 'Center, periphery, and hierarchy: gender in Southeast Asia,' in Sandra Morgen (ed.) *Gender and Anthropology: critical reviews for research and teaching*, Washington, D.C.: American Anthropological Association, pp. 294–312.

Peletz, Michael G. 1996 *Reason and Passion: representations of gender in a Malay society*, Berkeley, Los Angeles and London: University of California Press.

Wazir Jahan Karim 1992 *Women & Culture: between Malay adat and Islam*, Boulder: Westview Press.

Wessing, Robert and Ronald Provencher 1988 'On the historicity of a mysterious teungku in Cowan's *De Hikayat Malem Dagang*,' *Sari* (Journal of the Institute for Malay Language, Literature and Culture at the National University of Malaysia) 5, pp. 51–66.

Chapter 11

Dower, John W. 1986 *War Without Mercy: race and power in the Pacific War*, New York: Pantheon Books.

Haga Tōru et al. (eds) 1989 *Bigot Sobyō Collection* (A Collection of Bigot's Sketches), Tōkyō: Iwanami Shoten.

Ide Magoroku 1996 *Nejikugi no Gotoku: gaka, Yanase Masamu no kiseki* (Like the Minus Screw: the journey of an artist, Yanase Masamu), Tōkyō: Iwanami Shoten.

Ienaga, Saburo 1978 *The Pacific War, 1931–1945* (translated by Frank Baldwin), New York: Pantheon Books.

Ishiko Jun 1988 *Nihon Mangashi* (A History of Japanese Comics), Tōkyō: Shakai Shisōsha.

Ishiko Junzō 1994 (1975) *Sengo Manga-shi Nōto* (Notes on the History of Postwar Comics), Tōkyō: Kinokuniya Shoten.

—— 1970 *Gendai Manga no Shisō* (The Philosophy of Contemporary Comics), Tōkyō: Taihei Shuppansha.

Kasza, Gregory J. 1988 *The State and the Mass Media in Japan, 1918–1945*, Berkeley, CA: University of California Press.

Katayori Mitsugu 1980 *Sengo Manga Shisō-shi* (A History of Ideologies in Postwar Comic Art), Tōkyō: Miraisha.

Kimoto Itaru 1985 *Zassi de Yomu Sengoshi* (Reading Postwar History in Magazines), Tōkyō: Shinchōsha.

Minejima Masayuki 1984 *Kondō Hidezō no Sekai* (The World of Kondō Hidezō), Tōkyō: Seiabō.

Okamoto, Rei 1999 'Pictorial propaganda in Japanese comic art, 1941–1945: Images of the Self and the Other in a newspaper strip, single-panel cartoons, and cartoon leaflets,' Doctoral dissertation, Temple University.

—— 1997 '"Fuku-chan" goes to Java: images of Indonesia in a Japanese wartime newspaper comic strip,' *Southeast Asian Journal of Social Science*, 25 (1), pp. 111–123.

—— 1993 'The Japanese Comic Strip "Fuku-chan" (Little Fuku), 1936–1944,' *Philippines Communication Journal*, 2 (8), pp. 71–79.

Saitama Kenritsu Kindai Bijutsukan (The Museum of Modern Art, Saitama) (ed.) 1993 *Nippon no Fūshi* (Subtle Criticism: caricature and satire in Japan), Saitama: Saitama Kenritsu Kindai Bijutsukan.

Sakai Tadayasu and Shimizu Isao 1985 *Nisshin Sensōki no Manga* (Cartoons during the Sino-Japanese War), Tōkyō: Chikuma Shobō.

Schodt, Frederik 1983 *Manga! Manga!: the world of Japanese comics*, Tōkyō: Kodansha International.

Shillony, Ben-Ami 1981 *Politics and Culture in Wartime Japan*, Oxford: Clarendon Press.

Shimizu Isao (ed.) 1992 *Zoku Bigot Nihon Sobyōshū* (Additional Collection of Bigot's Sketches of Japan), Tōkyō: Iwanami Shoten.

—— 1991 *Manga no Rekishi* (A History of Japanese Cartoons), Tōkyō: Iwanami Shoten.

—— (ed.) 1987 *Wirgman Nihon Sobyōshū* (A Collection of Wirgman's Sketches of Japan), Tōkyō: Iwanami Shoten.

—— (ed.) 1986 *Bigot Nihon Sobyōshū* (A Collection of Bigot's Sketches of Japan), Tōkyō: Iwanami Shoten.

—— (ed.) 1985 *Nihon Manga no Jiten* (Dictionary of Japanese Comics), Tōkyō: Sanseidō.

—— (ed.) 1971 *Taiheiyō Sensōki no Manga* (Cartoons during the Pacific War), Tōkyō: Bijutsu Dōjinsha.

Teramitsu Tadao 1990 *Shōden Shōwa Manga: nansensu no keifu* (Comic Art during the Shōwa Period: genealogy of nonsense), Tōkyō: Mainichi Shimbunsha.

Usami Shō 1981 *Sayonara Nippon: ehon sakka Yashima Tarō to Mitsuko no bōmei* (Good-bye Japan: exile of a picture book creator, Yashima Taro and Mitsuko), Tōkyō: Shōbunsha.

CONTRIBUTORS

Laine Berman is a Research Fellow in the Center for Cross Cultural Research at the Australian National University. Her research is on popular culture, language and power, oppression, violence, and marginal communities in Indonesia. She has recently published *Speaking Through Silence: narratives, social conventions, and power in Java* with Oxford University Press, and is currently writing a book on popular culture in Indonesia.

John A. Lent is a Professor of Communications at Temple University and for 2000, Rogers Chair of Studies in Journalism and New Information Technology and Visiting Professor at University of Western Ontario. Author or editor of 55 books, he chairs the Asian Cinema Studies Society and two association divisions on comic art study. He is founding editor of *International Journal of Comic Art* and since 1994, editor of *Asian Cinema*.

Fusami Ōgi is a Lecturer in the Department of English at Chikushi Jogakuen University, a women's institution of higher learning. She earned an MA in English language and literature at Kyushu University and is a Ph.D. candidate in comparative studies at State University of New York, Stony Brook. Her dissertation title is 'Reading, Writing, and Female Subjectivity: gender in *manga*.'

Rei Okamoto is an Assistant Professor of Japanese at Northeastern University. She completed her Ph.D. dissertation at Temple University on Japanese comic art during the Pacific War and has published articles in *Southeast Asian Journal of Social Science*, *Journal of Asian Pacific Communication*, *Philippines Communication Journal*, and *Media History Digest*.

Ron Provencher is a cultural anthropologist who specializes in the study of complex societies. He has conducted ethnographic research in cities, towns, and villages of Malaysia, Thailand, and Indonesia. His publications include works on the evolution and nature of urban societies, cultures of Southeast Asia, Malay folklore, and humor as social and political commentary. He has been an avid reader of comics and cartoons for six decades.

Aruna Rao is completing a Ph.D. at Temple University, writing a dissertation on Indian comic books. Her work has appeared in three books and the *Journal of Asian Pacific Communication*. She has presented papers at Association for Asian Studies, Popular Culture Association, and other conferences.

Kuiyi Shen is an Assistant Professor in the Department of Art History, State University of New York at Buffalo. Among previous positions were teaching assignments in art and art history at the University of Oregon and Rice University and Curatorial Assistant, Solomon R. Guggenheim Museum, New York.

Shimizu Isao, born in Tōkyō in 1939, is Director of the Archives of Japanese Cartoon History, editor of *Fūshiga Kenkyū Quarterly*, Professor of Information Studies, Teikyō Heisei University, and Senior Curator of Kawasaki Museum.

Shu-chu Wei, a native of Taiwan with a Ph.D. in comparative literature from the University of Massachusetts at Amherst, is teaching at Whitman College in Walla Walla, Washington. Her major areas of interest include Chinese-western comparative drama and children's literature.

Yingjin Zhang received his Ph.D. from Stanford University and is an Associate Professor of Chinese, Comparative Literature and Film Studies at Indiana University. He is the author of *The City in Modern Chinese Literature and Film: configurations of space, time, and gender*, co-author of *Encyclopedia of Chinese Film*, editor of *China in a Polycentric World: essays in Chinese comparative literature* and *Cinema and Urban Culture in Shanghai, 1922–1943*.

INDEX

References to notes are italicized; those to illustrations are in bold type.

236

Fujimoto Yukari *186*
Fuji Shobō 141
Fujokai (Women's World) 137
Fukuzawa Yukichi 207
Fushiga Kenkyū 146

'Gajaman' 89
Ganbare Rikidozan 144, **146**
Gandhi, Indira 61
Gandhi, Mahatma 42, *63*
Gandhi, Rajiv 42, 61
Ganes TH 20–1
Gao Qifeng *136*
Gao Shanlan 73
Gara-Gara Sepatu 25
Gareng 23
gatal 196
gender 3, 8–10, 17, 19, 43–4, 46, 49–50; in
   Japanese comics 171–86; in Malaysia
   187–203
genres 3, 14–9, 100, 180, 183–5, *186,* 218
Gen Si Kaki Ayam 26
giga 219
Gila-Gila (Crazy about Mad) 4, 10, 187–8,
   192, **193**, 194, **195**, 198–200, **201–2**,
   202–3
Godzilla 144, **145**
Gojira Nippon wo Yuku 143–4, **145**
Gongzaishu 101
Good Housekeeping 202
Gordon W. Prange Collection, University
   of Maryland 145
Gramedia 27
Great Auntie 67–8
Great Britain 38, 42–3, 47, 82, 137, *149,*
   204, 206, 214–5
Griffiths, Gareth 65
Grimm 70, 74
group commentary cartoons 87, **88**, **89**, 94,
   97
Guangji Book Company 106
Guangtou Shentan 153
Gunung Agung book shop *36*
Gupta, Maneesh 58

Hagio Moto 180–1, **182**, 183–4, *186*
Haikara Ponchi **138**
Haishang Hua Liezhuan 124
Halbe, V.B. 61
'Halt' 88, **97**
Hamlet 161
Hana Monogatari 171, **172**, 173

'hana no 24 nengumi' ('Magnificent 24s')
   177, 179–83, *186*
Han Bangqing 124–5
Hang Jebat 199–201
Hang Tuah 199–202
Hapana 91, *99*
Harishchandra 44, **45**
Hasegawa Machiko 141
Hay, John *136*
Hayter, H.W.G. 130
He Linken 73
Hepburn, Audrey 178
heroines 49–50, **51**, 52, **53**, 66, *98,* 143,
   172, 174, 178, 184
heterosexuality 178–80, 184
Hettigoda, Winnie 85–8, 94–7, **97**
Hettigoda Industries *98*
Hideo Kikuchi 141
Himeshan 90
Hinduism 43–6, *62, 63*
Hinotori (Phoenix 2772) *150*
Hiroshima City Manga Library *185–6*
Hiru 86
history 39, 42, 46, 59, 69–70, 89, *219*
Hithawatha 90, 92
Hōhigassen (Farting Contests) 2
Hokusai Manga 219
Hollywood 56, 178
homosexuality 180–3, *186*
Honda Kinkichirō 137, 206
Honda Masuko 171
Hong Jianquan Children's Literature
   Awards *80*
Hong Kong 3–6, 8, 20
horror comics 56, 58–9
huaji hua 130
Hua Junwu 122
Huang Changhui 71
huangmao yatou 75
Huang Miaozi 117, 122, 132
Huang Wennong 111
Hu Die 107
huihui tu 100
huitu 122
Hu Kao 118, 122
humor 3, 25, *35,* 42, 55, 59, 68, 73, 82,
   158, 178–203, 208, 210
HumOr 15, *35*
humor magazines 2, 4, 10, 137; in
   Malaysia 187–203
"Hundred Appearances of the Old Gibbon,
   A" 109